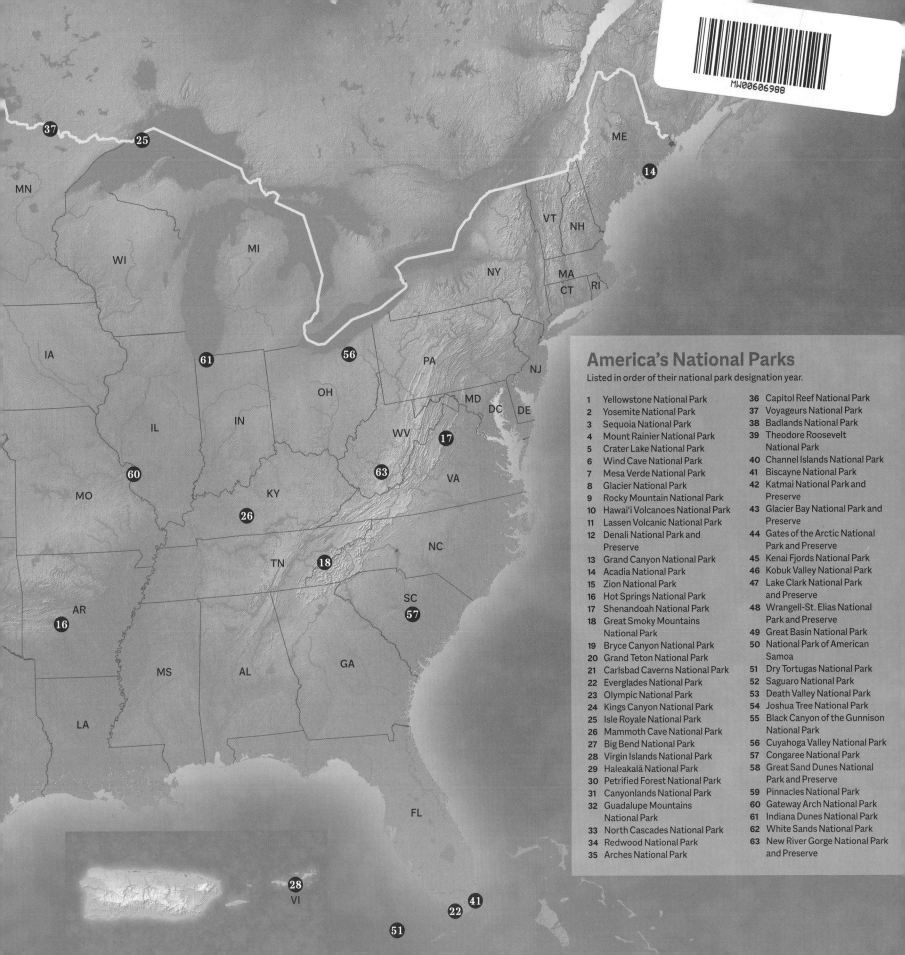

America's National Parks

Listed in order of their national park designation year.

1	Yellowstone National Park	36	Capitol Reef National Park
2	Yosemite National Park	37	Voyageurs National Park
3	Sequoia National Park	38	Badlands National Park
4	Mount Rainier National Park	39	Theodore Roosevelt National Park
5	Crater Lake National Park		
6	Wind Cave National Park	40	Channel Islands National Park
7	Mesa Verde National Park	41	Biscayne National Park
8	Glacier National Park	42	Katmai National Park and Preserve
9	Rocky Mountain National Park		
10	Hawai'i Volcanoes National Park	43	Glacier Bay National Park and Preserve
11	Lassen Volcanic National Park		
12	Denali National Park and Preserve	44	Gates of the Arctic National Park and Preserve
13	Grand Canyon National Park	45	Kenai Fjords National Park
14	Acadia National Park	46	Kobuk Valley National Park
15	Zion National Park	47	Lake Clark National Park and Preserve
16	Hot Springs National Park		
17	Shenandoah National Park	48	Wrangell-St. Elias National Park and Preserve
18	Great Smoky Mountains National Park		
19	Bryce Canyon National Park	49	Great Basin National Park
20	Grand Teton National Park	50	National Park of American Samoa
21	Carlsbad Caverns National Park		
22	Everglades National Park	51	Dry Tortugas National Park
23	Olympic National Park	52	Saguaro National Park
24	Kings Canyon National Park	53	Death Valley National Park
25	Isle Royale National Park	54	Joshua Tree National Park
26	Mammoth Cave National Park	55	Black Canyon of the Gunnison National Park
27	Big Bend National Park		
28	Virgin Islands National Park	56	Cuyahoga Valley National Park
29	Haleakalā National Park	57	Congaree National Park
30	Petrified Forest National Park	58	Great Sand Dunes National Park and Preserve
31	Canyonlands National Park		
32	Guadalupe Mountains National Park	59	Pinnacles National Park
		60	Gateway Arch National Park
33	North Cascades National Park	61	Indiana Dunes National Park
34	Redwood National Park	62	White Sands National Park
35	Arches National Park	63	New River Gorge National Park and Preserve

HIKING AMERICA'S
NATIONAL PARKS

HIKING AMERICA'S
NATIONAL PARKS

KAREN BERGER

Photography by JONATHAN IRISH • Foreword by SALLY JEWELL

RIZZOLI
NEW YORK

New York Paris London Milan

Contents

Foreword

SALLY JEWELL

I was just three years old in 1959 when my family arrived in the United States from England to start our adventure in a new country. My dad came six months before us, and in his early days he asked his colleagues what people did around our new home in Seattle. He was told they camped, hiked, and bought their gear from a little co-op downtown—REI. My earliest memories of family outings are of piling into Dinah, our old green station wagon, to travel into the mountains and camp in our canvas tent—usually in the rain. We were greeted by massive trees, rushing streams, and snow-capped peaks that were awe-inspiring and so foreign from the tidy gardens, hedgerows, canals, and estuaries of our homeland.

As our family adjusted to the culture and natural beauty of our new home, we embraced the spirit of American adventure and visited many national parks in Dinah and her often unreliable successors. We camped at Mount Rainier, Olympic, Crater Lake, and later national parks farther afield, such as Death Valley and Haleakalā, where our father's naivete with hot conditions and steep scree slopes provided fodder for great stories. Hiking was adventuring, and we roamed far and wide, or at least it felt that way when we were young.

In the one summer I didn't work during my college years—1977—I put 15,000 miles on my Fiat 128 by traveling between national parks and public lands from Seattle to Miami and up the East Coast to Acadia National Park. While in Maine, I enjoyed a rainy night in my tent eating lobster with Warren, my now-husband of 44 years, who had joined me for the final few weeks of my trip. Immersing myself in America's diverse landscapes, cultures, and history was a privilege that fueled my soul and nurtured a deep appreciation for the importance of protecting the treasures that are owned by all of us, not to mention providing a nice break before the decades of work to follow. When leaving Washington,

Bumpass Hell Trail,
Lassen Volcanic National
Park, California

DC, in 2017, to return to Seattle, Warren and I took a long, slow drive home, visiting public lands, wildlife refuges, and national parks, taking the less-traveled trails that I encourage you to discover, and appreciating our nation's diversity in so many dimensions.

As our country has grown, national parks and public lands have become more critical than ever to preserve and experience thoughtfully. This was so vividly evident as people sought breathing space in nature after being housebound by the COVID-19 pandemic. It was also clear that these places were not enjoyed equally, as many of our citizens lack the exposure and opportunity to feel comfortable and welcome in national parks and public lands. We all can play a role in inviting those who have not been privileged to experience our nation's extraordinary natural gifts to join us on an adventure. It might just change their lives.

During my time as secretary of the interior, we worked across the government to create the "Every Kid in a Park" pass, later codified into law by Congress as the "Every Kid Outdoors" pass, a rite of passage providing every fourth grader in the country free access to take their family and friends into national parks and other federal public lands for a year. Some of my most memorable experiences were witnessing the wonder of fourth graders from the Central Valley of California visit Channel Islands National Park to see the endangered island fox they had been studying in school, brought back from the brink of extinction through conservation efforts. And watching the youngsters from the Tohono O'odham Nation in Arizona hike up a trail in Saguaro National Park, where the park ranger stepped aside and their elder sang and spoke of their ancestors' signals in the rock petroglyphs. We worked with many youth conservation groups around the country to support their efforts to improve trails and visitor access, while also giving young people a connection to these

special places that will never leave them. I met youths who had turned their lives around by building their emotional and physical strength and finding meaning in their hard work, which benefits the rest of us. Please thank them when you meet them along a trail.

My four years as a public servant were challenging and rewarding. I enjoyed my time spent protecting and stewarding our nation's public lands, national parks, and wildlife for generations to come, while building trusting relationships and deep respect for those who have lived in harmony with these lands since time immemorial—American Indians, Alaska Natives, and Native Hawaiians. Our partnerships with tribal nations, private landowners, nonprofit organizations, scientists, businesses, communities, and citizens to understand our landscapes, protect adjacent lands to preserve ecosystem health and wildlife migration, and incorporate Indigenous wisdom were rich with commitment and enabled greater understanding of where and how to protect these places as our climate changes and the pressures of human development continue. When the job was daunting, I found solace in nature—walking or biking the C&O Canal to Great Falls, or hiking in Shenandoah, where the trees were green at the bottom, vividly colorful in the middle, and bare at the top before winter fully embraced the landscapes.

In this chapter of my life, introducing people to nature—especially taking my youngest grandchild on adventures, earning his Junior Ranger badges, and seeing his curiosity thrive—fills my heart and increases my resolve to champion access to nature for everyone.

As you read the experienced and engaging words of author Karen Berger and absorb Jonathan Irish's inspiring images of our national parks in the pages of this beautiful book, I hope you envision many more adventures for yourself in these special places. I also hope you visit them with respect and reverence, consider inviting a youngster or newcomer to share in their legacy, and help protect our nation's extraordinary bounty—the national parks—for generations to come.

Mother grizzly bear and two cubs,
Lake Clark National Park and Preserve, Alaska

Introduction

KAREN BERGER

"National parks are the best idea we ever had," writer Wallace Stegner famously said. "Absolutely American, absolutely democratic, they reflect us at our best rather than our worst."

That description has resonated for generations, not only because of the "best idea" bit, but also because of how Stegner articulated what the parks say about, and mean to, Americans. Whether we visit the parks or don't, whether we live right next door or hundreds of miles away, we have a feeling of connection, of ownership, of pride.

National pride was front and center at the first national parks I ever visited. Like many East Coast kids, my first national parks were not the behemoth western icons of Yellowstone and Yosemite, but rather New York City's Statue of Liberty National Monument and Philadelphia's Independence National Historical Park. Family trips helped me develop an interest in the outdoors as we explored nearby national park units: the Delaware Water Gap (a national recreation area on the Pennsylvania–New Jersey border), Assateague Island (a national seashore), Cape Cod (another national seashore), and the Appalachian Trail (a national scenic trail that can be considered the longest, skinniest continuous unit in the national park system). But it wasn't until I was an adult and could travel independently that I finally got to the big-ticket marquee parks: Shenandoah, Rocky Mountain, Kings Canyon, Sequoia, Yosemite, Yellowstone, Grand Canyon, Glacier, Mount Rainier, Great Smoky Mountains, Zion, Bryce Canyon, Crater Lake, and many more of the icons that are the most famous units in the system.

Each park was unique and exceptional, but as I accumulated more and more experiences, and more and more miles of hiking on national park trails, what struck me was a sort of cumulative effect: the staggering scope of a national park system that encompasses

every cliché in the great American songbook—sea to shining sea, purple mountains, fields of grain, mountains to prairies, oceans white with foam. America's seascapes and waterways include two oceans, the Gulf of Mexico, the Great Lakes, and countless rivers; its mountains range from Alaska's arctic monoliths to Hawai'i's volcanoes to ranges that are rocky, Cascadian, coastal, ancient, or still smoking from yesterday's—or this morning's—eruptions. We have sand dunes and prairies and caves and tropical forests; we have a 60-mile-wide river and a canyon that could hide the entire island of Manhattan. We have coral reefs and deserts and sculpted rock arches and buttes and towers. And we have evidence of 10,000 or more years of human settlement—and now, under the park system, protection that will reach indefinitely into the future. This land is your land, our land, everyone's land.

Our parks also belong to the world. Many of them represent critical ecosystems and habitats and are recognized as UNESCO world biosphere reserves and world heritage sites, IDA international dark sky parks, or Audubon important bird areas. Millions of visitors from all over the world come to camp, hike, paddle, climb, ski, bike, and auto tour in the parks each year. They take home their photographs and memories—and also inspiration. Since Yellowstone was established a century and a half ago as the first large-scale wilderness preserved in the public interest, the idea and ideals of the American parks have spread around the globe.

In the United States, the idea has also spread, and in the process, it has morphed and expanded. The park system began with the great wild, western parks—icons such as Yosemite, Sequoia, Mount Rainier, Glacier, and Crater Lake. But almost immediately, the definition of a national park became broader. Wind Cave took the park system underground to one of the longest and most complex cave systems in the

Trail through redwood trees, Redwood National Park, California

world. Mesa Verde, one of the premier examples of the ancient cliff dwellings that long predated European American settlement, entered the park system for its historic values. Later, Acadia brought national parks to the East Coast. And Everglades became the first national park to be established primarily to protect its ecological value.

Support for the parks came from a wide coalition of unlikely bedfellows with vastly different motivations. The activism of preservationists such as John Muir, the advocacy of organizations such as the Sierra Club, the commercial interests of railroads seeking to entice paying passengers, and the calculated actions of politicians all had a role in establishing the parks as Americans, now settled from coast to coast, began to understand the vast resources of the land they had claimed. In 1906, Congress passed the Antiquities Act, which gave the president the authority to establish national monuments on federal lands containing historic and prehistoric landmarks and structures, as well as other objects of historic or scientific interest. Theodore Roosevelt wasted no time. In 1906, he established Devils Tower as the first national monument, and followed up with another 17 national monuments, some of which later became national parks.

After the National Park Service was established in 1916, the system continued to expand, finally including—in addition to national parks and monuments—national seashores, national lakeshores, national rivers, national battlefields, national historic sites, national wildlife preserves, national reserves, national parkways, national military parks, national trails, and more. But the crown jewels in the system are the 63 units known simply as the national parks. Many of these units entered the national park system as full-fledged national parks; others were originally established in other categories, such as national monuments, recreational areas, or lakeshores, and then upgraded to national park status. This book introduces the parks in the order they were designated as national parks by Congress, regardless of when they first entered the system or were officially opened to the public. (Parks designated on the same date are ordered according to whether and when they were previously in the national park system in other categories, or alphabetically.)

Upon first glance, we may be hard-pressed to see what these 63 national parks have in common. Gates of the Arctic in Alaska and Gateway Arch in Missouri? One sprawls over more than eight million acres north of the Arctic Circle, the other barely takes up 91 acres in a major metropolitan city. What could Florida's wet and waterlogged Everglades have in common with California's desiccated Death Valley? Or Alaska's huge and wild Denali and Ohio's urban Cuyahoga Valley? The list goes on: Grand Canyon, American Samoa, Dry Tortugas, Badlands, Petrified Forest, White Sands, and Hawai'i Volcanoes. As we scan down a list of national parks, we see more differences than similarities.

But as different as all the national parks are, they do have something in common: their status as park royalty, which each park has earned because it occupies a place in our culture, ecology, history, geology, or geography that is unique and superlative. It's not enough to be a canyon, or a cave, or a mountain, or a nice place to relax on a Sunday afternoon. To be a national park means the place must be outstanding and important. There is nowhere like Yosemite Valley except Yosemite Valley. The simmering cauldrons of Yellowstone are different than those of Lassen are different than those of Hawai'i Volcanoes. There is no other canyon like the Grand, and when we compare it to the Black Canyon of the Gunnison—also a national park—we see two canyons that are as different as day and night, light and dark.

In many ways, the national park system was the product of a philosophical movement that evolved in the late 1800s and early 1900s as industrialization and urbanization cast their smoky pall over what had only a generation or two earlier been wild open spaces. Benton MacKaye, the conservationist who first proposed the Appalachian Trail (which runs through Shenandoah and Great Smoky Mountains National Parks), envisioned a trail that would connect the Appalachian Mountains to "serve as the breath of a real life for the toilers in the bee-hive cities along the Atlantic seaboard and beyond." It was almost as if he could look ahead 100 years to the COVID-19 pandemic and the explosion of interest in outdoor recreation as residents of those "bee-hive cities" sought escape from the cabin fever that set in as quarantine dragged on week after week.

Soaptree yucca, White Sands National Park, New Mexico

FOLLOWING SPREAD: Trail through Paradise Valley, Mount Rainier National Park, Washington

MacKaye's words—"We need the big sweep of sea or hills for our jaded nerves"—are as fresh as today's headlines. We indeed did find respite in the wild places, courtesy of the framework put in place by the early conservationists—John Muir, Benton MacKaye, Stephen Mather, Theodore Roosevelt, and many others. In first a stream, then a flood, Americans rediscovered the national parks and trails and wildernesses. National parks became our new safe spaces, among the few places where we could escape isolation and even despair. Trails became the conduits from which we could experience the parks up close and personal. Visitors who had never hiked before discovered that there was a whole world beyond the pavement. We learned that we could see the Grand Canyon from the rim, or we could descend into its depths and experience its steepness, its heat, its aridity, and its changing vistas for ourselves. We could watch Old Faithful from its boardwalk, or we could walk into the backcountry of Yellowstone and come upon a geyser with no guardrails or signs or schedules. Trails allowed us to touch the land—to feel it, hear it, smell it—and to walk away from the jangled, jagged nerves of an era recently fractured by political extremes and an invisible submicroscopic virus.

And that is what this book is about. Jonathan Irish has visited and photographed all 63 national parks. I have logged thousands of miles on national park hiking trails. Together, we take you away from the pavement and onto trails that lead to a whole new world. In a system made up of some of the greatest geographical, geological, and ecological wonders on the planet, we describe the even greater wonders available to visitors who are willing to walk beyond the next bend and over the next rise to the next viewpoint.

The first section of each chapter answers this question: What is it about this location that earned it a place in the exalted company of American national parks? I didn't attempt to cover the same information for each park, which would have turned the book into a boring litany with most of its word count devoted to lists of which park is on which list: world heritage sites, world biosphere reserves, important bird areas, and on and on. All of the national parks are unique and spectacular and have been recognized as such. Instead, I looked for each park's central feature: sometimes it was its

geography, sometimes its ecosystem, sometimes its history. Some parks are known for being home to a particular plant or animal species; others have well-known landmarks like mountains, caves, canyons, or glaciers; still others contain important historic sites, some with artifacts dating back hundreds or even thousands of years. And often, what makes a park special is its particular combination of those features—and many others. Pictures are worth a thousand words, and Jonathan's photographs will tell you a great deal more about each park's core reason for being.

Each chapter also contains information about trails that will take visitors to places where they can experience the superlatives of each park up close and personal. In many cases, I've drawn from my own experience, but no one person can hike every mile in every national park (though having said that, I'm sure someone will try someday). I've also depended on recommendations from fellow hikers, from the National Park Service, and from guidebook writers whose work I know and respect. Hikes range from half-mile nature walks on accessible boardwalks to strenuous full-day hikes to multiday backpacks. But these suggestions are only the tip of the iceberg, chosen to showcase the variety of experiences that are possible for people with vastly different interests: long trails and short trails, hard trails and easy trails, and trails to mountains, canyons, waterfalls, wildlife meadows, forests, wild-flowers, deserts, glaciers, volcanoes, beaches—the list goes on. The more you hike, the more favorite trails you will collect.

Each park is very different, so each chapter is very different—and so will be your experiences as you begin to visit the parks yourself. What you learn while visiting one park may not apply to the next park you go to. The trail systems in the national parks range from practically nonexistent (a handful of paved walking paths in St. Louis's Gateway Arch) to enormous (1,000 miles of trails in Yellowstone). Most of the parks fall somewhere in between. A few have limited trails, best for casual day hikers. Some don't allow backpacking at all. A handful of parks (such as Everglades, Dry Tortugas, and much of American Samoa, Virgin Islands, and Biscayne) offer far more water-based activities than hiking trails. The Alaska parks are mostly trailless, but cross-country

travel and backpacking are allowed. (Hard-core wilderness skills, or a guide, are required.) As different as they are, all the parks offer at least some opportunity (and more often, lots of opportunities) to experience the natural environment. As a general rule, the areas around park visitor centers and campgrounds have networks of trails that make for excellent day hiking and allow hikers to create interlocking hikes of various lengths.

A few practicalities are important to note. This is not a guidebook. Its intent is to inspire readers to decide which features of which national parks intrigue them, and to give trail suggestions that will be appropriate for a range of visitors, from first-time hikers to experienced adventurers. Each national park has an official website containing updated information on conditions, seasons, permit regulations, activities, park highlights, and trail recommendations. Use this book as a starting point, but check guidebooks for more details and visit the park websites, especially for permits and online reservations.

Trails vary greatly from park to park. In some parks, hikers may see nothing more terrifying than a mosquito. In others, it is possible to encounter grizzly bears, alligators, mountain lions, and wolves (though ticks and giardia lamblia—the invisible parasite that lives in some backcountry water—usually do far more harm). Other hazards can include weather, terrain challenges, ice and snow, stream and river crossings, rockfall, cliffs, and other natural hazards. Western parks are also subject to wildfires. Some of these issues are seasonal, so check park websites for current conditions.

Some parks have trails marked so well that following them is simply a matter of staying awake and paying a modicum of attention. But trails have a sneaky habit of changing character as they meander away from roads and parked cars. The farther afield one travels, the more essential it is to have paper maps and compasses, as well as the skills to use them. In many national parks, there is no cell phone service, which means that if you are depending on your smartphone for a map or to make a call for help, you could be out of luck. Even in parks where cell service is available, it may not be available everywhere—and dead batteries or a phone dropped in a river also render GPS apps useless.

The American love affair with national parks has been ongoing—the question of whether we are loving

Hole-in-the-Wall, Olympic National Park, Washington

FOLLOWING SPREAD: Towers of the Virgin, Zion National Park, Utah

our parks to death is at least several generations old. Many parks have long-standing permit quotas, timed entry systems, lotteries, and other policies in place to manage visitors and their impact on the land and one another. Permits are typically required for backcountry camping in national parks. For some popular trails, permits are doled out by lottery and can be difficult to get. Having flexibility regarding your intended hiking itineraries may save some frustration as you navigate the permit systems. If you are hiking a popular trail in a popular park (such as the John Muir Trail in the High Sierra parks, the Wonderland Trail in Mount Rainier National Park, or the down-and-up overnight to Bright Angel Campground in the Grand Canyon), check the park website to learn about the permit process for that trail. In addition, each park has its own regulations regarding food storage in the backcountry, as well as rules about whether and where pets are allowed.

Permits are not usually needed for day hiking on national park trails; however, even before the pandemic, some of the best-known trails in popular parks were becoming overcrowded (examples include Zion's Angels Landing and Yosemite's Half Dome Trail). Some of these trails now require permits; permits may also be required for popular tours and activities, such as the synchronous firefly displays in Great Smoky Mountains and Congaree National Parks and some cave tours. In addition, the combination of COVID-19 safety protocols and overcrowding has led to new policies as managers try to cope with issues such as facilitating adequate social distancing on park shuttle buses while infection rates vary and visitation numbers continue to climb. Each park's website will give updated information on these policies, which are constantly changing as the pandemic wears on.

It is worth noting that the less visited national parks often have far fewer restrictions and offer a quieter, more remote wilderness experience. It's also axiomatic that the farther you walk from a parking area, the more alone you are. Trails truly are the entryway to the heart of the wilderness. Seeking the road less traveled in the national parks can pay huge dividends for those seeking to connect with nature and escape the madding crowds.

Leave No Trace is a governing principle for back-country use, with basic tenets such as packing out all garbage, camping in areas that won't be damaged by the impact, and staying on marked trails (where they are available). In some parks, ecosystems are especially fragile and require special policies to minimize impact. But even a robust ecosystem can be damaged by overuse. Each park's website has information on its unique issues: how to hike across fragile desert soil crusts (which serve an ecological purpose, but regenerate slowly when broken), how to take precautions when touring caves to avoid bringing in plant and animal material from outside (which can affect the delicate ecosystem and infect bat populations), or how far to camp away from water (to avoid polluting it).

On a practical note, mileage numbers (for trails) and elevation numbers (for mountain summits) can be inconsistent from guidebook to guidebook, map to map, and website to website. Often this is because measurement methods have changed over time. So, for example, if you do a web search to learn the height of the summit of Mount Whitney (the highest peak in the contiguous states), your search will turn up a host of different answers: 14,494 feet, 14,501 feet, 14,505 feet, 14,508 feet—and more. I've tried to include the most recent numbers from the most reliable sources, usually the National Park Service or the United States Geological Survey. Trail mileages are similarly variable; sometimes the reason is that the hike can start or end at a different trailhead, or can follow a different spur, side trail, or loop. Sometimes relocations have changed the trail's routing, and hence, its mileage. Sometimes guidebook writers are unclear about whether the mileage they list is for the whole out-and-back hike or one way. I have specified one-way or round-trip mileage when giving distances, but this book is intended to be used for inspiration, not detailed planning. Always double check your maps for specific information about the trailheads and trails you are using.

Finally, and above all, these are your parks. Get some comfortable rugged hiking shoes, take lots of water, check in at the visitor center or ranger station for the most current information, then get out there and have fun in the best playgrounds on the planet.

PREVIOUS SPREAD: Island of Olosega, National Park of American Samoa, American Samoa

View of Teton Mountains from Schwabacher Landing, Grand Teton National Park, Wyoming

FOLLOWING SPREAD: Backpacker on Kennicott Glacier, Wrangell-St. Elias National Park, Alaska

PAGES 28-29: Big Bend National Park, Texas

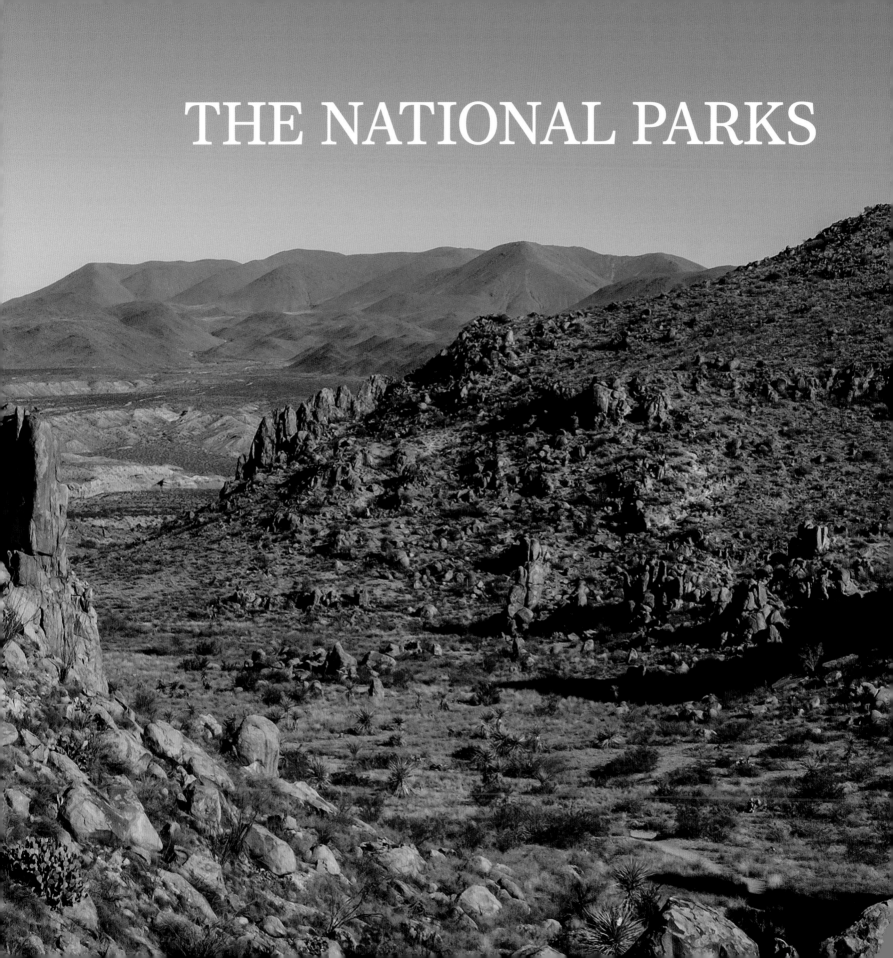

THE NATIONAL PARKS

Yellowstone National Park

IDAHO, MONTANA,
AND WYOMING

_____

Designated 1872

Thumb Geyser, with West
Thumb of Yellowstone Lake
in the background

You know what it looks like, of course. Even if you've never been there, in your mind's eye you can see Old Faithful gushing like clockwork. You can picture the terraces layered like wedding cakes at Mammoth Hot Springs, and the stinking, steaming mud pots and vents that hiss and burble, giving evidence of the continuing geothermal turmoil rumbling just beneath your feet. You might imagine the brilliantly colored circles—turquoise, cobalt, and sulfur yellow—that surround the simmering hot springs and fumaroles. Or perhaps your image of Yellowstone National Park takes a broader view of a vast plateau surrounded by mountain peaks that frame valleys where America's largest herd of bison chomp on the grasses, while elk, deer, and moose might wander about, and predators—grizzly bears, mountain lions, and wolves—lurk at the edges.

Indigenous peoples have inhabited, hunted, and lived in the Yellowstone region for some 10,000 years; its wonders were not news to them. But imagine what it must have been like for the earliest European American explorers to arrive here in the 1800s. Nothing could have prepared them for the earth rumbling as though hell were just beneath the surface, for geysers that shot into the air without warning, for the sizzling mud pots without the benefit of guardrails or boardwalks. They returned back east with accounts so improbable and descriptions so ridiculous that they were derided as liars or jokers or maniacs. Once in a while, tall tales eclipsed reality, as when explorer Jim Bridger described a petrified forest—filled with "petrified birds singing petrified songs." But even the unembellished truth—a cliff made of glass, plumes and explosions of steam a hundred feet high—seemed unbelievable. "We don't print fiction," read a rejection letter from staid *Lippincott's*, a respected journal of the 19th century, forgetting for a moment—or perhaps proving—that truth can be stranger than fiction.

As remarkable as the geology and ecosystem is the fact that the time and distance between European discovery and preservation was a fast, straight line. In the Wild West of exploitation, profiteering, gold rushes, water wars, and railroad land grabs, this was a remarkable anomaly. Yellowstone could have been developed, exploited, or destroyed, but something about its wonders outshone the lure of profit. The very act of preserving Yellowstone had ripples far beyond the northwestern corner of Wyoming; it created the foundation of the American national park system, which has since inspired and protected parks not only around the country but also around the world.

Encompassing some 2.2 million acres, Yellowstone takes up a large corner of northwestern Wyoming and spills into Idaho and Montana. That's about 3,500 square miles, more than the combined area of Delaware and Rhode Island. Admittedly, those are the two smallest American states, but look at it another way: Delaware and Rhode Island have a population of two million people, while Yellowstone has a population of about 700 grizzly bears.

The heart of Yellowstone is an 8,000-foot plateau that sits on what remains of an ancient caldera created by what geologists call a supervolcano. This is one of the most geothermally active regions on the planet, with more than 10,000 thermal features, including the world's greatest concentration of geysers, along with uncountable hot springs, mud pots, and steam vents. The landscape ranges from desertlike sagebrush scrub to lodgepole pine forests, from broad, grassy valleys to riparian habitats of canyons, rivers, and waterfalls, from fields of wildflowers to alpine summits at the 10,000-foot mark and above. Wildlife includes bison, elk, moose, mountain lions, deer, wolves, coyotes, and, most famously, bears. Yellowstone is home to a healthy population of black bears and the largest

number of grizzly bears in the Lower 48. Either kind of bear can become acclimated to humans and their food. To keep both humans and bears safe, hikers and campers should properly store all food, make noise in the backcountry to avoid surprising a bear, hike with others, and carry bear spray.

The main transportation artery in the park is a double-loop road in the shape of a figure eight, which takes visitors to the trailheads, campgrounds, scenic features, and visitor centers. Spurs leave the double loop and fan out to each of the park's five entrances. Many of Yellowstone's most famous scenic icons— Mammoth Hot Springs, Old Faithful, Artist Point, Lamar Valley, and Yellowstone Lake—are easily accessible from the main road loops. Some of the features are right on the roadside; others require short hikes on boardwalks, paved paths, or well-maintained walking trails. From some of these trail networks, other, longer trails veer off, accessing the backcountry for longer day hikes or for multiday trips.

The best way to experience the park is to walk away from your car, whether for half an hour or half a day or half a week or more. Trails lead to canyons, waterfalls, wildlife habitats, and backcountry thermal features. Even a short trail takes hikers into quieter parts of the park, away from guardrails, boardwalks, and crowds. Multiday backpack trips take hikers to remote reaches of the park that are seldom visited by tourists. In winter, cross-country skiing is a way for hardy visitors to experience a completely different aspect of the park.

Exploring the Park

As one of the largest and most popular national parks in the system, Yellowstone has multiple visitor centers and campgrounds. It also has the biggest trail system of all the parks. Yellowstone's fabled front-country attractions are so numerous that many visitors don't make it to the backcountry, which is a mistake. The park's thousand miles of trails lead to backcountry versions of the front-country wonders—geysers, waterfalls, wildlife sightings, and lakes. To explore them would take a lifetime; to describe them in any detail would take a book. To start, check out trail networks near the

major visitor centers, which offer plenty of opportunities to hike to some of the park's key features, as well as to create longer hikes by linking connecting trails and loops.

Old Faithful Visitor Education Center Area

➤ The 4.9-mile **Upper Geyser Basin** and **Old Faithful Observation Point Loop** includes many of Yellowstone's iconic thermal features, including, of course, Old Faithful.

➤ The **Lone Star Geyser Trail** is an easy hike to the largest backcountry geyser in Yellowstone. The trail meanders along the Firehole River through a dense lodgepole pine forest. Time the hike carefully: the Lone Star Geyser erupts for about 45 minutes, but only once every three hours (approximately). The 2.4-mile out-and-back hike means you won't have to share the spectacle with as many people as you do when visiting the features on the front-country boardwalks.

➤ At about 200 feet, **Fairy Falls** is the highest front-country waterfall in Yellowstone. An easy 5.2-mile,

OPPOSITE: Bighorn sheep near Lamar Valley (top left); Grand Prismatic Spring (top right); Midway Geyser Basin (bottom left); black bear in Hayden Valley (bottom right)

ABOVE: Artists' Paintpots

FOLLOWING SPREAD: Grand Canyon of the Yellowstone and Lower Falls of the Yellowstone River

round-trip hike starts at a trailhead about a mile south of Midway Geyser Basin. The trail passes Picture Hill, which is an Instagram-worthy spot for taking photos looking down on Grand Prismatic Spring, one of the most colorful thermal features in the park, and Excelsior Geyser.

Albright Visitor Center Area, near Mammoth Hot Springs

➤ The 1.75-mile **Mammoth Hot Springs Trail** explores the Upper and Lower Terraces, home to about 50 hot springs as well as Liberty Cap, a 37-foot-tall volcanic cone (said to resemble the caps worn during the French Revolution).

➤ Starting from a trailhead just southwest of Mammoth's terraces, the **Bunsen Peak Trail** climbs moderately to views of Yellowstone's Northern Range, the Gallatin Range, Mammoth Hot Springs, and the Yellowstone River Valley. The 4.6-mile round trip is well marked and well maintained.

➤ The 7.4-mile, round-trip trail to **Osprey Falls** starts from the same parking area as the trail to Bunsen Peak, but skirts around the peak and instead follows an old roadbed to a forest. From there, the trail switchbacks steeply down to the river, where Osprey Falls tumbles over the cliffs. Wildlife sightings—especially mountain goats and bighorn sheep—are frequent on this moderately strenuous hike.

➤ An easy 1-mile round-trip hike goes to 79-foot **Wraith Falls**. It starts from a trailhead at the Lava Creek Picnic Area on the Grand Loop Road just east of the Albright Visitor Center area. It leads through sagebrush meadows, marshlands, and conifer forests to the falls.

East Entrance Area

➤ The trailhead for 10,566-foot **Avalanche Peak** is located between the East Entrance at Cody, Wyoming, and the west shore of Yellowstone Lake. Heading north, the 2.1-mile, one-way trail switchbacks steeply up and crosses a scree slope to gain 2,100 feet of elevation. The reward is views of

Yellowstone Lake and some of the region's highest mountains, including the Tetons and the Absaroka Range. En route, the spruce, fir, and whitebark pine forests and meadows are habitat for grizzlies.

Canyon Visitor Education Center Area

➤ A trail to **Mount Washburn** (3.2 miles each way) is a popular day hike that starts from Dunraven Pass near the Canyon Visitor Education Center. The 1,400-foot climb leads to a summit fire tower, where a map identifies the landscape features in each direction. The views include Hayden Valley, several geyser basins, the Grand Canyon of the Yellowstone, the southern edge of the Yellowstone caldera, and, farther away, the Teton mountain range. Features include wildflowers (in July and August) and the possibility of seeing bighorn sheep, elk, and bears.

➤ The 9.6-mile, round-trip **Observation Peak Trail** starts just north of Canyon Village, approximately 1 mile north of the junction and visitor center on the **Cascade Lake Trail**. The flat starting section wanders through meadows filled with wildflowers and sometimes wildlife. The Observation Peak Trail veers off at Cascade Lake and climbs about 1,400 feet to reach the peak.

➤ There are trails on both the north and south rims of the 20-mile-long **Grand Canyon of the Yellowstone**. On the south side, Artist Point is one of the most photographed features in the park. The **Brink of the Lower Falls Trail** (about 0.7 miles round trip) descends steeply on switchbacks all the way into the canyon for a view of the falls.

Northeast Entrance Area

➤ The **Lamar River Trailhead** is located at Soda Butte in the Lamar Valley, about halfway between the East Entrance and the Tower Junction Ranger Station. From either of two trailheads, the 5-mile out-and-back hike crosses Soda Butte Creek on a footbridge to reach a meadow that is often populated by a herd of bison. The goal of this hike, the Lamar River, is a good lunch-and-fishing stop.

➤ The very arduous **Specimen Ridge Trail** also starts at Soda Butte, but it is a 17-mile one-way trail with 3,000 feet of elevation gain to reach a second trailhead located on the road almost all the way to Tower Junction. Hiking westward from the Lamar River trailhead means tackling the steep climb first. Highlights include wildlife along the Lamar River, the climb to 9,600-foot Amethyst Mountain, and views of Lamar Valley and the Grand Canyon of the Yellowstone.

Grant Village Area

➤ This 10.8-mile loop connects the **Lewis River Channel Trail** and the **Dogshead Trail**; the trailhead is about 5 miles south of Grant Village. Starting clockwise (on the Lewis River Channel Trail), follow the flat, forested path to Lewis Lake, the third-largest lake in the park. After leaving the lakeshore, the trail goes to the Lewis River, where there is a chance of seeing bears and bison, then to Shoshone Lake (Yellowstone's second-largest lake). Use the **DeLacy Creek Trail** to connect to the Dogshead Trail and loop back to the starting point.

Backpacking

➤ The **Continental Divide National Scenic Trail** follows the general arc of the divide across the southwestern part of the park. From the south, it enters the park from the Teton Wilderness. Heading north, it follows first the Snake River and then the Heart River to Heart Lake and Shoshone Lake. It leaves the backcountry smack in the middle of the throngs at Upper Geyser Basin and Old Faithful, then turns southwest and west to cross the Madison Plateau before exiting the park in Idaho. The section from the park's southern border to Old Faithful is the most interesting and diverse, with thermal features, lakes, and rivers. The section across the Madison Plateau is a lesson in wildfire and rejuvenation. This part of the park was badly burned in the epic firestorm of 1988, with some sections reaching the point of soil sterility from the heat and duration of the fire. New growth and abundant wildflowers show the process of fire recovery.

Mammoth Hot Springs (top left); bison near Old Faithful (top right); Great Fountain Geyser (bottom left); anglers along Yellowstone River (bottom right)

Yosemite National Park

CALIFORNIA

———

Designated 1890

If ever there was a park with multiple personality disorder, it would be Yosemite National Park. There is the Yosemite Valley front country, an enterprise so large it has hotels, tent cabins, campgrounds, restaurants, stores, a police station—and even a jail. There is Tioga Road, which climbs to Tuolumne Meadows: also front country, with a campground, tent cabins, and a store containing a post office, but no fancy restaurants, no hotel-style accommodations, no jail, and far fewer people. The Hetch Hetchy region, tucked into a quieter part of the park northwest of the valley, reminds us of the vulnerability of great landscapes. The dam that flooded this valley destroyed what John Muir called "one of Nature's rarest and most precious mountain temples." As impressive as the mountains, the enormous forests of the Mariposa Grove include the largest concentration of sequoias in the world. And for hikers, the pinnacle is the backcountry—the sacred mountain spires and cathedrals that Muir and Ansel Adams fought to preserve with their classic words and photographs.

As with Yellowstone, images of Yosemite are ground into our collective mental map of America. Approaching Yosemite Valley can almost feel like a homecoming, even for a first-time visitor, except that—unlike remembering your hometown from childhood—Yosemite seems even bigger in reality than in the imagination. And more brilliant as well: instead of being in the blacks and grays and whites of Adams's timeless portraits, the vertiginous landscape of swirling clouds, enormous skies, and precipitous towers, cliffs, walls, and spires is in full color.

Indigenous trails have crossed Yosemite for generations. When European American expeditions first arrived, the valley was settled by Ahwahnechee people, a subgroup of the Miwok nation that inhabited a swath of north-central California. Not long after

the first European American expeditions, sightseers arrived, followed by businesses that filled the need for lodging, food, trails, and guides to Yosemite's beauty spots. In 1864—eight years before Yellowstone became America's first national park, and 26 years before Yosemite entered the national park system—Congress enacted the Yosemite Grant Act, which set aside Yosemite Valley and Mariposa Grove as protected lands to be managed by the state of California. Interestingly, when Yosemite National Park was established in 1890, its original boundaries did not include those two parcels. They remained under state control until 1906, three years after Muir guided Theodore Roosevelt through the park and made his case for federal protection of the valley and the grove (as well as for the protection of many more of the noteworthy and unique landscapes of the American West).

Yosemite is part of an even larger Californian hodgepodge of national parklands, national forests, and wilderness areas in the High Sierra, including the Sierra, Inyo, and Stanislaus National Forests; Sequoia and Kings Canyon National Parks; Devils Postpile National Monument; and the Hoover, Emigrant, Ansel Adams, and John Muir Wildernesses. It is thus part of one of the largest and most spectacular backcountry mountain landscapes in the United States (except, as usual, for Alaska). Ninety-four percent of Yosemite is managed as wilderness. Elevations range from 2,127 to 13,114 feet, and a rain-shadow effect captures Pacific Ocean–fed rainfall on the western side, but leaves the eastern side drier. These variable conditions have resulted in some of the most diverse ecosystems on earth and ecological edge communities where species that don't usually live in close proximity to each other reside side by side.

The park's 1,187 square miles contain roughly 800 miles of trail. Today's trail system evolved from

View of Yosemite Falls from Yosemite Valley

ancient Indigenous routes, equestrian routes, and 19th-century toll trails built for visitors. Now, as then, the trails include gentle saunters and steep climbs to high mountains, waterfalls, and big trees, but not just any mountains, waterfalls, and big trees. Yosemite's trails include the famed cable-assisted scramble up to Half Dome, the 60 switchbacks that climb to Yosemite Falls (one of the tallest waterfalls on earth), and the forested paths through the giant sequoias of the Mariposa Grove.

Exploring the Park

For car campers and backpackers, it's important to note that generations of black bears have devoted themselves to the intense study of how to access food from hikers and campers. Food-storage protocols are strictly enforced in both backcountry and front-country campsites, where it is not unusual to see hungry bears making the rounds, and where the park's collection of photographs of ruined campsites and torn-apart cars shows exactly what kind of damage a determined and hungry bear can do. Seven-mile-long Yosemite Valley makes up only one percent of the park's land area, but it attracts the majority of its visitors. Walkers and road-trippers flock from one viewpoint to the next, checking off the well-known attractions. A network of trails allows hikers to form an endless combination of loops or out-and-back options.

Yosemite Valley

➤ The **Half Dome Trail** is the most popular in the valley (permits are required). Originally a behemoth ball of rock, the dome was cleanly sliced down the middle; half of it remains, and the rest was cracked into pieces by glaciers and carried away to who knows where. This trail is less a hiking trail and more a cable-assisted rock scramble that is both steep and exposed. It should not be attempted in rain or when lightning is forecast.

➤ On the north wall of the valley, the **Yosemite Falls Trail** is a 7.2-mile round trip to the top of the highest waterfall in the park (and among the tallest in the world). The trail, which gains 2,700 feet of

elevation, was built in the 1870s as a toll trail. It is steep and rocky, and visitors are advised to stay away from the treacherous edges. If you don't want to do the entire trail, consider going to Columbia Rock, a mile from the trailhead, which offers views of Yosemite Valley, Half Dome, and Sentinel Rock.

➤ The trail to **Vernal Fall** and **Nevada Fall** is one of the oldest trails in the park, with a bridge built across the Merced River in the 1860s to enable travelers to hike from the top of Vernal Fall to Nevada Fall. The trail to Vernal Fall is a 2.4-mile round trip with 1,000 feet of elevation gain; the hike to Nevada Fall is a 5.4-mile round trip (with an extra 1,000 feet of climbing). The trail is famous for slippery footing, waterfall spray, and for its 600 stone steps.

➤ The **Four-Mile Trail** on the south wall of the valley climbs 3,200 feet to Glacier Point, with far-flung views of the Sierra Range. The trail is actually closer to 5 miles because of improvements and switchbacks made since the trail was first named—and that's a one-way distance. But the extra distance and switchbacks soften the grade of the 3,200-foot climb.

➤ The paved 1-mile trail to **Mirror Lake** on the eastern side of the valley is popular with families; there's also the chance to tack on an additional 5-mile loop around the lake and **Tenaya Creek**, which feeds it.

➤ The 13-mile **Valley Loop Trail** follows remnants of early trails and wagon roads along the valley floor. A popular starting point is at Lower Yosemite Fall, heading west along the base of El Capitan and Cathedral Rocks.

➤ The northern terminus of the **John Muir Trail** is at Happy Isles in Yosemite Valley.

Tioga Road

➤ Tioga Road bisects the park, connecting its eastern and western slopes; just about in the middle is Tuolumne Meadows, where hikers can join up with the **Pacific Crest National Scenic Trail** and **John Muir Trail**, which split apart here after being contiguous for most of the High Sierra. The Pacific Crest Trail heads north to Sonora Pass; the John

Small river cascading over rocks near El Capitan Bridge (top left); hiker on Four-Mile Trail (top right); small pond along Northside Drive (bottom)

Muir Trail veers off to Yosemite Valley. There are also a number of trailheads along the road, many of which see far fewer hikers than the Tuolumne area. The **May Lake Trailhead** off of Tioga Road is only 1.3 miles from lovely May Lake, making the hike to this scenic area a great one for families. It is also possible to add on a climb of 10,850-foot **Mount Hoffmann** for a 5.4-mile round trip. The **Cathedral Lakes Trail** at Tuolumne Meadows is either a 7- or 8-mile round trip, depending on whether you go to Upper Cathedral Lake, Lower Cathedral Lake, or both. This hike also includes a bit of time on the John Muir and Pacific Crest Trails. Lower Cathedral Lake is the more popular beauty spot, surrounded by 10,000-foot granite peaks, but Upper Cathedral Lake is no slouch, framed by 10,912-foot Cathedral Peak.

Hetch Hetchy Area

➤ The Hetch Hetchy area is far less visited, but its trails give visitors an idea of what the valley might have been like before it was flooded by a dam. Hikes include the 2-mile round trip to **Lookout Point**, from which there is a viewpoint overlooking the flooded valley, and the trail to **Wapama Falls**, which is a moderate 5-mile round trip that includes two other waterfalls en route, plus wildflowers (spring is the best time for this one). The **Poopenaut Valley Trail** offers a short but strenuous 3-mile round trip. Longer hikes include **Rancheria Falls** (13.4 miles) and **Smith Peak** (13.5 miles).

Mariposa Grove and Wawona Areas

➤ Located near each other in the southwestern corner of the park, the Mariposa Grove and Wawona areas have a network of easy day-hiking trails. Most visitors come to this corner of the park to see the Mariposa Grove's giant sequoias (Sequoiadendron giganteum). A network of trails branches out from the arrival area, including the short and easy 0.3-mile wheelchair- and stroller-accessible **Big Trees Loop Trail** that wanders past the Fallen Monarch Tree, with interpretive panels on the life and ecology of giant sequoias. The Wawona area also offers popular hikes such as the 3.5-mile **Wawona Meadow Loop** known for its wildflowers, the 4.8-mile **Swinging Bridge Loop**, the strenuous 8.2-mile **Chilnualna Falls Trail** (which includes 2,400 feet of elevation gain), and the longer and more challenging 12-mile **Alder Creek**.

BELOW: Hiker on Panorama Trail, with Half Dome in the background (left); lupine in Yosemite Valley (right)

OPPOSITE: Hiker on precipice of Taft Point

Sequoia National Park

CALIFORNIA

_____

Designated 1890

There is some confusion about Sequoia National Park, so let's get that out of the way. Sequoia is America's second national park—certified just one week before Yosemite in 1890—but today it is jointly managed with adjacent Kings Canyon National Park, which was added to the park system in 1940. Ninety-eight percent of the two parks are managed as wilderness—900,000 acres of remote High Sierra high country with no roads or towns, accessible by about 1,000 miles of trails. This book covers the two parks separately because of their separate histories, and because their large land area and extensive trail networks give them some of the most interesting wilderness destinations for hikers in the 48 contiguous states.

Sequoia is named after its eponymous trees, which are the largest organisms on earth—although that depends on how you define "organism." Another contender for the title includes *Armillaria ostoyae*, a giant fungus in Oregon's Blue Mountains, which sprawls over and under the surface of 2,384 acres of soil and is estimated to possibly weigh as much as 35,000 tons. In the world of trees, there is another contestant as well: a male (yes, they have genders) quaking aspen (*Populus tremuloides*) named Pando that grew from a single seed to become a 106-acre grove of 47,000 genetically identical trees, connected via a root network and estimated to weigh 6,000 tons. Regardless of which organism eventually gets the title—or even if a new one is someday discovered—there is no getting around the impact of *Sequoiadendron giganteum*, let alone an entire grove of them. The 2,200- to 2,700-year-old General Sherman Tree stands 275 feet tall, has a 102-foot circumference, and contains an estimated 630,000 board feet of lumber that weighs 1,350 tons. The fungi and aspen might weigh more, and they might take up more space, but in terms of making an impression, they don't stand a chance.

The giant sequoia is distinct from the related but different coast redwood, *Sequoia sempervirens*, which has its own national park. While redwoods grow lower down and nearer the ocean, giant sequoias grow naturally only here on the western slopes of the Sierra Nevada, at elevations between 5,000 and 7,000 feet. Their lumber is noted for being brittle; nonetheless, their sheer size made them an attractive resource to exploit, and during the 19th-century Wild West land grabs for gold mines, homesteading, and logging camps, the giant sequoia was threatened by logging.

Sequoia National Park—along with the Mariposa Grove (which would later be added to Yosemite National Park) and General Grant National Park (which was later expanded and renamed to become Kings Canyon National Park)—was formed to protect the trees from logging, fires, and visitor abuse, such as carving tunnels and graffiti into the trunks of living trees. Later, the National Park Service expanded its preservation efforts beyond maintaining charismatic representatives of impressive species; the focus today is on protecting all aspects of entire ecosystems, including the role of wildfire in rejuvenating the ecosystem and returning nutrients to the soil.

If the park were simply about the trees, it would be impressive enough, but Sequoia National Park has a landscape as striking as its giant forests. Indeed, the park's eastern slope includes Mount Whitney, which, at 14,500 feet (give or take; official measurements dating from the early 1900s to the present have ranged from 14,492 to 14,508 feet), is the highest peak in the contiguous United States. The surrounding mountains and high passes include some of the most spectacular alpine scenery in the world, famous from the photography of Ansel Adams and the writings of John Muir. But the only way to see most of this park's high country is on foot.

Trail through Giant Forest

FOLLOWING SPREAD: Tharp's Log (top left); hikers along Big Trees Trail (middle left); Tunnel Rock (bottom left); Crescent Creek through Crescent Meadow (right)

Exploring the Park

Hiking and exploring Sequoia National Park is about trees, mountains, cascades, and, above all, wilderness. A few of the park's famous features are accessible to day hikers and visitors who don't wander far from their cars, but the majority of the park is best enjoyed via its hundreds of miles of backcountry trails. The most extensive network of day-hiking trails is found between the Giant Forest Museum and the Lodgepole Visitor Center on the park's western side.

➤ In the Giant Forest, several easy trails lead to the General Sherman Tree. The paved 2-mile **Congress Trail** is a popular, easy hike that takes one to two hours and is wheelchair accessible. The shorter 1-mile **Main Trail** is also paved, but has more elevation and some stairs. Other short trails in the Giant Forest area are the accessible, paved **Big Trees Trail** (less than a mile around Round Meadow), with its interpretive signs about sequoia ecology; the 0.5-mile, out-and-back **Moro Rock Trail**, which climbs 300 feet to the top of a granite dome to give a view of the Great Western Divide; and the 3.4-mile, round-trip trail to **Tokopah Falls**, which starts just past the Marble Fork Bridge in Lodgepole Campground and follows the Marble Fork of the Kaweah River to granite cliffs and a 1,200-foot waterfall in Tokopah Canyon.

➤ Longer day hikes include the trail to **Mist Falls** (8 miles round trip, including a varied series of ecosystems: forest and chaparral, along with creeks with rapids, cascades, and the falls themselves). The **Alta Peak Trail** is perhaps best for serious hikers who can manage the mileage (14 miles out and back) and elevation (the summit of Alta Peak is 11,204 feet). The trail offers views of the Great Western Divide, which splits the park's eastern and western sides.

➤ Two of the most spectacular backpacking trails in the park are a segment of the **John Muir Trail** (which is mostly contiguous with the **Pacific Crest National Scenic Trail**) and the **High Sierra Trail**. The southern terminus of the John Muir Trail is on the summit of Mount Whitney. From there, it descends the west side of the mountain and heads north. At 13,153-foot Forester Pass (the highest point on the Pacific Crest Trail), the trail leaves Sequoia National Park and enters Kings Canyon National Park. The trail then continues north through the Sierra to Yosemite Valley. The John Muir Trail is one of the most iconic backpacking trips in the world; permits are required and can be hard to get. The summit of Mount Whitney can be reached via a day hike from the eastern side; permits are also required for this strenuous climb, and they are in high demand as well. The equally spectacular but far less traveled High Sierra Trail was built as a thoroughfare for rangers in order to connect the park's eastern and western sides when the park was expanded in 1928. Its western terminus is in the Giant Forest. Heading east, it crosses the Kaweah Divide to join the John Muir Trail and climb Mount Whitney, then exits the park via the Whitney Portal Trail. One popular shorter overnight trip is to do an out-and-back hike from the High Sierra Trail's western terminus to Bearpaw Meadow, a popular camping area.

OPPOSITE: Hiker among giant sequoias

BELOW: Moro Rock Trail

Mount Rainier
National Park

WASHINGTON

———

Designated 1899

It is the most distinctive natural feature in the Pacific Northwest. For 100 miles in any direction, 14,411-foot Mount Rainier towers over the landscape, as out of scale as Godzilla at a children's party.

The mountain's name is a matter of debate. In 1792, British Captain George Vancouver named the mountain after his "great friend Rainier." Then a rear admiral in the British Navy, Rainier had never seen the mountain, and to add insult to injury, he also fought for England during the American Revolution. The Indigenous peoples of the region have other names for the mountain, most of which reference the mountain's snow, water, and height. The Puyallup and other nations around Puget Sound called it Tacoma (pronounced "Taquoma"), while most nations near Yakama called the mountain Tahoma. Today, there is a move to restore one of the original names to the mountain (and hence, the park), but the process is long, requiring not only agreement among Indigenous peoples, but also approval by the U.S. Board on Geographical Names and—quite literally—an act of Congress.

Mount Rainier (the current official name) looks sleepy under its mantle of snow, but it is considered one of the most dangerous volcanoes in the world. A mere 500,000 years old, it's a baby by the measure of mountains, but like a toddler with tantrums, it has erupted thousands of times since it was formed. The last eruption was in 1894—yesterday, in geological terms. According to the U.S. Geological Survey, it earns its "most dangerous" status because of its height (it is the second-highest peak in the contiguous United States), frequent earthquakes, active hydrothermal system, and extensive glaciers, and also because its path of debris from previous eruptions (which predicts how the debris might flow in the future) lies in areas that are now densely populated.

View of Mount Rainier
from Reflection Lake

A northern location and proximity to the Pacific Ocean give Mount Rainier an entirely different character than California's Mount Whitney. Whitney, the highest peak in the contiguous states, is far to the south but about 100 feet taller. Where Whitney is a high, dry, alpine desert, Rainier is covered by 26 glaciers, with steep volcanic ridges, deep ravines, and an annual snowmelt that creates impressive waterfalls. Like the mountains of the Sierra, Mount Rainier also boasts enormous ecological diversity, courtesy of elevations that rise from a low point of 1,600 feet to the 14,411-foot summit. Natural wonders range from massive (old-growth forests of enormous Douglas fir, western red cedar, and western hemlock) to miniscule (stunning wildflowers that bloom with wild abandon in the alpine meadows as they try to cram their entire reproductive cycle into the short, snow-free summer).

Soon after settlers arrived in the Pacific Northwest, the old-growth forests attracted the interest of timber companies, and cleared land was turned over for farming. An unlikely coalition of interests lobbied for the protection of the national park: the Sierra Club wanted to conserve it, the National Geographic Society wanted to study the volcanoes, and railroad companies wanted an attraction that people would travel to via train. Today, the park is essentially a big box around the peak.

Exploring the Park

With the exception of its roads and visitor services areas, Mount Rainier National Park is mostly managed as wilderness, with about 360 miles of hiking trails. Large networks of trails and loops are found near all the visitor centers, enabling day hikers to combine trails to create itineraries of various lengths, difficulties, and features.

➢ The 93-mile **Wonderland Trail** circumambulates the mountain and is a bucket-list adventure for many hikers, but it's not an easy undertaking. The available permits can't meet the demand, so most of them are doled out by lottery, with a few reserved for walk-ins (first come, first served). But the real difficulty is the 22,000 feet of elevation gain (and loss) as hikers ascend and descend the many ridges that radiate down from the summit. Hiking itineraries range from seven to 14 days, with about 10 days being average for backpackers who can manage more than 2,000 feet of elevation gain (and loss) every day. Stream and river crossings are also a challenge, especially during and just after snowmelt. Day-hiking sections of the Wonderland Trail can be accessed from multiple trailheads along park roads; the trailheads are marked on the National Park Service's online map. In addition, the Wonderland Trail passes close to the major visitor centers.

➢ A portion of the **Pacific Crest National Scenic Trail** wanders back and forth over the eastern boundary of the park, from Chinook Pass in the north to Laughingwater Creek in the south.

➢ Paradise, on the mountain's southern slope, is the most visited area of the park; Longmire is just a few miles away to the southwest. Both are renowned for their wildflower meadows and views. At Paradise, the trail names tell visitors what to expect: **Avalanche Lily**, **Waterfall**, **Moraine**, **Skyline**, and **High Lakes**. At Longmire, it's possible to combine the **Trail of the Shadows**, the **Rampart Ridge Trail**, and a section of the **Wonderland Trail** to form a 5-mile loop. It's also possible to hike from Longmire to Paradise via 6 miles on the Wonderland Trail.

➢ At 6,400 feet, Sunrise is the highest point in the park reachable by road and the park's highest visitor center. Sunrise Point features nearly 360-degree views of glaciers, the summit, Mount Adams to the south, alpine meadows, and lakes. The easy 2-mile, round-trip **Silver Forest Trail** leads to a spectacular view of the Emmons Glacier, the largest in the contiguous United States.

➢ The **Mowich Lake** area in Rainier's northwest corner is a quiet area of the park, accessible via a mostly unpaved and often rough road. There are numerous opportunities for hikes of varying lengths around the park's largest and deepest lake, with views of glaciers, wildflower meadows, and both old-growth forest and temperate rain forest.

Myrtle Falls (top left); hikers on trail down from Panorama Point (top right); alpine lake in Paradise Valley (bottom left); Christine Falls (bottom right)

The trails in the Ohanapecosh area are best known for wildlife, waterfalls, and old-growth forests. A highlight is the 1.5-mile **Grove of the Patriarchs Trail**, where 1,000-year-old trees in the old-growth forests reach heights of 300 feet or more.

Finally, **Mount Rainier** is a climb, not a hike. Because of its glaciers and northern latitude, the mountain requires ropes, ice axes, crampons, and the skills to use them. Professional guide services are available, where would-be climbers with no experience can learn the basics of rope handling, self-arrest, and rest stepping before being guided to the top. John Muir climbed Mount Rainier in 1888, and reported that although he enjoyed the view, he thought the mountain was better appreciated from below.

BELOW: Fallen tree along Grove of the Patriarchs Trail

OPPOSITE: Hiker on Sourdough Ridge Trail

Crater Lake
National Park

Designated 1902

It's never a good thing when a rejected lover also happens to be a god. Legends of the local Klamath and Umpqua people vary in the details, but each relate a saga of Llao—a god who lived below the world, inside what we have retroactively named Mount Mazama. At 12,000 feet, it was once one of the high peaks of the Cascade Range. About 7,700 years ago, Llao fell in love with the daughter of a local chief. When she rejected his offer to come and live with him in the guts of the mountain, he rained fire and ash and destruction on the local people. In the Umpqua telling, the god Skell got involved in the epic battle, climbing atop Mount Shasta and unleashing its fury to protect the people from Llao. At the end, Llao's anger was spent and he was chased back inside Mount Mazama, which collapsed. The crater that remained filled with rain and became Crater Lake. It is considered a place so holy that many Indigenous people think that even to look upon it is disrespectful, or worse, can cause an early death.

The European Americans who arrived in 1853 had no such inhibitions. The Oregon and California Trails were bringing thousands of people to the West Coast, and a mining party made the first record of the body of water they unimaginatively, but accurately, named the Deep Blue Lake. But early European American reports of the lake were mostly ignored. The area was largely unexplored by European Americans, and while those who did visit returned with compelling descriptions of the sapphire lake, there were no reports of the all-important gold mines. Later explorations in the 1860s were more widely reported, and in 1870, a newspaper article about the lake attracted the interest of a young man from Kansas, who decided he needed to see it for himself. It was 15 years before William Gladstone Steel finally reached Crater Lake, but apparently his experience was worth the wait. He embarked on a lifelong

Wizard Island within
Crater Lake

commitment to preserving the lake and making it, and the region surrounding it, a national park.

Today, the park is a rectangle around the lake, accessible from the south, west, and north. Much of the park is old-growth forest of ponderosa pines, lodgepole pines, western white pines, hemlocks, and Shasta firs; wildlife includes black bears, mountain lions, coyotes, bobcats, foxes, marmots, elk, and deer.

Crater Lake is 1,943 feet deep—the deepest lake in the United States, and the seventh-deepest lake in the world. Poking out of the lake near the western shoreline is Wizard Island, a 763-foot cinder cone created when the volcano collapsed. The lake's brilliant blue waters are some of the clearest in the world, which is even more remarkable because it has no inlet and no outlet. Its rainfall is almost exactly balanced with its evaporation, maintaining a fairly constant level. But the lack of inlets and outlets means that there is

BELOW: Bluebird on a snag along Rim Drive

OPPOSITE: Hillman Peak

no natural way to flush contaminants; whatever is dropped into the lake—a child's sneaker, used toilet paper, an orange peel, a cigarette butt—stays there. Unfortunately, in recent years, especially when the COVID-19 pandemic drove many Americans to the outdoors and the national parks, the threats of contamination to the lake have increased.

Exploring the Park

Crater Lake National Park's 90 miles of trails are split between front-country hikes to various viewpoints and backcountry trails. Rim Drive encircles the lake, offering plenty of day-hiking trailheads and viewpoints.

➤ Of the park's trails, 33 miles are on the **Pacific Crest National Scenic Trail.** However, the trail entirely misses Crater Lake, which is the whole point of the national park. So most hikers actually veer off the official route near Dutton Creek to pick up the **Rim Trail**, which tracks alongside the crater's rim, affording plenty of views, before rejoining the Pacific Crest Trail northwest of the lake.

➤ **Wizard Island** is one of the park's outstanding and unique experiences. To get there requires about a mile-long hike. Visitors descend to the boat launch at Cleetwood Cove, then take a boat shuttle (reserved in advance) to the island, where they can spend about three hours exploring, swimming, or hiking on several trails that can be combined to create hikes of varying lengths. By far the most impressive is the 1-mile, 750-foot climb to the summit, featuring a miniature crater and a 360-degree panoramic view of the lake. The return requires visitors to trek the mile back (climbing, this time) from the boat launch to the parking area.

➤ The park's high point is Mount Scott at 8,929 feet, accessible from a parking area on Rim Drive on the east side of the lake. The **Mount Scott Trail** is a 5-mile round trip with about 1,500 feet of elevation gain (figure a half day or more). Views from the top extend 100 miles south to Mount Shasta in California, and 85 miles north to the Three Sisters. The trail is only accessible in summer—and even then, some parts may still have patches of snow.

Wind Cave National Park

SOUTH DAKOTA

—

Designated 1903

Trail leading into Wind Cave National Park

FOLLOWING SPREAD: Inner cave along main cave trail (left); bison in grasslands above ground (top right); view of rainbow from Elk Mountain Campground (bottom right)

The earliest national parks—Yellowstone, Sequoia (along with General Grant, which later became Kings Canyon), Yosemite, Mount Rainier, and Crater Lake—set a pattern. To begin with, national parks were all about big western mountains filled with peaks, lakes, cascades, and a picture-perfect vista at every turn.

The next one, Wind Cave National Park, broke that pattern. At only 34,000 acres, it was small by western park standards. And it was located in the Black Hills of western South Dakota under a mixed-grass prairie with barely a mountain in sight. Wind Cave is all about what lies beneath the earth.

Established on January 3, 1903, it was the first cave in the world to become a national park. And though Mammoth Cave (established as a national park in 1941) surpasses it in terms of sheer size, Wind Cave has its own claims to fame. It has the densest network of mapped passages of any cave in the world (measured by miles of passage per cubic foot of cave). Its 154.2 miles of explored passages (as of 2021; there may be many more in years to come) make it the seventh-longest explored cave system in the world, and the third-longest cave in the United States, behind Mammoth Cave and Jewel Cave (a national monument, also in South Dakota). It contains 95 percent of the world's so-called boxwork, unusual formations of calcite in a honeycomb pattern that project from cave walls, looking, in the eyes of early explorers, like post office boxes.

Frequent visitors to caves know that the temperature and airflow at a cave's entrance can be dramatically different above and below the surface, especially when the barometric pressure above the surface changes. Wind Cave's small natural entrance, no more than an 18-inch hole in the ground, funnels the air flowing in and out of the cave to equalize the pressure. The resulting sounds—almost as if the cave is inhaling and exhaling as air currents move through the entrance—gave the cave its name.

A prairie ecosystem covers the cave with a soft blanket of grasslands. Located at the edge of the midwestern prairie and the Rocky Mountains, Wind Cave's aboveground ecosystem contains a rich assortment of wildlife common to both: bison, prairie dogs, pronghorn antelope, elk, deer, and black-footed ferrets (one of North America's most endangered mammals).

Exploring the Park

Below ground, visitors can choose among several tours of varying lengths, which lead to the cave's highlight features. Above ground, 30 miles of trails are notable for the prairie landscape and the chance to spot wildlife.

➤ From the shortest (and least arduous) to the longest (and most arduous), the **Garden of Eden**, the **Natural Entrance**, and the **Fairgrounds** underground cave tours last from an hour to an hour and a half.

➤ Specialty tours—such as an accessible tour, a "wild" tour (think crawling around in the mud and scrambling through narrow passages), and a candlelit tour (exploring the caves the old-fashioned way)—are available with advance reservations.

➤ Above ground, the **Rankin Ridge Nature Trail** is a mile-long loop to a lookout tower atop the highest point in the park. The **Prairie Vista Nature Trail** is another easy trail, a mile-long round trip through grasslands, passing the natural entrance to the cave.

➤ Longer trails include the **Lookout Point Trail** to Beaver Creek (2 miles), a section of the **Highland Creek Trail** combined with the **Centennial Trail** (a 4.5-mile loop), and the **Highland Creek Trail** itself (an almost 9-mile round trip).

Mesa Verde
National Park

COLORADO

————

Designated 1906

It was Wind Cave that introduced the underground to the national park system; Mesa Verde, the seventh national park, broke the mold again. The previous parks had caught the American imagination with unique geological and ecological features, from the geysers of Yellowstone to the giant sequoias of the western Sierra Nevada. In contrast, Mesa Verde (the name means "green table" in Spanish) was the first national park to celebrate the human history and archaeological values of a landscape. It was added to the system to "preserve the work of man," in the words of Theodore Roosevelt.

The "green table" was the home of Ancestral Puebloans, who inhabited Mesa Verde and the surrounding region for more than 700 years, from approximately AD 550 to AD 1300. The park houses more than 4,700 archaeological sites, including 600 cliff dwellings and the remains and ruins of other structures that supported an ancient culture of settled peoples who farmed and hunted in the dry tablelands of what is now southern Colorado.

The cliff dwellings are the best-known feature at Mesa Verde—entire apartment-like complexes built into rock alcoves, which are themselves overhung by shade-producing cliffs. But for the first six centuries that the ancient Puebloans lived here, they inhabited the tops of the tablelands, growing corn, squash, and beans; raising turkeys; hunting deer, rabbits, and squirrels; making pottery; and studying the stars. It was only in the final century of their habitation here—sometime around the beginning of the 13th century—that they set to the task of using sandstone bricks and mortar to construct their elaborate multistory cliff dwellings, creating structures that ranged from simple single-room storehouses to villages of more than 150 rooms.

And then they left. The reasons they left are debated by everyone from Puebloan elders to academic

View of Cliff Palace from Overlook Trail

archaeologists to computer modelers. Explanations have been proposed: perhaps a drought, or social strife, or overhunting, or deforestation, or resource scarcity. For whatever reason, the ancient inhabitants moved, perhaps mixing with other peoples and becoming the forebears of some of today's Puebloans in Arizona and New Mexico. Puebloan oral histories provide evidence of connections and linguistic analyses and etymologies that connect today's Puebloans with the ancients of Mesa Verde. At the same time, a host of scientific analyses enabled by data-crunching software and computer-modeling technologies examine a wide swath of data—climate trends, the DNA of ancient turkeys, the crop yields of prehistoric corn-farming methods—to learn what stressors contributed to the migration, and to theorize how the Puebloans of the ancient cliff dwellings are related to the Puebloans of today. In the meantime, what is left are the ruins—housing that fits seamlessly into the landscape and inspires visitors to imagine what life must have been like centuries before Europeans even heard of a continent across the ocean.

Mesa Verde's 30 miles of mostly short hiking trails ramble over expansive mesas and into rugged canyons, giving visitors a broad sense of the landscape as well as an up-close view of the region's ecology, which changes as the trails move from the sunbaked tablelands into the cool, shaded canyons. The trails combine spectacular views with the chance to explore ancient cliff dwellings, petroglyphs, and other archaeological sites. The routes through the ruins challenge visitors with steep ladders and (potentially) head-banging tunnels and entryways, while the trails through the surrounding landscape challenge those not accustomed to the high, dry climate. Bring plenty of water and salty snacks to prevent electrolyte depletion and dehydration.

Exploring the Park

Most of the trails are concentrated in three areas of the park, though a few roadside pullouts have trailheads for hikes leading to overlooks and other features. Note that some trails, and some of the ruins, are only open when rangers are available and on-site. Entering some of the cliff dwellings requires tickets, which must be purchased at the entrance station.

➤ The Morefield Campground area is just south of the park entrance. In addition to the campground, this area includes several trails that are known more for views than for dwellings and ruins. The **Point Lookout Trail** takes hikers to the top of a geological formation that guards the park entrance; the lookout also offers views of the San Juan and La Plata Mountains. The **Knife Edge Trail** was originally a road, built 100 years ago and known for its steep overhangs. And the **Prater Ridge Trail** offers several paths that can be combined in various ways to add up to a 7.8-mile hike along the edge of the mesa with expansive canyon views.

➤ Chapin Mesa, with its archaeological museum and access to the famed Cliff Palace, is the don't-miss destination in the park, with interconnected auto loops winding around several of the park's best-known features. The trails include the popular but rugged trail to **Petroglyph Point**, a challenging scramble that rewards hardy hikers with both views and ancient rock art; the steep and switchbacked **Spruce Canyon Trail**; and several other shorter trails to viewpoints and archaeological features.

➤ Wetherill Mesa is located at the end of a tricky, narrow, curvy road that is open only between May and October. This corner of the park draws far fewer people, most of whom come to visit the Long House (tickets are required). The 5-mile **Long House Loop** paved trail (no autos are allowed, but bicycles are fine) circles the area, leading to several hiking spurs to viewpoints or other ruins, notably the Step House (open only when rangers are present), the Badger House Community (four excavated mesa-top villages that were in use for 600 years), and the Nordenskiöld Site No. 16 (a 50-room dwelling that can be viewed from outside but is not open to visitors).

Sun Temple (top left); lone tree on trail to Montezuma Valley Overlook (top right); view of Mancos Valley from Montezuma Valley Overlook (bottom left); sculpture depicting Ancestral Puebloans at visitor center (bottom right)

Glacier National Park

MONTANA

———

Designated 1910

Glacier National Park brings a unique international element to the national park system. In addition to being a park in its own right, it is partnered with Canada's Waterton Lakes National Park; together, they make up Waterton-Glacier International Peace Park and World Heritage Site. The partnership, established in 1932, symbolizes US-Canadian cooperation. Perched on what is referred to as the "Crown of the Continent," the two parks protect nearly 1,130,000 acres of the Northern Rockies ecosystem—just over a million acres in Montana's Glacier, and 125,000 acres in Alberta's Waterton Lakes.

The parks comprise a wide range of scenic landscapes and ecological communities: mountains, glaciers, lakes, cascades, rivers, meadows, prairies, and forests. The Continental Divide (which separates the Atlantic and Pacific watersheds) and the Laurentian Divide (which separates the Atlantic and Arctic/Hudson Bay watersheds) meet in the park atop Triple Divide Peak, from which waters flow to one of three destinations: the Atlantic, the Pacific, or the Arctic Ocean via Hudson Bay. Environments range from arctic tundra to cedar-hemlock forests to lowland prairies that support populations of some of North America's best-known wildlife species, including grizzly and black bears; mountain lions and lynx; moose, elk, mule deer, and white-tailed deer; bighorn sheep and mountain goats; coyotes and gray wolves; and mink, otters, badgers, beavers, porcupines, bald eagles, and peregrine falcons.

Human history in the region dates back at least 10,000 years. Today, two of the main regional Indigenous populations are the Blackfoot, just east of the park, and the Kootenai, to the west. European American explorers arrived in the early 1800s, initially in search of animal pelts, but later expanding their interests to include mining, railways, and logging. The conservation movement of the late 1800s resulted in the establishment of Waterton

Wild Goose Island within
St. Mary Lake

Lakes as Canada's fourth national park (in 1895); Glacier became the eighth American national park in 1910.

For visitors doing most of their sightseeing by car, the park's premier attraction is the 50-mile Going-to-the-Sun Road, which bisects the park from the St. Mary Visitor Center on the east side to the Apgar Visitor Center on the west side. Stephen Mather, the first director of the National Park Service, believed that making parks accessible created supporters; Going-to-the-Sun Road takes visitors past prime examples of the park's geological, ecological, and historical features. It is listed on the National Register of Historic Places, as well as the list of National Historic Civil Engineering Landmarks. The road crosses the Continental Divide at 6,646-foot-high Logan Pass and offers a series of scenic lookouts into the heart of the park's Continental Divide. Numerous trailheads along the road give access to footpaths that lead into the park's interior. If driving yourself, plan about two hours to travel the full length of the road, not counting stops. The park also has a free hop-on, hop-off shuttle (though COVID-19 and overcrowding have changed how it operates, so visitors should check in advance).

Ninety-three percent of Glacier National Park is managed as wilderness, meaning that it is inaccessible by roads and permanent human-made structures are not allowed (with the exception of the pole-and-cable system hikers must use in campsites to keep their food safe from bears). Glacier is the fourth-largest national park in the contiguous states, and the 10th most visited, with more than three million visitors a year. Most of those visitors are compressed into the short, snow-free summer window and cluster in the nine percent of the park not designated as wilderness, so the park—particularly the front country—can have an overcrowded feeling.

To combat overcrowding, which impacts both the environment and the visitor experience, and to manage issues pertaining to COVID-19 (increased visitation at outdoor destinations and social-distancing requirements), the park has implemented various reservations, ticketing, and permit systems for back-country camping, front-country campgrounds, and even for driving on Going-to-the-Sun Road or taking the free shuttle buses. High demand for campsites means visitors need to plan ahead and be flexible regarding their preferred campsites and trail itineraries. Current details are available on the park website; double check any information from nonofficial websites, as much of it was written before the new regulations were in place.

Exploring the Park

With 700 miles of trails, and the fact that the backcountry is managed as wilderness, Glacier National Park is one of the park system's premier destinations for day hikers, backpackers, and campers. Because it is only possible to scratch the surface, this list covers some of the park's most iconic hikes. Those seeking solitude might ask rangers for suggestions about more off-the-beaten-track itineraries.

➤ Glacier is the only national park that hosts the termini for two national scenic trails. **The Pacific Northwest National Scenic Trail** begins at Goat Haunt, on the south (US) shore of Waterton Lake, and heads west to exit the park at the Polebridge Ranger Station. **The Continental Divide National Scenic Trail** has two northern termini: the terminus at the Belly River Trailhead near the Chief Mountain Customs Station, which can be used by those who don't have passports or who are concerned about high snow levels, and the terminus at the US-Canadian border at Waterton Lake, preferred by many for its scenic drama. The two termini can be connected. Hikers can park at the Belly River Trailhead near the Chief Mountain Customs Station and hike 26.6 miles to Goat Haunt via the **Stoney Indian Pass Trail**. Boat and park shuttles take care of the return journey to Chief Mountain.

➤ Numerous trailheads on Going-to-the-Sun Road (GTTSR) allow access into the heart of the park for both day hikers and backpackers. The shuttle system allows hikers to get from some starting trailheads to some ending trailheads. Starting at Logan Pass, the **Highline Trail** is one of Glacier's legendary hikes, with views of the Continental Divide, the Garden Wall, and glaciers. One popular option is to do a 15.6-mile out-and-back overnight

Canoes on dock of Swiftcurrent Lake (top left); Apikuni Falls (top right); hiker at Iceberg Lake (bottom left); tipi on eastern side of park near Blackfeet Indian Reservation (bottom right)

FOLLOWING SPREAD: Grinnell Glacier Trail (left); moose in Upper Two Medicine Lake (top right); trail near Logan Pass (bottom right)

from the Logan Pass Visitor Center to Granite Park Campground, staying either at the Granite Park Chalet or the campground. This hike can also be done as an out-and-back day hike for very strong hikers, or as a shorter horseshoe, which returns to GTTSR via the **Granite Park Trail**. Beyond Granite Park, it is possible to make a three- or four-day hike by continuing on the Highline Trail to Fifty Mountain Campground, then looping back to GTTSR via the **Flattop Mountain Trail**. The 19-mile **Gunsight Pass Trail** is another spectacular path that leaves from GTTSR and goes to Lake MacDonald; do part of it as an out-and-back hike, or go all the way, using the shuttle system to get from one trailhead to the other. The 5.3-mile, out-and-back **Hidden Lake Trail** is a scenic hike that takes off from the east side of GTTSR.

➤ The Many Glacier area on the east side of the park is one of the most populated areas, with a lodge, campground, and miles of trails that head off into the heart of the park. It is possible to create hikes of varying lengths by combining different trails according to your itinerary and what permits are available. **The Continental Divide Trail** stops by the campground here, then follows the **Swiftcurrent Pass Trail** 2,400 feet up to Swiftcurrent Pass. For strong day hikers, **Ptarmigan Lake** and **Iceberg Lake** are two outstanding trails (each is about a 10-mile round trip from the campground; both are extremely popular). There are also opportunities for shorter hikes that take off from trailheads at or near the campground.

➤ Trailheads accessible by automobile are found along all park roads and campground areas: St. Mary Lake, Polebridge, Waterton Lake (on the Canadian side), West Glacier, and Two Medicine. The northwest corner of the park has typically been less visited, although it too has become more popular in recent years. Trails to two lakes— **Bowman Lake** and **Kintla Lake**—can be combined to form a 48-mile horseshoe hike, but getting from one trailhead to another will require two cars or a hitchhike. Either lake is worth its own independent out-and-back hike.

OPPOSITE: McDonald Falls

BELOW: Lake McDonald

Rocky Mountain
National Park

COLORADO

———

Designated 1915

At about 265,000 acres, Rocky Mountain National Park is not in the national park big leagues, at least not by size. (It comes in somewhere in the middle of the pack, at number 26.) And its 350-mile trail system is smaller than those of some of the other parks famed for hiking and wilderness: Glacier (700 miles), Great Smoky Mountains (800 miles), Yosemite (750 miles), or Yellowstone (1,000 miles). But a *USA Today* survey rated Rocky Mountain as having the best hiking trails in the entire national park system, and visitation numbers support the verdict. With more than 4.6 million visitors, Rocky Mountain is the third-busiest national park. Most of it is designated as wilderness.

Only 55 miles northwest of Denver, the park sits on the Front Range of the Rocky Mountains, bisected by the Continental Divide. Surrounded by a sea of peaks and bordered by about 250,000 more acres of the Arapaho, Roosevelt, and Medicine Bow-Routt National Forests, it has the feeling of a much larger wilderness. With 77 peaks jutting above 12,000 feet and elevations ranging from just under 8,000 feet to 14,259-foot Longs Peak, Rocky Mountain is one of the highest-elevation parks in the system. Fully one-third of the park is above the 11,500-foot tree line, making it a poster child for American mountain wilderness. This is a high-country extravaganza of nonstop scenic fireworks, with open tundra framed by glaciated peaks that tower over alpine meadows, glacial lakes feeding streams that tumble in cascading waterfalls, and deep green conifer forests that blanket the lower elevations. The variation in elevations, the angles and directions of the slopes, the different exposure to prevailing winds, and the patterns of how moisture moves in different parts of the park lead to an immense variety of microclimates and ecological communities.

Designated in 1915, Rocky Mountain National Park is in the rarefied club of the 10 inaugural national parks,

Dream Lake, with Hallett Peak in the background

FOLLOWING SPREAD: Alluvial Fan (left); autumn colors along Old Fall River Road (top right); Big Thompson River through Moraine Park (bottom right)

all of them representative of a different aspect of the scenic drama and landscape icons of the American West. Here, the focus is on elevation. One of the park's most famous features is Trail Ridge Road, the highest continuously paved road in the country. Built by the Civilian Conservation Corps in the 1930s, Trail Ridge Road crosses the Continental Divide and spends 11 miles above the 11,500-foot tree line to connect the eastern and western sides of the park. Most visitors enter the park from one of the two entrances on the eastern side near Estes Park; there is also an entrance on the southwestern side of the park, near Grand Lake.

The park can be loosely divided into five zones. The region near Grand Lake is known for its meadows, with wildflowers and wildlife sightings of moose and elk. The alpine area comprises the subarctic tundra and the peaks of the high country. One of the unique aspects of Rocky Mountain National Park is that these alpine areas are accessible not only to hardy back-packers, but also to casual day hikers because of the numerous outlooks and trailheads on Trail Ridge Road. The remaining three regions are accessed from the two entrances near Estes Park. Highway 34 enters the park via Old Fall River Road and becomes Trail Ridge Road, with trailheads that give access to the park's northern wilderness region. Slightly to the south of Old Fall River Road, Park Entrance Road (Highway 36) gives access to Bear Lake Road, which leads into the "heart of the park" region, with its popular campgrounds and well-known trails. About half an hour's drive south of Estes Park on secondary roads, the southeastern region of the park is noted for waterfalls and for the trailhead to iconic Longs Peak.

Exploring the Park

Trailheads are found along all the main roads and around the campgrounds. Recently, Rocky Mountain National Park began experimenting with different ticketing and permit systems to regulate visitor traf-fic. As a result, access to some parts of the park—even for road trips and day hiking—may require reserva-tions for timed-entry tickets. Most of the trails listed here are either out-and-back hikes (where day hik-ers can turn around at any point) or loops and spurs that can be connected in various ways, so mileages are variable.

➤ The park's southwestern entrance is hardly a secret, but it is less trafficked than the eastern entrances, which are a shorter drive from Denver. The **Continental Divide National Scenic Trail** crosses the southwestern part of the park for about 30 miles, first on the **East Shore Trail**, then on a route to the west of the actual Continental Divide. Hiking highlights in this "moose and meadows" section of the park include the Big Meadows area, with its lush grasses and colorful wildflowers, which is reached via the **Onahu**, **Green Mountain**, or **Tonahutu Trails** (the latter is briefly contiguous with the Continental Divide Trail). Rocky Mountain National Park holds the headwaters of the Colorado River; from the western side of Trail Ridge Road, the **Colorado River Trail** heads off to explore them.

➤ For accessing the high country, Trail Ridge Road offers numerous trailheads. The **Ute East** and **Ute West Trails** (not connected) are both accessible from the road. Unpaved Endovalley Road connects the easternmost and westernmost segments of Trail Ridge Road; on the western side of the road, near the Alpine Visitor Center, is the trailhead for the **Chapin Pass Trail**.

➤ The northern wilderness of the park is reached from the Fall River Entrance near Estes Park, from secondary roads just north of Estes Park, and from the eastern side of Endovalley Road. North of Estes Park, the **Lumpy Ridge Trail** and **Black Canyon Trail** lead into a less traveled wilderness area. From the eastern end of Endovalley Road, the **Lawn Lake Trail** heads off, with a choice of heading toward Mummy Mountain, Lawn Lake, and Crystal Lake, or toward Ypsilon Lake.

➤ The "heart of the park"—as might be expected from its nickname—is the most heavily trafficked area of the park. Access is from the Park Entrance Road. Turn south onto Bear Lake Road. From Bear Lake Road, Moraine Park Campground Road leads to a large network of short trails around the campground. Beyond that is the Fern Lake Trail

Snow-covered path to Dream Lake (top left); fall foliage along Bear Lake Road (top right); hiker on Ute Trail (bottom)

access road and the **Fern Lake Trailhead**. The Glacier Basin Campground on Bear Lake Road has its own network of trails. Continuing farther down Bear Lake Road leads to some of the park's most popular (and crowded) trails: the **Storm Pass Trailhead** and **Bierstadt Lake** (a big loop is possible) and the alpine lakes wonderland accessed by **Bear Lake Trailhead**, with paths to Bear Lake, Dream Lake, Nymph Lake, Emerald Lake, and Lake Haiyaha.

➤ Finally, south of the main park entrance, back roads lead to the southeastern sector of the park, notable for its waterfalls, for its lack of crowds, and for the most commonly used trailhead to **Longs Peak**. Warning, this 15-mile, out-and-back trail is an all-day strenuous climb, not a hike, with exposed rock scrambling and the very real possibility of being caught out on a high ridge in an afternoon thunderstorm.

BELOW: Elk near Beaver Meadows Entrance Station

OPPOSITE: Bear Lake, with Hallett Peak in the background

Hawai'i Volcanoes
National Park

HAWAI'I

———

Designated 1916

Rainbow over Hawai'i
Volcanoes National Park

FOLLOWING SPREAD: Rock
cairns on Pu'uloa Petroglyphs
Trail (top left); lava in
Halema'uma'u Crater (middle
left); hiker on Chain of
Craters Road (bottom left);
Hōlei Sea Arch (right)

Flying plumes of ash, fiery rivers of lava crashing into the Pacific Ocean, steaming and hissing vents of stinking gas that smell of the bowels of the earth: Hawai'i, the Big Island of the Hawaiian Archipelago, is one of the most dynamic volcanic zones on earth. Sitting on top of a geological hot spot, this youngest and largest of the Hawaiian Islands is still being formed, shape-shifting as lava erupts and then creates new landforms or falls into the sea to solidify. Perhaps one day in the distant geological future, it will accumulate and poke out of the ocean to form the rock on which new ecosystems will come to life. Mauna Loa, the most massive mountain on earth measured from its base on the ocean floor to its summit, towers over the park.

Nearer to the park entrance, and far more accessible for most visitors, is hyperactive Kīlauea, which makes up for its skimpy 4,000 feet of elevation by erupting almost continuously since 1983; it is the longest continuously active volcano in historic recorded times. In 2018, a new eruption featuring tens of thousands of earthquakes and towering ash plumes led to the collapse of the Kīlauea Caldera and the destruction of park buildings (including the Jaggar Museum, which focused on volcanology) and hundreds of nearby homes.

Several factors contribute to making Hawai'i Volcanoes National Park one of the most diverse parks in the system, with a unique combination of ecological and geological features. Its remote location of the Hawaiian Archipelago—in the middle of the Pacific Ocean more than 2,000 miles from the next landform—means that its ecosystems evolved in isolation. Some 90 percent of the plants and animals are endemic, having been brought here by wind, waves, and water and left to evolve independently. The environment to which these species had to adapt might seem at first glance to be a gentle tropical paradise, but closer examination reveals extremes ranging from sizzling lava to snow

and ice. The nearly 14,000-foot range in elevation from sea level to summit is one of the greatest differentials in the entire national park system. Around 150 miles of trails showcase the resulting diversity: black sand beaches, rough and desertlike fields of ‘a‘ā (brittle and rough lava) and pāhoehoe (smoother, rounder lava that is easier to walk on), arid and subtropical lowlands, rain forests on the mountain slopes, and an alpine zone where temperatures can drop below freezing and hikers might feel snowflakes tickling their noses.

The park was originally added to the system in 1916 as Hawai‘i National Park, which then included both this park and Maui's Haleakalā. In 1961, the parks were split to become Hawai‘i Volcanoes National Park and Haleakalā National Park.

Exploring the Park

Hawai‘i offers day hikers a choice of landscapes, from lava tubes to seaside vistas to an active volcanic crater. Tent sites for backpackers offer similar diversity, from beaches to high mountains, and several cabins and shelters are spread throughout the park (permits are required). Half of the park is managed as wilderness. Challenges include high-altitude acclimatization and weather that can range from scorching to tropical rain to snow and ice. Trails through lava fields can be occasionally hard to follow, but are often marked by alu, the Hawaiian word for cairns. Volcanic activity can close roads and trails. Check when you arrive; depending on what Pele (the fiery goddess of the Native Hawaiians) is doing on any given day, some paths may give you access to parts of the park where eruptions are happening and you can watch as earth's newest land is being formed.

➤ Visitors can orient themselves by starting on Crater Rim Drive, which passes near the visitor center and intersects with Chain of Craters Road, which goes all the way to the ocean. Crater Rim Drive is centered around the active Kīlauea volcano, with several viewpoints showcasing its myriad features. The **Crater Rim Trail** follows the general direction of the road, making about a 270-degree circle around much of the caldera, and can be hiked starting and ending at different trailheads along the rim. It also intersects with several other trails, enabling day hikers to make loops of varying lengths. One combination is to take the Crater Rim Trail to the Thurston Lava Tube (Nāhuku to the Hawaiian people), where you can walk through a tunnel made of lava. Also in this area is the **Devastation Trail**, a paved path through a stark landscape that was buried by cinder that fell from 1,900-foot-tall lava fountains that erupted in the Kīlauea Iki explosion in 1959. Nearby, the Uēaloha (Byron Ledge) divides the Kīlauea Caldera and the Kīlauea Iki crater, offers excellent views of the Pu‘upua‘i cinder cone, and leads to the **Kīlauea Iki Trail**, where you can descend 400 feet onto a solidified lava lake on the floor of the Kīlauea Iki crater. Features include cinder cones, steaming vents, spatter cones, and beautiful wildflowers whose colors provide bright contrast to the black and gray volcanic ground. Mileages vary, depending on how the trails are combined.

➤ Leaving the Kīlauea area and heading toward the ocean puts you on Chain of Craters Road, where two popular trails stand out. For serious hikers and trail runners, the 11.8-mile **Nāpau Trail** is a beautiful but challenging path to the Nāpau Crater, with notable wildflowers. Near the ocean is the much easier **Pu‘uloa Petroglyphs Trail**. This 1.5-mile, out-and-back hike follows a boardwalk over a 550-year-old lava field to reach the largest collection of rock art in the Hawaiian Islands, with more than 23,000 ki‘i pōhaku, illustrations engraved in stone to represent daily life.

➤ For the adventurous, a trek up 13,681-foot Mauna Loa can be rewarding but poses a significant challenge. There are several options ranging from day hiking the 12.8-mile, round-trip **Observatory Trail** to a full-fledged 40-mile backpack trip (four days recommended) with a 7,000-foot elevation gain. The trail is nearly entirely above tree line across a lava landscape. Ahu, or cairns made of lava rock, mark the route but can be difficult to follow in rainy or foggy conditions. There is little vegetation, almost no shade, and no reliable water except for catchments at two cabins.

Kīlauea Iki Trail

Lassen Volcanic
National Park

CALIFORNIA

———

Designated 1916

Lassen Volcanic National Park is a land created by fire. It is one of only a few areas in the world where the four different kinds of volcanoes—plug dome (also called lava dome), shield, cinder cone, and stratovolcano (also called composite)—can be found near one another. At 10,457 feet, eponymous Lassen Peak is the largest plug-dome volcano in the world, and the southernmost peak of the chain of volcanoes that make up the Cascade Range in the Pacific Northwest.

The park began as two separate national monuments: Cinder Cone National Monument and Lassen Peak National Monument. Between 1914 and 1917, a series of eruptions spewed steam, lava, ash, and mud into the air, destroying nearby forests and landing on earth sometimes as far as 200 miles away. In 1916, in response to the dramatic geology, the two monuments and the area surrounding them were combined into a single national park that showcased the raw and active volcanic landscape. Hydrothermal sites like the bubbling mud pots of Bumpass Hell, as well as fumaroles and hot springs, attest to the ongoing plate tectonic activity that gives rise to explosions and earthquakes. In the contiguous United States, Lassen's thermal features are second only to those of Yellowstone.

Like all the Cascade Volcanoes, Lassen is part of the Pacific Ring of Fire, the horseshoe-shaped chain of volcanoes that roughly encircles much of the coast of the Pacific Ocean. So Lassen is, however distantly, geological cousins with Japan's Mount Fuji, Indonesia's Krakatoa, and Mexico's Popocatépetl, as well as active volcanoes as far-flung as New Zealand, the Philippines, Alaska, and Chile.

Most recently, the park has been shaped by fire of a different sort. The catastrophic Dixie Fire of 2021 burned for more than three months before being completely suppressed. One of the biggest wildfires in California history, Dixie burned nearly one million

Lassen Peak reflected in meadow stream

FOLLOWING SPREAD: Bumpass Hell (left); trail to Bumpass Hell (top right); trail down from Lassen Peak (middle right); trail down from Bumpass Hell, with Lassen Peak in the background (bottom right)

acres in Northern California, including 69 percent of Lassen's 106,000 acres. Fire is a natural part of the western forest ecosystem, periodically clearing out old deadwood, opening the canopy, and encouraging new growth. But this fire crossed the line between regenerative and destructive, impacting soil composition in some areas, as well as destroying buildings and closing many of the trails. After the fire was suppressed, restoration work began, with trails reopening as they could be cleared, but the damage remains evident. Still, it is a natural process, and in the timeline of a forest's life span, regeneration is already underway. Flowers and shrubs create colorful contrast with the burned ground, and tiny conifer seedlings take advantage of the newly available sunlight to sprout. But full recovery will be a slow process, and in some parts of the park, hikers will see the impact of the fire for years, even decades, to come.

BELOW: Painted dunes near Cinder Cone

OPPOSITE: Trail to Cinder Cone

Exploring the Park

As a general rule, Highway 89, which curves around the western half of the park in a generally south-to-north direction, marks the boundary of the fire. Many of the park's thermal features are easily seen at viewpoints and parking areas along the highway. The western side of the park is the most heavily used by visitors and was the least impacted by the fires. The eastern side was more severely burned.

➤ Right through the middle of the park, 17 miles of the **Pacific Crest National Scenic Trail** cross Lassen's wilderness. The terrain features forests, lakes, and streams in a landscape at the intersection of the Cascade Range to the north, the Sierra Nevada mountains to the south, and the Great Basin to the east. But the Pacific Crest Trail was badly damaged by the fires. According to the Pacific Crest Trail Association, the Dixie Fire burned more miles of the trail than any other fire in the trail's history.

➤ The park's northwest corner, near the Manzanita Entrance Station, has visitor services such as a campground, tent cabins, and a trail network that includes a 1.7-mile loop around **Manzanita Lake**, a 0.6-mile loop around **Reflection Lake**, the short 0.5-mile **Lily Pond Interpretive Trail**, and longer trails to **Crags Lake** and along **Manzanita Creek**.

➤ In the southwest region of the park, the **Lassen Peak Trail** is a strenuous 5-mile round trip to the park's high point, with an elevation gain of nearly 2,000 feet, some of which switchbacks through loose rock and sandy volcanic cinder. The mountain has two high points; the trail ends at the first, lower summit, where there are interpretive signs and excellent views. Hikers can then scramble to the true summit or climb down into the crater. This is a harsh environment. Much of it is shadeless, with snowbanks that can persist into summer and some tricky footing, along with variable weather. The high altitude can also be a challenge for unacclimated hikers. Also in the southwest area of the park, the 4.6-mile, round-trip hike to **Ridge Lakes** (1,000 feet of elevation gain, with mountain lakes as the reward) and the 7.6-mile, out-and-back **Brokeoff Mountain Trail** (considered one of the most scenic in the park) were unaffected by the fire.

OPPOSITE: Trail to Kings Creek Falls

BELOW: View of Lassen Peak from Manzanita Lake

Denali National Park and Preserve

ALASKA

———

Designated 1917

Open meadow along Denali Park Road

FOLLOWING SPREAD: Braided river near Teklanika River Campground (left); grizzly bear mother and cubs in the backcountry (top right); willow ptarmigan near Denali Park Road (middle); ground squirrel near Teklanika River Campground (middle right); pair of moose near Wonder Lake (bottom right)

A funny thing about place names: they can represent thousands of years of cultural history, or they can be the result of whim, cronyism, self-aggrandizement, honor, mistake, politics, or accident. In 1896, a gold prospector returned from the Alaskan wilderness, perhaps a bit addled by the sheer size and scale of everything Alaskan. A hulking mass of a mountain rose 20,000 feet into the clouds; the lands surrounding it stretched endlessly, holding out a promise of riches and gold. Ignoring the fact that the mountain already had a name—Indigenous people had long known it as Denali, or "the high one"—the newcomer proposed that the peak be named for an Ohio politician. Republican presidential candidate William McKinley had never been to Denali—nor would he ever—and his only connection to Alaska was that his political platform included linking the value of American currency to the value of the gold Alaskans and newly arrived prospectors were finding in the wilds of the far northern outpost. Nonetheless, the proposal gathered support and was adopted in Washington; the 25th president's name was superimposed on the mountain and, later, on the national park that included it. Not until 2015—by an executive action that was bitterly contested by Ohio Republicans—was McKinley's name removed and the name used by Native Alaskans and nonnatives alike restored to the peak.

At 20,310 feet above sea level, Denali is not only the highest mountain in North America, but also one of the most prominent and isolated peaks on earth. Its topographic prominence (the height of its summit relative to the lowest contour line that encircles it) is a whopping 20,194 feet and its topographic isolation (its distance from the nearest peak that is higher) is 4,621.1 miles; a crow would have to fly clear to Aconcagua in South America to find a loftier perch.

For mountaineers, Denali presents even more obstacles than those numbers suggest. It rises 17,000 feet above the landscape that immediately surrounds it (for comparison, Mount Kilimanjaro rises 14,000 feet and Mount Everest 13,000 feet). Climbers on Denali typically fly to Kahiltna Glacier, from which they ascend 13,000 feet to the summit. That elevation differential is actually bigger than that of Mount Everest, where climbers on the most commonly used Nepal route trek to a 17,600-foot base camp, then climb 11,400 feet to the summit. While Denali is not anywhere near the 26,000-foot "death zone" of the high-elevation Himalayan peaks, its extreme northern latitude gives it brutally cold weather similar to that found on Himalayan peaks. Barometric pressure is also lower at high elevations near the poles, which reduces the amount of oxygen available. Climbers use Denali as a training ground for the Himalayan peaks.

With such scale, it seems only fitting that the mountain would be protected as one of the first national parks. However, the park's origin story begins not with the mountain, but with a species of sheep. Dall sheep—guides tell tourists to look for "white dots with legs"—hide from predators by clinging to sheer crags and cliffs; once in a while, the males emerge to clash heads in testosterone-fueled, horn-to-horn combat. More than 100 years ago, conservationist and hunter Charles Sheldon traveled in Alaska and became concerned that the wild white sheep were being commercially overhunted to feed gold miners, railroad workers, explorers, and settlers. He lobbied Congress for a game refuge; Congress responded with a national park that was designated as a wilderness and just happened to contain one of the most impressive mountains in the world.

In 1980, the Alaska National Interest Lands Conservation Act (ANILCA) was passed. ANILCA established more than 100 million acres of federal land in Alaska, including seven new national parks, and more than

doubled the size of the entire national park system. It also expanded the original Mount McKinley National Park, bringing it to 6.1 million acres (only Wrangell-St. Elias and Gates of the Arctic are larger). Today, Denali National Park and Preserve contains the original Mount McKinley National Park allotment (still reserved for recreation; no subsistence hunting or sport hunting is permitted), the new park lands (where subsistence uses are permitted), and the new preserve lands (where subsistence uses and sport hunting are both permitted).

Sheldon would be pleased that Denali continues to provide wild habitat for the Dall sheep, which are now an object of study; they are one of the few populations of wild sheep that live in a system with intact populations of large predators. The park is also the site of other ongoing scientific studies dealing with climate change, including receding glaciers, the thawing of the permafrost, and rising tree lines.

Denali may be enormous, but in some respects, planning a trip there is simpler than planning a trip to many smaller parks. By Alaska standards, it is reasonably easy to get to Denali via roads, buses, rail, charter plane, and even tours from cruise ships. Inside the park, there is only one road (mostly dirt and gravel). For day hikers, the choices are not overwhelming; all hikes are accessed from that one road. For backpackers, the only limits are how far you can walk and if you will resupply (and if so, how you will make the necessary arrangements) via food caches stashed in areas where caching is permitted. The road enters the park from the east and runs 92 miles on the north side of the peak. Private cars are only allowed on the first 15 miles; to travel farther into the interior requires taking one of the guided tour buses or transit buses, which start outside the park or at the visitor center near the entrance. Six campgrounds are available in the park, and lodgings are available nearby.

The main activities for visitors include bus tours, wildlife and landscape photography, bicycling, hiking, backpacking, climbing (for the brave of heart), and, in season, dogsledding; the park has the only sled-dog kennel in the national park system.

Alaska national parks are different in several ways from any of the other parks in the system, and much of the information regarding Denali (with predictable variations owing to location, weather, season, and any other park's individual differences) can be applied to other Alaskan parks too. Unlike most parks in the Lower 48, which squeeze a lot of trail mileage into their (usually) smaller acreages, Alaskan parks have enormous acreages but relatively few marked and maintained trails. Alaska takes the idea of wilderness to an exponential level, eschewing trails, markers, mileages, and developed campsites. The ethic and aesthetic here is for backcountry travelers to truly be self-reliant and make their own path; rangers may suggest areas of the park to visit but will rarely recommend specific routes.

Also note that the weather is frequently bad enough to make navigation and travel difficult; it can be impossible for pilots to fly to prearranged pickup points, in which case hikers need enough food and fortitude to sit out whatever Mother Nature is dishing out. Self-rescue, first aid, navigation, food storage, and communication skills are all essential. Cell phones rarely work in Alaska wildernesses; mirrors, ground-to-air signals, VFG radios (which enable emergency communication with pilots who are in proximity), and satellite phones are tools used instead. Bear encounters are not uncommon; all hikers need bear spray, and backpackers need bear-proof food-storage containers. For less experienced hikers, numerous guide services offer a margin of safety and valuable local intel, which even experienced backpackers might appreciate.

Exploring the Park

There are two ways to hike in Denali National Park—on one of the marked trails, or off-trail in nearly any direction you choose. Many of the marked trails are located near the visitor center at the park entrance; others start from trailheads on the main park road. Trails near the entrance can be used year-round, but farther inside the park, trails can only be accessed by vehicle when the buses are running, which means before snow sets in for the winter. For backpackers, knowledge of the park's bus system and permit system are both necessary; the park is divided into units, with quotas limiting how many campers are allowed in each on any given day. Beyond the marked day-hiking trails, all backcountry travel is off-trail. The National Park

Caribou near Eielson Visitor Center (top left); rainbow over small lake in the backcountry (top right); hikers exploring the backcountry (bottom)

Service website has exhaustive information on each unit, including its challenges, its highlights, and what skills are required. Most backpackers will travel to their hike embarkation point by the park's camper bus (it's a slow ride; the full 92 miles to the road's end takes six hours one way). Rangers recommend that backpackers come prepared with several itineraries and be amenable to suggestions from the rangers, especially if their preferred unit is already booked.

➤ The trails in the network near the park entrance can be combined in numerous ways. The **Taiga Trail** acts as a connector from which many other popular trails head out in ever-expanding spurs and loops. **The Roadside**, **Rock Creek**, **Mount Healy Overlook** (a tough hike, but good views of Denali), **McKinley Station**, **Horseshoe Lake**, and **Triple Lakes Trails** are just a few, and they can be combined in all sorts of ways to fashion hikes that can take anywhere from half an hour to all day.

➤ About 15 miles inside the park, the Savage River area can be accessed by private car or the Savage River shuttle bus. For an easy hike, the 2-mile **Savage River Loop** is a mostly flat walk along the river. The 4-mile, one-way **Savage Alpine Trail** has views of Denali and connects the Savage River area with the Savage River Campground; the return to the starting trailhead or to the park entrance can be done via the Savage River Shuttle.

➤ Eielson Visitor Center is at mile 66; start early, because the bus ride to get there takes time. The reward is great views of Denali from most of the trails. The **Tundra Loop** is around a third of a mile through alpine country, very close to the visitor center. The **Eielson Alpine Trail** climbs more than 1,000 feet in just under a mile to Thorofare Ridge, with especially impressive mountain views. The **Gorge Creek Trail** descends 600 feet to the Gorge Creek and Thorofare River bars, with access to numerous day-hiking opportunities and backcountry camping areas.

➤ Located at mile 85, the Wonder Lake area can be reached from early June to mid-September by a Wonder Lake or Kantishna shuttle bus. The 5-mile, round-trip **McKinley River Bar Trail** leads from Wonder Lake Campground to the McKinley River, with negligible elevation gain but good views. The trail travels through spruce forest and past several small ponds, where hikers might see waterfowl but will definitely see (and hear and feel) mosquitoes. Head nets and bug spray are essential.

OPPOSITE: Small stream along Denali Park Road

BELOW: Fireweed, with Alaska Range in the background

Grand Canyon
National Park

ARIZONA

———

Designated 1919

A full mile deep, big enough that you could fit all of Manhattan in it and still have room for several more of the world's biggest cities, and a river that carved a canyon out of two-billion-year-old rock: the scale and drama of the Grand Canyon still befuddles modern-day visitors, even though they know what lies ahead from pictures and film.

It seems almost unbelievable today, but Grand Canyon National Park almost wasn't. In 1882, then-senator Benjamin Harrison introduced a bill to establish the national park. But logging and mining interests prevailed, and the bill failed. He introduced two more bills, which also failed. And that might have been the end of it, except that, in 1888, Harrison won the presidency. In 1893, he settled for creating the Grand Canyon Forest Reserve, which gave the canyon some level of protection, even though mining and logging were still permitted. President Theodore Roosevelt picked up the torch, establishing the Grand Canyon Game Preserve in 1906 and the Grand Canyon National Monument in 1908. More Senate proposals to create a national park were introduced again—and defeated again—in 1910 and 1911. It wasn't until 1919 that the Grand Canyon National Park Act finally passed and was signed by President Woodrow Wilson.

The Grand Canyon has been inhabited for centuries. Cliff dwellings and petroglyphs still tucked into the canyon walls talk to us across the intervening years, giving us an image of daily life in the canyon. The first European reported to have visited was García López de Cárdenas from Spain, who arrived in 1540. Looking into the maw that opened a mile beneath his feet, Cárdenas could make no sense of the size and scale of what he was seeing. He thought the river was a trickle. But when his men tried to climb down to bring back water, they made it only a third of the way and returned with tales of great difficulties that had not

Hiker on South Kaibab Trail

FOLLOWING SPREAD: Pack mules on trail into the canyon (top left); hiker on South Kaibab Trail (bottom left); view of South Rim from Hopi Point (right)

been visible from above. His full report is lost to time, but it didn't encourage anyone to return. It would be 300 years before the next serious European American expedition arrived at the South Rim in the 1850s.

By the end of the 19th century, public sentiment had changed dramatically: miners of uranium, copper, and silver poked away at the ancient rock, and timber barons cast covetous eyes on the ponderosa pines at the canyon's higher elevations. But ultimately, tourism was the moneymaker. The enterprising Fred Harvey Company, which ran the concessions in the park, offered mule rides, along with hotels, restaurants, and gift shops. Today, the Grand Canyon draws some six million visitors a year to gape at geological history laid bare. And even though today's visitors have a mental image of the Grand Canyon from television, film, and photographs, the canyon, when seen up close and in person, still has the power to confound.

The park has two main visitor areas, the North Rim and the South Rim. Additional iconic tourist spots, Havasu Falls and the Grand Canyon Skywalk, are found on the adjacent Havasupai and Hualapai Indian Reservations just to the west. The North Rim is about 1,000 feet higher than the South Rim. That 1,000 feet means the difference between passable and not passable in winter; visitor facilities on the North Rim are closed from October 15 until May 15. The North Rim tends to be less crowded. The South Rim is open year-round.

For decades, the accepted way to travel through the canyon was to ride a mule. Mule rides are still offered, but today the vast majority of visits into the canyon are on foot.

Exploring the Park

Grand Canyon trails are divided into four categories: corridor trails, threshold trails, primitive trails, and wild (off-trail) routes. The corridor trails are the best maintained, most often patrolled, and most used (especially within a mile of the trailheads). Difficulties and dangers include falls, dehydration, heat exhaustion, rough footing, and misjudging the effort required to regain the elevation lost when descending into the canyon. Rangers strongly encourage first-time visitors—especially those with little or no experience hiking in

desert climates—to stay on one of the corridor trails until they have the skills to tackle more difficult options.

➤ Corridor trails include the **South Kaibab** and **North Kaibab Trails**, which connect the South Rim and the North Rim. These routes are part of the border-to-border **Arizona National Scenic Trail** and are commonly used for rim-to-rim cross-canyon treks. One of the park's most popular overnight hikes is to descend to the river via the steep and view-filled South Kaibab Trail, then spend the night at the bottom of the canyon in a tent at Bright Angel Campground (or, alternatively, in a bed at nearby Phantom Ranch; reservations are required for both). To return, most hikers take the **River Trail** (another corridor trail) from the campsite to the **Bright Angel Trail**, which leads back up to the South Rim, but on a longer, less steeply graded path. Some hikers spend a second night at the Havasupai Garden (formerly Indian Garden) Campsite, then finish the remaining 4 miles of the climb the next day.

➤ Another corridor trail is the **Plateau Point Trail**, which is a short side trail that is accessed from Havasupai Garden. For day hikers, this would require hiking 4 miles down to the campsite, then another 1.5 miles to Plateau Point—an ambitious 11-mile round trip. But for those already staying at the campsite, it is an easy add-on.

➤ Most appropriate for beginning hikers is to trek some of the 13-mile **Rim Trail**, which runs from the South Kaibab Trailhead to Hermits Rest. The trail is served by plenty of shuttle bus stops that allow hikers to plan a walk of any length. Much of the trail is paved and mostly flat; it offers multiple overlooks with different dramatic views into the canyon.

➤ Rated "primitive," the 95-mile **Tonto Trail**, also on the south side of the canyon, offers excellent multiday backpacking opportunities with views in all directions. The Tonto Trail crosses many of the rim-to-interior-canyon trails (of varying difficulty levels), allowing hikers to create hikes of varying lengths. When calculating mileage, don't forget to add the mileage from the rim to

Hikers admiring view of Grand Canyon (top left); Bright Angel Trail (top right); hiker on South Kaibab Trail (bottom)

your starting and ending points on the Tonto Trail itself. The trail largely follows the canyon's wide, flat-when-seen-from-a-distance, sage-green Tonto layer, occasionally dropping down to the river (and then, of course, climbing back up again). The Tonto Trail is suitable for backpackers with extensive desert and navigation experience.

➤ Last, **Grand Canyon river-rafting trips** are bucket-list adventures for outdoors lovers from all over the world. While the adrenaline thrill of the rapids is the big dramatic draw, most trips include quieter hikes into remote slot canyons accessible only from the river.

BELOW AND OPPOSITE:
Colorado River, at bottom of the Grand Canyon

Acadia National Park

MAINE

———

Designated 1919

In 1919, the national parks finally arrived in the eastern United States. Acadia National Park takes its name from Greece by way of New France; Arcadia, in ancient Greece, referred to a part of the Peloponnese peninsula that was imagined to be an unspoiled wilderness. The name came to the New World in the 1500s. Giovanni da Verrazzano, a Florentine who explored for the French, used the name to refer to North America's mid-Atlantic and northern coast. In the 1600s, Samuel de Champlain followed suit, but dropped the "R"; he used the name Acadie to refer to a northeastern province of New France in what is now Maritime Canada. Today, the terms Arcadia and Acadia refer to French culture in northeastern North America, as well as in Louisiana.

As for Acadia National Park, it first gained protection in 1916 as Sieur de Monts National Monument, then was renamed in 1919, when it became Lafayette National Park. In 1929, it was renamed yet again, and this time the name stuck. Acadia National Park celebrates exactly what Arcadia (or Acadia) originally meant: wilderness that is pure, rural, idyllic, and far removed from the stresses of cities and urban life.

Acadia National Park protects the coastline of central Maine, a landscape of high rocky headlands, beaches, and 26 identifiable mountains. Lichen-covered, pink-granite Cadillac Mountain, at 1,528 feet, is the highest mountain along the entire Atlantic coast of the United States. The park includes about half of Mount Desert Island, part of the Isle au Haut, the tip of the Schoodic Peninsula, and parts of more than a dozen other islands.

The landscape has been shaped by ocean, wind, and glaciation, evidenced by the park's exposed granite domes, glacial erratics, and U-shaped valleys. This is a place where different environments and habitats merge—mountains, lakes, streams, wetlands, forests, meadows, and a coastline consisting of cliffs, cobbles,

Sunrise at Bass Harbor Head Light Station

FOLLOWING SPREAD: Shore of Schoodic Peninsula (top left); Boulder Beach (middle); hiker resting along Ocean Path (bottom left); rocky shoreline along Ocean Path at dusk (right)

and sand beaches—to create ecosystems that support diverse communities of plants and animals.

Acadia National Park's human history begins—as did the human history of the earlier western national parks—with more than 10,000 years of human settlement by Indigenous peoples. European exploration and settlement followed; in the 19th and early 20th centuries, the newcomers here were wealthy summer visitors looking for exactly the kind of escape from their urban lives that the ancient Greeks dreamed about when they considered the idea of Arcadia. Many of these visitors built "cottages" (that's New England–speak for lavish country estates). But some looked beyond their personal summer-house luxuries to the land itself, and considered its value, not only to themselves, but to future generations and the public. John D. Rockefeller Jr., for example, financed Mount Desert Island's now-historic carriage-road system, while George B. Door, who became known as the father of the park, worked to have the land protected by national park status.

Today, Acadia is one of the 10 most visited parks in the system, even though it is nowhere near a major popular center; the nearest big city, Boston, is five hours away. Nonetheless, 3.5 million people a year find their way here. The park is small by national park standards—only about 50,000 acres—so it can be congested, especially during summer. From the spring through the autumn high season, recreational activities include auto touring; walking, bicycling, and horseback riding on carriage roads (where motor vehicles are prohibited); hiking and rock climbing; kayaking and canoeing on lakes and ponds; sea kayaking on the ocean; and boat tours, swimming, and beachgoing. In winter, road access is limited, but the park is open for cross-country skiing, snowshoeing, snowmobiling, and ice fishing. Because of its small size and large visitor numbers, it is one of the few national parks where backpacking and backcountry camping are not permitted.

The vast majority of Acadia's hiking trails are on Mount Desert Island (the biggest section of the park), but there is also a small network of trails on the Schoodic Peninsula. In total, more than 150 miles of hiking trails intersect and loop with each other as they climb to some of the park's high points, traverse the coastline and beaches, and wander into the forests and meadows. Some trails are annually closed in spring to protect peregrine falcons from human disturbance during the nesting season; the carriage road is closed (and that includes for walkers) during the spring mud season.

Exploring the Park

Acadia's hikes can be divided into short, easy, family-friendly hikes, more strenuous day hikes, and climbs that present challenges such as rock scrambling, exposure, and the need to use iron aides (ladders, cables, and rungs) to go straight up rock obstacles and cliffs.

➢ Two of the most popular short hikes in the park are the **Ocean Path**, a 2-mile, one-way coastline hike from Sand Beach to Otter Point. Intermediate parking areas allow access at different points. The **Cadillac Mountain Summit Loop** is an easy 0.5-mile trail around the summit, giving those who drive up a chance to stretch their legs; driving to the summit before sunrise to catch some of the first rays to hit the North American continent is a ritual at the park. Another interesting and easy hike is the 2-mile, out-and-back trail across the long, shallow sandbar that runs between **Bar Harbor** (the town) and **Bar Island**. During low tide, the bar becomes dry, allowing visitors to hike to the island (also part of the national park). Check tide tables for coming and going!

➢ More strenuous day hikes include the **South Bubble Mountain Trail** to Bubble Rock, a balancing rock that sits on an incline, seemingly ready to heed gravity's call to fall down the cliff. Hikers can take a mile-long out-and-back trail or a 1.7-mile loop; both have some noticeable climbing. The 6-mile round trip to **Pemetic Mountain** takes hikers into a world of granite cliffs and unblocked, dramatic views. The 2.8-mile **Acadia Mountain Trail** loop is less trafficked than trails on the busier east side of the island, but offers beautiful views of Somes Sound and can be combined with the trail to **St. Sauveur Mountain** to make a longer 3.9-mile hike.

Sunset over Cadillac Mountain (top left); trail around Jordan Pond (top right); waterfall below a stone bridge (bottom left); Ocean Path (bottom right)

Finally, there are Acadia's trademark exposed climbs and iron-assisted scrambles. Not appropriate for small children, or for anyone with acrophobia, these trails ask the question: When does a hike become a climb? The **Beehive Trail** is one of the most famous, with granite steps, iron ladders, and handrails leading to premium views. The **Precipice Trail** can't be accused of false advertising. Located roughly a mile north of the Beehive Trail, it ascends Champlain Mountain, one of the tallest peaks in the park. The trail takes its cliffs straight on, with iron rungs, ladders, handrails, and wooden bridges. Less well known (and hence, not quite as jammed up with hikers with sudden-onset acrophobia) is the **Beech Cliff Trail**, which rises to the top of the Beech Cliff, with views of Echo Lake and the ocean in the distance.

BELOW: Hiker on Jordan Pond Path

OPPOSITE: Jordan Pond, with North Bubble and South Bubble in the background

Zion National Park

UTAH

———

Designated 1919

Located in southwestern Utah, Zion National Park sits on the edge of the Colorado Plateau, where the conifers of the high country live next door to the cacti of the lower desert. Zion is not huge—in a list of national parks ranked by size, it comes in right in the middle of the pack. But its location and reputation make it one of the most visited parks in the country. Zion is accessible from airports in St. George, Cedar City, and Las Vegas. It's also on the road-trip itinerary that can be made between Arizona's Grand Canyon and Utah's four other national parks (Canyonlands, Arches, Capitol Reef, and Bryce Canyon).

Zion's big attraction is rock, whether it is rock that pokes into the sky (Angels Landing) or rock that blocks the sky (slot canyons such as the famous Narrows). Either way, Zion's vertical towers, sculpted side canyons, and ancient petroglyphs recall elements of Yosemite, Grand Canyon, and Mesa Verde National Parks.

From about AD 500 to AD 1200, Zion was inhabited by Puebloan people whose homes were cliff dwellings nestled in rock alcoves. When European American pioneers and settlers first arrived in 19th-century Utah, the canyon had become home to the Southern Paiute people; John Wesley Powell reported that its name was Mukuntuweap, a "straight canyon" in the Paiute language. In the mid-19th century, Mormon settlers moved in. Mormon pioneer Isaac Behunin is credited with renaming the canyon, writing "a man can worship God among these great cathedrals as well as in any man-made church—this is Zion." As more Mormons arrived to farm (among other things) tobacco, sugarcane, and fruit trees, the Paiute gradually left, were forced out, or were killed by disease.

In 1909, Mukuntuweap National Monument was established, named in recognition of the Paiute. But Mormons appealed that decision, and National Park Service officials sided with them on the grounds that the

View of the Watchman from Canyon Junction Bridge

FOLLOWING SPREAD: Canyon Overlook Trail (left); Emerald Pools (top right); hiker on trail to Canyon Overlook (bottom right)

Paiute name was too difficult to pronounce and would discourage visitors from coming. In 1918, Mukuntuweap was changed to Zion. In 1919, the national monument was upgraded to a national park.

Today, Zion attracts millions of visitors with its iconic rock formations, many of which have names that continue to reference Mormon traditions and religion: Towers of the Virgin, Court of the Patriarchs, Cathedral Mountain, Temple of Sinawava, the Great Temple, Angels Landing, the Watchman, and Great White Throne. In addition to the cliffs and peaks, Zion is famous for its slot canyons. These passages through high towers of rock began as hairline cracks that were expanded and finally broken under the pressure of eons of flash floods. Zion's slot canyons are among the park's most popular and most photographed attractions.

A warning: Zion National Park is a dramatic landscape, but in the outdoors the difference between drama and danger can be as slim as the park's famous slot canyons. Deaths in the park have been caused by falls, especially after rain when the sandstone is slick, or when visitors misguidedly take selfies while posing at the edge of a thousand-foot cliff. Other factors include environmental hazards such as heat, cold, lightning, and rockfall. In the slot canyons, drowning and flood-related falls are also a risk.

Exploring the Park

Hiking trails range from short, flat strolls to seriously challenging rock scrambles to wet-footed wading through canyons so narrow you can touch both sides with outstretched arms. To reach the main trailheads in the heart of the park requires using shuttle buses; for most of the year, no private cars are allowed on Zion Canyon Scenic Drive, which starts near the visitor center at the park's South Entrance.

➤ The **Zion Canyon Overlook Trail** is a short (just under a mile) out-and-back hike that delivers what its name promises: an overview of Zion Canyon. Another short view-filled hike is the **Watchman**, a 2.7-mile out-and-back trail that begins at the park's South Entrance, wanders past overhanging cliffs, and affords views of Bridge Mountain, the Watchman, and the Towers of the Virgin.

➤ The **Emerald Pools Lower**, **Middle**, and **Upper Trails** are among the park's most popular day hikes. It is possible to hike just one of these trails for a short 1.2-mile out-and-back hike, or to connect the trails to the pools with the **Kayenta** and **Grotto Trails** to create a hike of up to about 6 miles. Note that the water-covered sandstone can be dangerously slippery.

➤ One of the park's most iconic hikes is **Angels Landing** (permits are required, even for day hikers). The first mile or so is nothing too notable, and first-time visitors might wonder what the fuss is about. But that changes on Walter's Wiggles, a series of 21 seemingly impossible switchbacks constructed into an almost vertical cliff. And then the real fun begins—a chain-assisted rock scramble on a knife-edge rock bridge with a drop of more than 1,000 feet on either side. The view is worth the terror, but this is no place for acrophobes, and the danger is real. Since 2004, 13 people have fallen to their death from this popular trail.

BELOW: Hiker on trail to Valley View

OPPOSITE: Angels Landing Trail (top left); striated rock in upper canyon (top right); bridge at start of Angels Landing Trail (bottom)

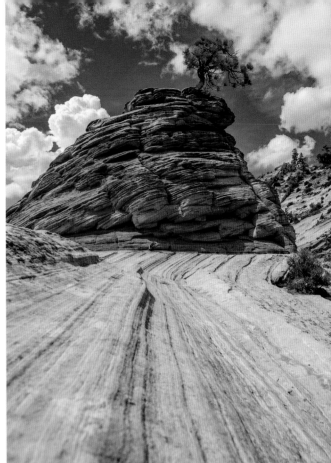

Zion's other iconic trail is the **Narrows**, which can be hiked from the bottom up (an out-and-back hike of the lower part of the canyon). The mandatory turnaround point is 5 miles in, but hikers can turn around before that wherever they like. No permit is required. The 17-mile top-down option goes one way down the canyon and can be done in one day or as an overnight backpack trip; permits are required for both. Never forget that these slots were created by flash floods. Before entering the Narrows, or any other slot canyon, check the regional weather conditions and get current advice and warnings from the ranger station. Flash floods can originate from many miles upstream, even if it is sunny in the park. But it's not all wild and dangerous: the first 1.1 miles of the trek is the **Riverside Walk**, a flat, paved trail along the Virgin River, which ends with spectacular views of the beginning of the Narrows.

For those whose idea of hiking does not involve jostling around hundreds of other people, the park's backcountry network of trails offers the chance to create up to about a 50-mile, trans-Zion backpacking trip. Combining the **East Rim**, **West Rim**, **Wildcat Canyon**, **Connector**, **Hop Valley**, and **La Verkin Creek Trails** can give intrepid hikers up to about six days in the park's more remote areas. For a shorter hike, choose one, two, or more. If you don't have two cars to shuttle to either end, local outfitters can help with transportation logistics, but they can be expensive.

OPPOSITE: Hiker at the Subway

RIGHT: Waterfall along trail to the Subway (top); Angels Landing Trail (bottom)

Hot Springs National Park

ARKANSAS

_____

Designated 1921

Here's another layer of debate to the question of which is the oldest park in the national park system: Hot Springs National Park sits on land that was set aside as a "special reservation" for preservation and recreation by President Andrew Jackson in 1832, 40 years before Yellowstone was designated a national park. But it wasn't until 1921 that it formally entered the system. Today, Hot Springs is billed as the "oldest area in the national park system." At 5,500 acres, it is also the second smallest.

Jackson was far from the first person to appreciate the hot spring water that flows down from Hot Springs Mountain in the Ouachita range of Arkansas. Indigenous peoples, including the Caddo, Cherokee, Choctaw, Quapaw, and Tunica, and, further back in precontact history, their forebears, are thought to have used the springs as a peaceful gathering spot, perhaps as long as 10,000 years ago. In 1541, Hernando de Soto became the first European to come upon the springs; as more Europeans arrived in the decades that followed, the springs gained a reputation for their healing properties. Jump forward three centuries: after the United States claimed the land, the city of Hot Springs became a successful spa town. Bathhouse Row consists of eight ornate Victorian buildings that were constructed between 1892 and 1923. The area was designated a National Historic Landmark District in 1987. Two of the original bathhouses have been updated to offer modern spa services. Other buildings have been repurposed; one is used as an art gallery, and another has become the park's visitor center.

Exploring the Park

The main features of this park are historic, with the bathhouses taking center stage. But 26 miles of hiking trails wander around the park's 5,000 acres, mostly through forested landscapes, passing streams and brooks and natural hot springs. The two networks of interconnected trails are centered around two sections of the park.

➤ The scenic **North Mountain Trails** are conveniently accessible from Bathhouse Row and sprawl out to the campground at Gulpha Gorge.

➤ The less traveled **West Mountain Trails** offer more opportunities for wildlife sightings.

➤ The two networks are connected by the 10-mile, one-way **Sunset Trail**, the park's most remote trail, which can be combined with other **North** and **West Mountain Trails** to form longer loops of between 15 and 17 miles.

Grand Promenade

FOLLOWING SPREAD:
Thermal waters near Hot Springs Visitor Center (left); original porcelain sink in a bathhouse (middle); pond along Sunset Trail (top right); stone bridge along Sunset Trail (bottom right)

Shenandoah
National Park

VIRGINIA

———

Designated 1926

Shenandoah National Park has a slightly different origin story than its wild western counterparts. The impetus behind the western parks was protection and preservation. The impetus behind the establishment of Shenandoah was to provide a recreational resource in the east and to restore and reforest a land that had been homesteaded, farmed, hunted, trapped, mined, lumbered, and milled for 200 years. In the West, the establishment of many of the parks displaced Indigenous peoples; in Shenandoah, Indigenous peoples had long since been pushed out by European Americans. Now, the establishment of the park displaced and sometimes forcibly bought out those same settlers, some of whose families had lived in these hills and "hollers" for 200 years.

Shenandoah farmers had a hard life as they fought to wrest a living from the stingy Appalachian mountain soil. Their lives became even harder when the chestnut blight of the early 1900s killed trees that were an important component of their subsistence lives. Chestnuts were used as food; the wood was turned into railroad ties, house siding, and roof shingles, or was sold as lumber.

Meanwhile, the Shenandoah Mountains were coming to the attention of residents of the growing eastern metropolises. As early as the late 1800s, urbanites seeking respite from cities all over the East Coast had begun flocking to the mountains to find their escape. Washington, DC, was only 75 miles from the Shenandoah Mountains. Capitalizing on clean water, cool breezes, big views, and quiet, developers began building vacation resorts. At the same time, the new national park system was gaining popularity. But while the list of parks in the West was steadily growing, as of 1920 only one national park had been established east of the Mississippi River, in part because much of the eastern United States was under private ownership.

Hawksbill Summit overlook

In 1926, Congress authorized Shenandoah National Park, but specified that no federal funds could be used for land purchases. So the state of Virginia began acquiring land, in some cases condemning land and evicting local inhabitants in a massive application of eminent domain. Remnants of the park's history as farmland are found in the ruins of cabins, cemeteries, and the stone walls that once marked the boundaries of fields and orchards.

It took until 1935 before the park was actually established, which put the opening of the park right in the middle of a debate about Jim Crow laws. The National Park Service sidestepped the issue by deciding to defer to local and state laws, meaning that the Old Dominion's Jim Crow laws were in full force. Separate campgrounds, visitor centers, and picnic areas were designated for African American visitors. Today, visitors might come upon a remnant of a "Negro only" sign; an exhibit at the Harry F. Byrd Sr. Visitor Center is dedicated to the history of segregation in the park.

Today, nearly 90 years after the designation of the park, Shenandoah is largely reforested, and its new growth of trees and shrubs blanket the remains of most of its history. Its main hiking features are waterfalls and rocky peaks like Hawksbill and Old Rag Mountains, some of which rise 3,000 feet above the Shenandoah River Valley to the west. Prominent wildlife species include deer, coyotes, foxes, bobcats, and black bears. Much of the visitor infrastructure—trails, bridges, overlooks, picnic areas, campgrounds, and even Skyline Drive—can be dated to the 1930s and the work of the Civilian Conservation Corps, the work-relief program that employed millions of young men on environmental projects during the Great Depression.

Exploring the Park

Shenandoah National Park is a 100-mile-long, north-south sliver that sits along the spine of the Appalachian Mountains. Skyline Drive runs the length of the park, along or parallel to its central ridgeline; the locations of most park amenities are given by mileage number along the parkway. The park's 500-mile network of hiking trails is accessed from numerous trailheads, most of which are found along the drive. Other trailheads can be accessed from Route 231 (east of the park) and Route 340 (west of the park), although if Skyline Drive is closed (as it sometimes is during and after winter storms), it's a fair bet that park trails are in tricky condition too. The park is especially beautiful in spring and fall. Spring features wildflower displays from mountain laurel, dogwood, azalea, and redbud; fall boasts brilliant foliage as the hardwoods turn colors. The National Park Service has an extremely useful "Plan Your Visit" web page that organizes hikes by mileage and features.

➤ The **Appalachian National Scenic Trail** runs the length of the park, frequently crossing Skyline Drive. In many places, it is possible to start a hike on another trail at a trailhead somewhere along the parkway, then link with the Appalachian Trail to make a loop back to your car. To hike the entire 115 miles of the Shenandoah segment of the Appalachian Trail usually takes a week to 12 days, depending on pace and fitness. Backpackers (permits are required) can sleep in shelters and campsites found every few miles along the trail. In addition, the Potomac Appalachian Trail Club operates several locked cabins that can be rented.

➤ The park's high point is 4,051-foot Hawksbill Mountain in the middle of the park (mile markers 45 to 48), which can be accessed via hikes of varying lengths, depending on which Skyline Drive trailhead you use and how you combine the **Upper and Lower Hawksbill Trails** with other adjacent paths. Trails to **Marys Rock**, **Chimney Rock**, **Hightop Summit**, **Blackrock Summit**, and **Stony Man** are other notable day hikes leading to some of the park's best views.

➤ The park's history is largely hidden beneath its second-growth forests, but exploring on foot takes visitors to remnants of the park's past. In the middle of the park is the **Brown House**, once used by President Herbert Hoover as his country office. Hikes of various lengths—either out-and-back trips or loop hikes—take visitors from various points on Skyline Drive (mile markers 51 to 55) to **Rapidan Camp**, which has historic exhibits and, sometimes, guided tours.

Dark Hollow Falls (top left); overlook along Skyline Drive (top right); trails through fall foliage just off Skyline Drive (bottom left and right)

➤ Trails to waterfalls are among the park's most popular, and the shorter trails make great destinations for families with small children. More than a dozen trails lead to falls; some of them are short and sweet, and some are more challenging rock scrambles. At 93 feet, **Overall Run Falls** is the highest in the park, though it dries up during the summer. Other popular waterfall trails are **Dark Hollow Falls** and **Whiteoak Falls**, both in the middle of the park. The best season for waterfall lovers is spring, when snowmelt feeds the cascades.

➤ Perhaps the best-known hike in the park is nowhere near Skyline Drive. **Old Rag Mountain** is named after the ragged rocks near its summit. The 9-mile loop is a full day's work; there is as much scrambling and climbing over, around, and through fields of granite boulders as there is walking. The vista at the top is expansive, with views down to circling hawks and falcons.

BELOW: Trail to Stony Man

OPPOSITE: Dark Hollow Falls in winter

Great Smoky Mountains
National Park

NORTH CAROLINA AND TENNESSEE

———

Designated 1926

BELOW: Tree in Cades Cove

OPPOSITE: Trail along Max Patch

FOLLOWING SPREAD: Mountain stream with moss-covered rock

The Cherokee people called these mountains "Shaconage," or "place of the blue smoke." When European Americans arrived here in the early 1700s, they called them the "Smoky Mountains," and later added the word "great." Much has changed in the intervening years. Between 1830 and 1850, the Cherokee, along with other southeastern Indigenous nations, were forcibly evicted from the region and relocated to Oklahoma on the infamous Trail of Tears. Farm communities grew, then succumbed to economic pressures and the establishment of the national park. More recently, acid rain and pest infestations have killed trees. The lands just outside the park have changed too: formerly near-subsistence Appalachian communities developed tourist attractions that cater to the more than 12 million people who come to the park every year. Great Smoky Mountains is the most visited national park in the system.

But the mountains—some of the oldest on earth—remain a constant: the place of blue smoke. Or rather, they remain the land of blue volatile organic compounds (VOCs). It's a less poetic moniker, but it more scientifically explains the mountains' famous blue fog.

It's all about the plants. The combination of abundant rainfall with elevations that range from 850 to 6,643 feet give Great Smoky Mountains National Park an astonishing biological diversity, with more than 19,000 recorded species—more than any other park in the United States—including 100 species of native trees and 1,500 species of flowering plants. Plants release oxygen, but they also give off VOCs, natural gases that react with other substances in the air to create vapors. Molecules in these vapors scatter wavelengths of light at the blue-violet end of the spectrum. In most places, this effect is negligible. In the Smokies, the abundance of plants creates so many VOCs that a bluish haze is formed, which in turn is spread by air saturated with rainfall and humidity.

Biodiversity has earned the park designation as a World Heritage Site. In addition to its diverse plant life, the park is home to 63 mammal species, nearly 70 species of native fish, more than 80 kinds of reptiles and amphibians, about 240 species of birds, and about 19 species of fireflies, one of which puts on a springtime synchronous display that lights up the forest and draws visitors from around the world (if, that is, they are lucky enough to get one of the tickets, drawn by lottery). Great Smoky Mountains National Park is also home to some 1,500 black bears, many of which have learned that they like hiker food better than bear food. The park provides a bear-proof cable system for food storage.

The park's location puts it within easy road-tripping distance for urbanites from southeastern cities.

Its sits almost exactly astride the Appalachian Ridge, one of only three parks that straddle state lines. Highway 441 goes through the middle of the park, linking the North Carolina and Tennessee sides. Entrance is free, courtesy of a restriction placed on the deed when Tennessee transferred land for the park and the highway that crosses it to the federal government.

The park is open year-round. In winter, some roads are closed, and others can be temporarily impassible, so not all trailheads will be accessible to hikers. Additionally, winter ice and snow can make trails difficult to navigate, especially at higher elevations. Summers are hot and humid. Spring and fall offer more comfortable temperatures.

Exploring the Park

About 850 miles of trails wind around the park's 850 square miles. Features include mountain balds and outcroppings, deep forests, and plenty of cascades and waterfalls.

➤ Seventy-three miles of the **Appalachian National Scenic Trail** traverse the spine of the park. Northbound, the Appalachian Trail climbs from Fontana Dam to the ridge that forms the border between North Carolina and Tennessee, then stays right there for the rest of the park. The Appalachian Trail offers a relatively remote experience because there are only three convenient access points to it: the trailhead near Fontana Dam, Highway 441 at Newfound Gap, and a side trail from the Big Creek Ranger Station on the western side of the park. On either side of Newfound Gap, Appalachian Trail hikers will have plenty of company. Two of the park's most popular trails are the paved hike to **Clingmans Dome** (a developed monument that is the highest point in the park) or the hike to **Charlies Bunion**, a famed lookout about 4 miles from Newfound Gap.

➤ An annual four-day **Spring Wildflower Pilgrimage** offers programs and guided hikes that celebrate the profligate blooms characteristic of the southern Appalachians: catawba rhododendron, mountain laurel, flame azalea, dogwood, and redbud.

North Carolina Side

➤ Near Newfound Gap, the 3.5-mile, round-trip hike to the open, grassy expanse of **Andrews Bald** starts at the Clingmans Dome parking lot, with a total elevation gain of around 900 feet. Balds are a characteristic formation in the southern Appalachians—summits that are not high enough to be above tree line, but nonetheless have no trees. The reasons are unknown; proposed theories have included fire, wind, Indigenous land use, geologic forces, and destruction from Ice Age mammals like woolly mammoths.

➤ Near Bryson City, a short 2-mile loop near the Deep Creek Ranger Station goes to three waterfalls—**Tom Branch Falls, Indian Creek Falls, and Juney Whank Falls**—making it a great family hike.

➤ A strenuous 11.8-mile, round-trip hike to **Mount Cammerer** starts at the Big Creek Ranger Station on the North Carolina side. The trail, part of which is on the Appalachian Trail, gains about 3,000 feet. The view from the fire tower is the reward.

Tennessee Side

➤ Off Highway 441, **Mount LeConte**, at 6,593 feet, is the third-highest peak in the park. Conveniently located trailheads, great views, a resort (where day hikers can purchase snacks), and multiple trails to the summit—all of which offer beautiful features en route—make this area a hiker favorite. The 11-mile, round-trip **Alum Cave Bluffs** route is steep, with interesting geologic formations (the 80-foot-high bluff, about halfway to the summit, is a popular turnaround point). Two other routes to the summit are accessed by Cherokee Orchard Road: the **Rainbow Falls Trail** passes 80-foot falls named for the rainbows created by a combination of waterfall mist and afternoon sun, and the **Trillium Gap Trail** passes Grotto Falls, a 25-foot waterfall that hikers can walk behind. The round-trip hike to the summit is a moderate 2.6 miles through old-growth forest and alongside a mountain creek. At the summit, nearby Myrtle Point and Cliff Top offer panoramic views.

➤ Cades Cove is one of the park's highlights, containing remnants of historic buildings that were once part of a thriving rural community and meadows known for wildlife viewing; bear sightings can slow traffic down to a New York City snarl. The 5.2-mile **Abrams Falls Loop** goes to an impressive 20-foot-tall waterfall (swimming is prohibited). The 8.5-mile **Rich Mountain Loop**, especially lovely in spring, is known for its diverse wildflowers.

➤ The 2.6-mile **Laurel Falls Trail**, about 3.5 miles from the Sugarlands Visitor Center on the road to Cades Cove, is a family favorite, but don't be confused if you see it described as paved. It's only partially paved, and places are steep and slick, making it unsuitable for strollers. Supervise kids closely here; the tempting rocks can be dangerously slippery. The 80-foot falls have an upper and lower tier, and if you hike in May, you'll be surrounded by the laurel the trails are named for.

BELOW: View of Forge Creek from Forge Creek Road

OPPOSITE: Dan Lawson Barn in Cades Cove (top left); Laurel Falls Trail (top right); deer near Big Meadows (bottom left); Mingus Mill (bottom right)

Bryce Canyon
National Park

UTAH

Designated 1928

"A hell of a place to lose a cow." That was how Mormon pioneer Ebenezer Bryce responded when a neighbor asked him back in 1875 how he liked that big red canyon at the back of his Utah homestead.

The hell of a place he referred to was Bryce Canyon and its hoodoo-filled amphitheaters. The giant rocks, spires, and bluffs stand guard like sentinels made of stone, looking every bit as fanciful and weird as their name. Thousands of them are arrayed in various formations, most of them nameless, like soldiers on parade. A few break ranks, demanding attention: Thor's Hammer, the Poodle, the Chinese Wall, Queen Victoria, and the Sinking Ship. Hoodoos are irregular spires of rock that can be found all over the world, from New Mexico to New Zealand, from Turkey to Taiwan, from Canada to the Canary Islands. But nowhere are they as concentrated as here in southern Utah, where they stand in the thousands. And nowhere are they as dramatic. Bryce Canyon's hoodoos rise to 200 feet, the result of terrain that was uplifted by tectonic movement, then carved into fantastical shapes. A combination of freezing and thawing cycles split the rock; then rain, snow, and ice found its way into the crevices, where it cut and carved and expanded, creating the rock statues. The colors—shades of beige, orange, white, and buff—change with the weather and the angle of the sun as it moves through its daily and seasonal cycles.

Despite its name, Bryce Canyon was not carved from the unrelenting pressure of the flow of a river, so it is not a true canyon. Rather, it is a 20-mile-long series of natural amphitheaters that were sculpted out of the edge of the eastern side of the Paunsaugunt Plateau. Just south of the main entrance, Bryce Amphitheater is the main attraction at the park, with visitor services such as a lodge, campground, store, shuttle stops, ranger station, and four of the park's

Queens Garden Trail

best-known viewpoints: Bryce Point, Inspiration Point, Sunset Point, and Sunrise Point.

The main road in the park is Rim Road, an 18-mile, one-way scenic drive built by the Civilian Conservation Corps during the Great Depression. It leads to the less visited southern end of the park, en route offering numerous outlooks and unlimited Instagram fodder. A number of trailheads lead into the amphitheaters themselves. In addition to hiking, activities include photography, stargazing, and wildlife viewing (prairie dogs, mule deer, elk, black bears, and—if you are very lucky—bobcats and mountain lions). While peak season is from May to September, the park is also beautiful in the winter, when snow coats the hoodoos, creating a winter fairyland. Rim Road becomes a snowshoe and cross-country skiing route; some trails may be closed due to ice and snow. Bring crampons or other traction devices if you intend to try winter hiking. The ice that split the ancient rock into its hoodoo formations can just as easily cause a human bone to break from a fall.

Exploring the Park

The park's 60 miles of hiking trails are the main draw at Bryce Canyon National Park. Day hikers have numerous ways to combine trails in various combinations of difficulty, length, and elevation gain. Because this is a relatively small park, backpacking trips are limited to only a few days, but watching the sun set and rise in this spectacular landscape makes even a short trip a pinnacle experience. The daily freeze-and-thaw cycles that created the hoodoos also create challenges for hikers. Bring layers; for 200 days a year, daily temperatures fluctuate above and below the freezing point. Elevations range from about 7,000 to 9,000 feet, and the altitude can challenge those who are not yet acclimated. Since the trails lead downhill from the rim, they require climbing back uphill on the return. Keep both your water supply and your endurance in mind as you descend, because the return is going to require more energy and more water.

➤ For day hikers, one of the classic routes is the **Rim Trail,** which winds near the mesa top for 5.5 miles (one way) between Bryce Point and Fairyland Point. This hike goes past all the main car-accessible viewpoints, but adds many other viewpoints along the way. It also connects with other trails in Bryce Amphitheater.

➤ Other popular day-hiking trails are **Queens Garden Trail** and the **Navajo Loop**, which can be hiked separately or combined. The 1.8-mile Queens Garden Trail is the easiest hike that goes into the amphitheater and back up; the Navajo Loop is shorter, at 1.3 miles, but steeper, with views of Thor's Hammer, Two Bridges, and the bottom of Wall Street. One of the park's easiest trails is found at its highest elevation, at 9,000 feet on the far south end. The 1-mile **Bristlecone Trail** takes hikers to thousand-year-old trees perched on the edge of the plateau, from which there are expansive views of the canyon. For more ambitious hikers, the **Fairyland Loop** (8 miles) and the **Peek-A-Boo Loop** (5.5 miles) are spectacular, steeper, and less crowded.

➤ For backpackers, the 23-mile **Under-the-Rim Trail** runs from Rainbow Point at the south end of Rim Road to Bryce Point in Bryce Amphitheater at the northern end of the park. Following the forested base of the Paunsaugunt Plateau, it offers views of the hoodoos up-canyon and to the west. The trail intersects all the rim-to-valley trails between Rainbow Point and the Bryce Amphitheater, allowing hikers to create trips of varying lengths. Campsites must be reserved, and permits are required.

Natural Bridge (top left); views of hoodoos from Rim Trail (top right and bottom left); hiker on Fairyland Loop Trail (bottom right)

Grand Teton
National Park

WYOMING

———

Designated 1929

With 310,000 acres, Grand Teton National Park is only middling in size, but its famed mountain landscape takes center stage among the iconic images of the American West. Even among such scenic heavy-hitters as Yosemite, Kings Canyon, Sequoia, Rainier, and North Cascades National Parks, Grand Teton holds its own; the view of the three granite Tetons rising above the surrounding plains to pierce the sky is one of the best-known vistas in the national park system. The park contains the 40-mile Teton Range, along with Jackson Lake and the northern part of the Jackson Hole Valley.

With more than three million visitors annually, Grand Teton is among the 10 most visited national parks. Within easy reach of Jackson's commercially served airport, it is also a straight shot from Yellowstone, only 10 miles away. The John D. Rockefeller Jr. Memorial Parkway, named after one of the park's early founders and benefactors, connects the two parks.

Despite Grand Teton's popularity, the backcountry ecosystem is almost pristine, with dozens of species of mammals and more than 300 species of birds (an impressive number considering the region's challenging climate). Geologically, the park contains some of the oldest rocks on earth—some dating back as much as 2.7 billion years. Glaciers are part of both the scenery and the ecology, but they are receding. The park's 12 named glaciers have been steadily shrinking, and some may be in the process of losing their status as glaciers. (Glaciers are defined as moving blocks of permanent snow and ice; when a glacier no longer has enough heft to move, it is classified as a stationary snowfield.)

Human history in the park dates back at least 11,000 years, to nomadic Paleo-Indians who seasonally hunted in the region. When European Americans arrived in the early 1800s, Shoshone people were using the area. European use of the land began with fur trading; the name of the mountain range is thought to have been

Beaver dam at Schwabacher Landing, with Teton Mountains in the background

FOLLOWING SPREAD: Oxbow Bend (left); view of fall foliage from Highway 191 (top right); cow and bull moose near Gros Ventre Campground (middle right); T. A. Moulton Barn on Mormon Row (bottom right)

given by French trappers, who referred to the peaks as the *trois tetons* (three teats). The arrival of more permanent white settlers in the 1880s coincided with the designation of Yellowstone National Park and the beginnings of the conservation movement that would lead to the development of the National Park Service. Efforts to preserve the region as a national park began in the late 19th century, and the park was designated in 1929.

The original park protected only the Teton Range's major peaks; the surrounding valley of Jackson Hole remained in private ownership and was threatened by the prospect of damming and development. John D. Rockefeller Jr. was one of the proponents of expanding the park. In the 1930s, he and other conservationists began purchasing land they hoped to add to the existing national park. However, the expansion was controversial. A coalition of local business owners successfully lobbied Congress and managed to prevent the expansion. Finally, in 1943, President Franklin D. Roosevelt made use of the Antiquities Act, which gave him the right to take executive action without congressional approval. He accepted land donated by Rockefeller's Snake River Land Company and established Jackson Hole National Monument. In 1950, the monument was abolished and most of its land was added to Grand Teton National Park.

The national park is a popular destination for camping, mountaineering, hiking, backpacking, birdwatching, wildlife viewing, and world-renowned trout fishing. Six drive-in campgrounds offer more than 1,050 campsites, and more than 200 miles of hiking trails lead to the park's backcountry camping areas.

Exploring the Park

The short, snow-free season, especially at the higher elevations, coincides with summer vacation, meaning that the vast majority of visitors come between the end of June and Labor Day. But the park also attracts winter-loving backcountry skiers and snowshoers.

➤ Jenny Lake, near the park's southern entrance, contains many of the park's best-known and most popular trails. A dense network of trails enables both backpackers and day hikers to create numerous loops of varying lengths. Favorite day hikes include **Inspiration Point**—a famed viewpoint with a short side trip to **Hidden Falls** and **String** and **Leigh Lakes** (2 miles)—and the **Jenny Lake Loop** (8 miles). For strong day hikers or backpackers, **Lake Solitude** is a 14- to 18-mile round trip (depending on the trailhead selected). For hikers looking for bigger mileage, the terrain west of Jenny Lake features a network of scenic trails that lead into the high country: two favorites are the **Cascade Canyon Trail** to Lake Solitude, or a combination of the **Cascade Canyon** and **Paintbrush Canyon Trails**, which form a longer loop.

➤ Jenny Lake is also near the starting trailhead for one of the park's classic hikes. The 40-mile **Teton Crest Trail**—often considered one of the most scenic trails in the country—winds around the southwestern section of the park, sometimes wandering over the park boundary as it heads to a trailhead just south of Teton Village. But it is rated difficult, with nearly 11,000 feet of elevation gain. (Mileage depends on trailhead choices; figure three to five days, with options to shorten the hike by veering off on side trails.)

➤ South of Jenny Lake, trails connect south to **Taggart** and **Bradley Lakes**, and then to **Phelps Lake**. Some of the popular hikes from these three lakes include the **Death Canyon Trail** and the **Phelps Lake Overlook Trail** (which can be combined), and the trail to **Amphitheater** and **Surprise Lakes**.

➤ Farther north in the park, the 2-mile **Lakeshore Trail** starts from Colter Bay Visitor Center at Jackson Lake. For backpackers seeking more isolation, the **Glade Creek Trailhead** off of John D. Rockefeller Jr. Memorial Parkway offers the opportunity to connect the **Glade Creek Trail** with the **Berry Creek Trail**, the **Owl Creek Trail**, the **Owl-Berry Cutoff Trail**, and the **Webb Canyon Trail** to form trips of varying mileages in the park's more difficult-to-reach northwestern sector.

Fall foliage near Oxbow Bend (top left); hiker on trail around Jenny Lake (top right); fall foliage, with Teton Mountains in the background (bottom left); chipmunk on a tree trunk near Snake River Overlook (bottom right)

Carlsbad Caverns National Park

NEW MEXICO

———

Designated 1930

BELOW: Bat Flight Amphitheater and entrance to Carlsbad Caverns

OPPOSITE: Just inside the entrance to the caverns

Above the surface in southeastern New Mexico, the Guadalupe Mountains and the Chihuahuan Desert intersect in a harsh mountain desert landscape. Plant life is mostly prickly here: prickly pear cactus and—also prickly—cholla, agave, barrel cactus, and ocotillo. In between, the opportunistic, deep-rooted creosote plants suck water from deep beneath the ground. Animal life—tarantulas, lizards, scorpions, rattlesnakes, javelinas, and golden eagles—are adaptable, but not generally cuddly.

Below the surface, the world morphs into the opposite of what lies above. The gloom of the underworld replaces the glare of the sun, cave walls sweat water to quench the memory of the scorching dryness above, and temperatures drop, sometimes as much as 50 degrees cooler than the air outside. This is an entirely different world, a maze of enormous underground chambers and stunning displays of speleothems—the scientific name for rock art created by minerals, water, and time. The stunning formations include all manner, shapes, and sizes of stalactites and stalagmites, along with formations named for their shapes: columns, cave popcorn, tubes, spires, ribbons, drapes, totem poles, and soda straws. Some are huge and imposing; others are as delicate as the finest needlework.

Carlsbad Cavern itself is only one of the 119 caves in the eponymous Carlsbad Caverns National Park, and that only counts the caves that have so far been discovered; there could be many more. It is also the park's "show cave." In caver lingo, that means a cave that has been developed to be accessible to the public for guided tours and visits, with safety and accessibility features such as constructed walking routes, handrails, lights, steps, and, in this case, even elevators, a gift shop, a snack shop, and restrooms. Calling Carlsbad a "show cave" is no exaggeration: its most famous attraction is the so-called Big Room, an enormous cavern that stretches out for 8.2 acres; it is one of the largest underground caves developed for touring in the world. Its features come in every imaginable size and shape, their colorful names giving hints as to what to expect—for example, Bottomless Pit, Temple of the Sun, and Hall of Giants.

The system of caves at Carlsbad Caverns was created by three completely unrelated geological events—the drying up of an inland sea, the movement of tectonic plates, and the presence of an underground oil field. The first two are commonplace in the formation of caves; the oil field is the wild card. About 250 million years ago, this part of New Mexico was under an inland sea that dried up and left behind the remains of a reef. Tectonic action lifted the reef to form some of the features of the Guadalupe Mountains. But it was hydrogen sulfide gas from the underground oil field that created the vast and extensive underground world; as

the gas rose and reacted with oxygen from the groundwater, it formed sulfuric acid, which is what dissolved the limestone and created caves on such a grand scale.

The caves are huge; they are also fragile. A feature that takes millions of years to form can be damaged or destroyed in any number of ways. Vandalism, graffiti, and litter are obvious issues, but even well-meaning visitors can have an impact. Tourists are asked not to touch anything in the caves (oil from fingers can restrict natural growth of cave features, and lint from skin and clothing can turn the cave walls brown and attract insects). During the COVID-19 pandemic, the closed spaces and high visitation numbers resulted in some policy modifications, including cancellation of guided tours of the park's other caves, which had previously been available, and a requirement that reservations be made in advance to enter the caverns.

Above ground, two-thirds of the park is managed as wilderness, and only backcountry camping is permitted. Bird-watchers should make a side trip to the noncontiguous Rattlesnake Springs section of the park, which, as an oxymoronic "desert wetland," is known for its large populations of reptiles and hundreds of species of year-round and migrating birds. Another wildlife spectacle is the nightly emergence of some 400,000 Brazilian free-tailed bats; evening ranger programs from late May through October share information about cave ecology and the bats.

Exploring the Park

The park offers opportunities both above ground and below ground. The engineering that was required to create safe, accessible passages through the tortured underground maze is as impressive as the caves themselves.

➢ Exploring the Carlsbad Caverns "show cave" can be done via two self-guided tours. An elevator leads from the visitor center 754 feet down a shaft of solid limestone to the **Big Room Trail**, a serpentine loop that winds around the main features of the room. Alternatively, hikers can descend through Carlsbad's natural entrance, via the 1.25-mile **Natural Entrance Trail**, which descends 750 feet to join the Big Room Trail.

➢ Above ground, the 0.5-mile, one-way **Chihuahuan Desert Nature Trail** is a mostly paved, mostly flat path with markers explaining the flora of the region. For more avid day hikers, the Rattlesnake Canyon area offers the chance to combine various trail segments and trailheads on the Desert Loop Road to make hikes of different lengths. For a longer hike, the 10.6-mile, round-trip **Slaughter Canyon Trail** begins at the parking lot for the **Slaughter Canyon Cave Trail**. The Slaughter Canyon Cave Trail is a short but rugged mile-long round-trip hike that branches off to the west, leading to a good view of the Slaughter Canyon Cave. The longer Slaughter Canyon Trail is a rugged hike that climbs 1,850 feet to the Guadalupe Ridge Trail.

➢ For backpackers, just over 20 miles of the **Guadalupe Ridge Trail** cross Carlsbad Caverns National Park from west to east. The Guadalupe Ridge Trail is a 100-mile national recreation trail that connects Guadalupe National Park (and the highest point in Texas) to Carlsbad Caverns National Park. The trail is rugged; in addition to climbs and rocky trail, heat and lack of water are two major challenges.

OPPOSITE: Big Room Trail within the caverns

BELOW: Chihuahuan Desert Nature Trail above ground

Everglades
National Park

_____

Designated 1934

The water is sapphire colored, glinting. Sawgrass undulates in the breeze, sometimes emerald green, sometimes gold; it depends on the season and the light. Water and grasses stretch for miles in any direction; occasionally, the wind ripples the water, but otherwise, all is still.

Seemingly motionless, sometimes 60 miles (or more) wide, flowing down an almost nonexistent gradient at the barely perceptible rate of 100 feet a day, the Everglades does not look like a river, but in fact it is. Starting with water that flows out of Lake Okeechobee, then creeps toward the sea, it is sometimes called the world's widest river.

The first 21 national parks protected landscapes, most often for scenic and recreational values, and later, in the case of Mesa Verde, for historical values. Everglades National Park was the first to be preserved primarily as an ecological preserve, with the goal of protecting its biological diversity from the threat of development in South Florida. Its 1.5 million acres makes it the third-largest park in the contiguous states—after Death Valley and Yellowstone. Even so, the park protects only about 20 percent of the original Everglades ecosystem, much of which continues to be compromised by development and large-scale agriculture.

Most of the park is wilderness. Marjory Stoneman Douglas's 1947 book, *The Everglades: River of Grass*, redefined the Everglades from the worthless swamp it was thought to be to a treasured river and ecological resource. It is the largest tropical wilderness in the United States. With 1.3 million acres officially designated as wilderness (and another 167,000 acres managed as de facto wilderness), it is also the largest wilderness of any kind east of the Mississippi River. Yet it is within an hour's drive of the Miami waterfront; an average of one million people visit the park each year.

American white pelicans on a sandbar

The Everglades fulfill an essential role in a state with unique geography and hydrogeology. Surrounded on three sides by water, Florida's state high point (not counting Miami skyscrapers) is a mere 345 feet above sea level. In the Everglades, the elevation range is even less, usually between eight and 12 feet above sea level.

Rain that falls in Florida has to go somewhere: it can flow down the barely perceptible gradient, it can seep underground, or it can flood. The Everglades does all three. Beneath the land—such as it is—lies a layer of limestone formed by fossilized deposits of calcium-rich coral, sand, shells, and other marine detritus; this permeable layer acts as a giant sponge and holds a freshwater aquifer. When the limestone sponge is fully saturated and the lumbering river can't handle any further rains, seasonal flooding occurs, covering what little dry land there is, as well as boardwalks, trails, and the park's few roads.

The Everglades are a prime example of an ecological edge—an ecosystem formed at the point of environmental or geographic intersection. They sit at the intersection of climates (a temperate climate to the north; a tropical climate to the south), as well as at the intersection of aquatic environments (fresh water from the interior; salt water from the ocean). The visual image most commonly associated with the park is the freshwater slough—the slow-moving river covered with undulating grasses. But the Everglades also encompass interdependent and related ecosystems: marl prairies (waterlogged sawgrass similar to the slough, but with still instead of moving water), tropical hardwood hammocks (where a mere few inches of elevation provide enough dry land for trees to grow), fire-adapted pinelands, cypress and mangrove swamps, coastal lowlands, and marine and estuarian environments.

The intersecting ecosystems allow animals and plants that usually inhabit entirely different environments to live side by side. As a result, the Everglades boast some of the richest wildlife on earth. Birds range from seabirds and waders like herons, egrets, roseate spoonbills, ibises, and brown pelicans to woodland birds such as barred owls, woodpeckers, northern cardinals, and southern bald eagles. Mammals include red and gray foxes, mink, marsh rabbits, and white-tailed deer. And Florida's famed megafauna are also in residence, including the Florida black bear, the critically endangered Florida panther, manatees, the fresh water–loving alligator, and the salt water–loving American crocodile.

Exploring the Park

Most of the park is accessible only via private boats, rented or chartered boats, or boat tours that begin near the Flamingo or Gulf Coast Visitor Centers. Strict rules apply concerning the use of motorized boats. To access the wilderness interior, canoes or kayaks give the best vantage points for viewing the wildlife and vegetation from a water-level perspective. Hiking and walking trails are mostly short—some paved and accessible, some on boardwalks, and some on dirt and limestone—and offer opportunities for bird-watching, wildlife spotting, and photography, usually near the visitor centers. Note that some trails are not regularly maintained to avoid disturbing wildlife; check with the visitor center for current conditions.

➤ On the southeast side of the park near the Ernest F. Coe Visitor Center, trails spread out from the Main Park Road. They include the **Anhinga Trail** (a short boardwalk through a wetland of slough and sawgrass, with the possibility of seeing alligators), the **Gumbo Limbo Trail** (a paved trail through junglelike hardwood hammocks), the **Pineland Trail** (a short, paved, wheelchair-accessible loop through pinelands), the **Pahayokee Overlook** (a wheelchair-accessible elevated boardwalk with sweeping river-of-grass views), and the **Mahogany Hammock Trail** (a boardwalk through a dense, junglelike hardwood hammock that includes the largest living mahogany tree in the United States).

➤ Trails in the Flamingo area at the southern tip of the park showcase a variety of ecosystems. Just east of the Flamingo Visitor Center, the **Snake Bight Trail** (1.6 miles, one way) runs through tropical hardwood hammocks to a scenic bayside view with good bird-watching; it can be linked with the **Rowdy Bend Trail**, an overgrown roadbed through shady buttonwoods and open coastal prairie. Also east of the visitor center, the

Brown pelican on a pole (top left); canoe on shore of one of the Ten Thousand Islands (top right); mangroves near Gulf Coast Visitor Center (bottom)

Christian Point Trail, 1.8 miles each way, wanders through dense mangroves and buttonwoods full of bromeliads to coastal prairies and the shore of Snake Bight. Closer to the visitor center, the 0.5-mile **Eco Pond Trail** loops around a pond that is home to wading birds, shorebirds, and the occasional crocodile. The **Bayshore Loop Trail** connects the **Bayshore Trail** with a short segment of the **Coastal Prairie Trail** to make a 2-mile loop. For a longer hike, the 7.5-mile, one-way **Coastal Prairie Trail** goes through open prairies and buttonwoods before reaching the shore of Florida Bay.

➤ On the northern side of the park, Shark Valley offers the 15-mile paved **Tram Road Loop** (which makes for a longer hike than most people are

willing to do, but bicycle rentals and tram tours are available). There is an observation tower at the halfway point; possible wildlife sightings may include alligators, herons, egrets, deer, and turtles. Below the Observation Tower is a short trail through a tropical hardwood hammock. Two short side trails, the **Otter Cave Hammock Trail** and the **Bobcat Boardwalk,** also veer off from the Tram Road to explore features of the surrounding hammocks, limestone, and ecosystems.

➤ For paddlers, the **Wilderness Waterway** is 99 miles long and takes approximately seven to 10 days by canoe or kayak. Many well-marked shorter water trails exist, including the **Hells Bay Canoe Trail** and the **Nine-Mile Pond Canoe Trail.**

BELOW: Mangrove pathway through the park

OPPOSITE: Kayaker on a paddling trail

Olympic National Park

Crashing waves, enormous old-growth forest, and alpine meadows: Olympic National Park contains all three of the marquee natural features of the Pacific Northwest. At the high elevations, flowers in brilliant profusion scramble to live their entire life cycle in a few short, snow-free months. Lower down, in ancient forests, enormous, sky-blocking trees grew from seedlings sprouted a millennium ago. Just off the coastline of the Pacific Ocean, sea lions and whales pass by.

Sprawling over the center of the Olympic Peninsula, a short hop across Puget Sound from the Seattle metropolitan area, the park attracts some three million visitors a year, putting it on the top 10 list of most visited parks. But despite the park's popularity, its interior is quiet and remote. Most visitors flock to those areas that are accessible via the park's few roads. However, the interior contains the largest wilderness area in Washington, accessible only on foot. This is one of the state's prime backpacking destinations, especially for those on multiday hikes. Other activities include day hiking, boating, rafting, and fishing. In winter, snowshoers, skiers, and snowboarders can access the backcountry or even—on days when Hurricane Ridge Road is open—a small lift-served alpine ski area.

Olympic National Park can be roughly divided into four sections. Each of them is part of the mosaic that makes this national park a microcosm of Washington's scenic extravagances.

Smack in the park's center are the glaciated and snow-covered high peaks, surrounded by meadows. Glaciers feed streams that flow into lakes colored sky blue, sapphire, or the milky turquoise of glacial meltwater, depending on the weather and the angle of the light. The size of the park and the lack of roads that penetrate the middle means that it takes several days of hiking to access the high country in the park's interior.

Hall of Mosses Trail in
Hoh Rain Forest

The lower elevations of the western region catch much of the rain blowing in from the Pacific Ocean and use it to feed a primeval temperate rain-forest ecosystem containing, according to the park's foundation document, the finest samples of old-growth Sitka spruce, western hemlock, Douglas fir, and western red cedar in the entire United States. Trails here lead into the maze of the rain forest, where plants grow over one another, and 50 shades of green—from emerald moss to deep spruce to brilliant fern—vie for attention. It's a rain forest, so take that name literally—though July, August, and September often have long dry spells.

The third major ecosystem of the park contains the drier, sparser forests of the lower elevations on the eastern side of the park. During wet weather, the eastern side of the park gets the least rain; it is also the most easily accessible from Seattle.

Finally, discontinuous with the rest of the park, the fourth ecosystem is a long, thin slice of shoreline that hugs the rugged coast. The long, narrow coastal strip provides suitable terrain for a multiday beach backpack trip, but it's a rugged hike, not a stroll on the beach. Hikers must check tide tables; in some places, high tide can trap an unprepared hiker between hell (the rocky cliffs) and high water (the raging ocean). Conditions range from sand to mud to overgrown brush to slick boulders and rock scrambling around the promontories, sometimes assisted by fixed ropes.

Exploring the Park

Many of the most popular day hikes in Olympic National Park are concentrated around the Hoh Rain Forest area in the west and in the Hurricane Ridge area in the east. Backpackers can use these trails as access points to reach the park's interior, with its glacier, alpine lakes, and peaks.

➤ The **Pacific Northwest National Scenic Trail** spends about 140 miles in Olympic National Park. Going east to west, it traverses the park; after leaving the Hoh Rain Forest area on the park's western side, it reenters the park at the coastal strip and heads north to Cape Alava. For backpackers, the trail offers the chance to experience all four of the park's

major ecosystems. For day hikers, it offers a sampling of park environments, accessible from trailheads at Rialto Beach, Third Beach, and Oil City, and from Olympic Hot Springs Road, the **Elwha to Hurricane Hill Trailhead**, **Boulder Hot Springs Trailhead**, **Happy Lake Ridge Trailhead**, and the **Whiskey Bend Trailhead**.

➤ The Hurricane Ridge area on the northeast side is one of the most visited sections of the park, with views into the mountainous interior and numerous trail options, including the popular 3.2-mile, round-trip **Hurricane Hill Trail**. Other popular short trails in this region are **Sunrise Point Trail** (a short connector trail) and **Klahhane Ridge** (accessible from several trailheads). It is also possible to combine trails and loops of varying lengths, and to embark on longer backpacks into the heart of the park—for example, by combining the **Elwha to Hurricane Hill Trail** with the **Pacific Northwest Trail** and the **Wolf Creek Trail**. Also on the eastern side of the park, but at the southern edge, is the less used Staircase Entrance, which gives access to the 2.8-mile **Staircase Rapids Loop** and the 6-mile, out-and-back **Wagonwheel Lake Trail**, with 3,200 feet of elevation gain.

➤ The alpine middle of the park is best reached by endurance trail runners or multiday backpackers because of the distances and the challenging elevation gains. Hikes of varying lengths can be designed by combining sections of the **High Divide Trail** (contiguous with the **Pacific Northwest Trail**) and the **Sol Duc River Trail** to circle around Seven Lakes Basin. These trails can also be linked to the **Hoh River Trail**, which connects the western, rain-forest side of the park (via the **Hoh Lake Trail**) with the mountainous interior. The **Skyline Ridge Trail** in the south-central part of the park is an alpine trail that is more remote and hence less frequently used.

➤ The Hoh Entrance Station on the southwestern side of the park leads to trailheads accessing the dense, fecund, shaded groves of ancient trees in the Hoh Rain Forest. Popular short choices include the **Hall of Mosses**, **Sol Duc Falls**, **Spruce Nature**, and **Sitka Nature Trails** (each about a mile long), the 1.8-mile **Marymere Falls Trail**, and the 2.2-mile **Sol Duc**

Sol Duc Falls (top left); Hall of Mosses in Hoh Rain Forest (top right); Hoh River Trail (bottom left); waterfall along Sol Duc River Trail (bottom right)

Falls Trail. A longer day hike, and one of the most popular trails in the park, is the 4.7-mile **Mount Storm King Trail**. For backpackers, the much longer **Hoh River Trail** heads 17.4 miles into the heart of the park and can be linked via the **Hoh Lake Trail**, which connects with trails leading to the central and east side of the park.

➤ Olympic's coastal segment attracts both day hikers and backpackers, but many sections are challenging, with sand to slog through, tidal charts to watch for, and rock scrambles. Popular choices include **Cape Flattery** (the northwesternmost point in the contiguous United States, right up at the Strait of Juan de Fuca), **Shi Shi Beach** (with tidal pools and rock scrambling), **Third Beach** (combines a forest hike with a stunning coastal beach), and **Ruby Beach** (reddish sand and dramatic sea stacks).

BELOW: Tidal pools near Rialto Beach

OPPOSITE: Sea stacks near Rialto Beach

Kings Canyon National Park

In October of 1890, just one week after Sequoia National Park was established in the High Sierra, two other nearby parks were added to the nascent system. The first was Yosemite, destined to become one of the crown jewels of the national park system. The second new park was General Grant, a mere 4 square miles, located adjacent to Sequoia. Established with the express purpose of preserving the Grant Grove of giant sequoias and protecting the second-tallest sequoia tree in the world (also named for the Civil War general), General Grant National Park was set up as its own discrete unit, managed in conjunction with Sequoia.

Yosemite, of course, is now one of the most iconic parks in the system. But General Grant National Park is no more. Instead, we have Kings Canyon National Park: a grown-up, expanded, unrecognizable version of the original 4-square-mile parcel.

Kings Canyon owes its designation to wilderness advocates of the 1930s who lobbied for the protection of the Sierra Nevada's stunning mountain landscapes. Among them were Ansel Adams, whose classic wilderness photographs communicated as eloquently as any orator. Putting these images on the desks of Secretary of the Interior Harold Ickes, President Franklin D. Roosevelt, and US congressmen had the intended result: in 1940, a mountain wilderness about the same size as Sequoia was added to the national park system. The new Kings Canyon National Park incorporated the preexisting General Grant National Park.

Kings Canyon's 462,000 acres are largely managed as wilderness, with very little road access and few tourist facilities. As a result, it has only half of the visitors to Sequoia National Park and about one-sixth of the visitors to Yosemite. Its tourist facilities are concentrated in the Grant Grove area and in the Cedar Grove area, which is the road access that goes farthest into the interior of the park.

Kings Canyon may not attract the hordes that frequent Yosemite Valley, but it is well known to hikers. Named after a mile-deep glacier-carved valley, the park features giant sequoias (on the western side), impressive (though potentially dangerous) snow-fed rivers, alpine meadows, and 13,000- and 14,000-foot peaks.

The park has only two road entrances. The Grant Grove entry leads to the original General Grant National Park, which is separated from the rest of Kings Canyon but is bordered by Sequoia. The entrance to the rest of Kings Canyon National Park—the vast majority of it—is via the Cedar Grove entry. The Grant Grove area is more popular with day hikers interested in the park's giant sequoias, while the Cedar Grove area is a debarkation point for day hikers and backpackers headed for the high country. Note that much of the park's high interior is snowbound from October through June (depending on the elevation and the snowfall in any particular year).

Exploring the Park

Kings Canyon day hikes include mountain and canyon hikes and big trees hikes. Backpacking trails include perhaps the national park system's best-known and most iconic trail: the John Muir Trail (which is contiguous with the Pacific Crest National Scenic Trail in the park). The most popular trails can be crowded, which makes permits hard to get. Plan well in advance and have flexible dates. Hikers looking for a more remote experience might veer off from the main trunk trails and explore some of the out-and-back trails that lead into the secret corners of the high country.

➤ From the Grant Grove area, the **General Grant Tree Trail** is short (only 0.5 miles long), flat, paved, and close to the visitor center, so it is hardly a

Hiker on Paradise Valley Trail

wilderness experience. But it leads to the General Grant Tree, one of the reasons General Grant National Park was founded in the first place. Also on this trail is the Fallen Monarch Tree, which toppled perhaps a thousand years ago, but now demonstrates the resiliency of sequoias, which resist decay for hundreds of years. The network of trails around the Kings Canyon Visitor Center and campground can be combined to explore many of the groves that led to the protection of the sequoias; the appeal of the 0.5-mile paved **Panoramic Point Trail** is self-explanatory. For less traveled trails, drive on the Generals Highway going first south, then west to the Redwood Canyon area, where the interconnecting **Redwood Canyon Loop**, the **Hart Tree and Fallen Goliath Loop**, the **Sugar Bowl Loop**, and the **Big Springs Trail** lead through huge tracts of sequoias of the original General Grant National Park. (Some of these acres were burned by fire in 2021; check with the ranger station for current status.)

➤ In the Cedar Grove area, a dead-end road leads into the heart of the mountain landscape of the park. Near the main entrance, visitor center, and campground, a network of short trails interlace around the river. With its convenient location near the entrance and an achievable-but-challenging 6-mile length, the **Hotel Creek Loop** is a popular day hike (add another 0.8 miles to go to and from the Cedar Grove Overlook). The loop is formed by connecting the **Hotel Creek**, **Lewis Creek**, and **River Trails**; backpackers can hike to the junction of the Hotel Creek and Lewis Creek Trails, then take the Upper Lewis Creek Trail north into the backcountry.

➤ From Cedar Grove to the Road's End Permit Station, the main park road follows the South Fork of the Kings River for about an hour (by car). Numerous trailheads allow access to the **River Trail**, as well as to offshoot trails such as the **Zumwalt Meadow Loop** or the short, paved trail to **Roaring River Falls**. Hikers interested in a longer foray into the high country should head to the **Road's End Permit Station and Trailhead**. For day hikers,

Mist Falls is a popular 9-mile hike (longer options are available for those who want to continue farther up to Paradise Valley).

➤ For backpackers, the **Bubbs Creek-John Muir Trail-Paradise Valley Loop** starts at the Road's End Permit Station. It is an unparalleled multiday loop that includes a section of the John Muir Trail over Glen Pass and past Rae Lakes. It can be hiked either clockwise or counterclockwise. Visitors should note that high temperatures and sun exposure can be challenging in midsummer.

➤ The **Pacific Crest National Scenic Trail/John Muir Trail** segment enters Kings Canyon from the south at 13,153-foot Forester Pass (the highest point on the entire Pacific Crest Trail), then continues over five more scenic passes, each higher than 11,700 feet: Glen Pass, Kearsarge Pass, Pinchot Pass, Mather Pass, and Muir Pass. On the north side of the park, the trail exits the park at the border of the Sierra National Forest. Visitors who want to hike any part of the Pacific Crest Trail/John Muir Trail in Kings Canyon must therefore use side trails to get to it. Also note that most of the high passes have snow until at least early July.

OPPOSITE: Hiker on path through the forest (top left); Roaring River Falls at dusk (top right); Zumwalt Meadow Trail (bottom left); General Grant Tree (bottom right)

BELOW: River through Paradise Valley

Isle Royale National Park

MICHIGAN

_____

Designated 1940

Isle Royale is the least visited national park in the contiguous states, with fewer than 30,000 annual visitors. (Compare that to the more than 12 million who have visited Great Smoky Mountains National Park in recent years.) Isle Royale's remote location in Lake Superior puts it closer to Canada than to the United States. Getting there requires driving to far northeastern Minnesota or to the Upper Peninsula of Michigan, then taking a ferry, boat, or seaplane.

Isle Royale is part of an archipelago in Lake Superior that was created by a combination of volcanic forces and glaciation. Formed about 20,000 years ago, the Great Lakes began as basins scoured out by great ice sheets that pushed enormous quantities of rocks and debris as they advanced southward across the continent. When the climate warmed and the ice sheets receded, the basins left behind were filled with meltwater. The lakes only reached their present shapes and sizes about 3,000 years ago—mere infants in geological time.

The main island is about 45 miles long and (at its widest point) 9 miles wide. Additionally, the park includes some 450 nearby smaller islands, as well as the surrounding marine environment, adding up to a total of about 850 square miles. In 1940, Isle Royale became a national park; 99 percent of the park is protected as a federally designated wilderness area.

In 1980, the park also became an international biosphere reserve, in part because it is home to one of the longest-running wildlife studies in the world. Since 1958, scientists have been examining the predator-prey relationship between the island's moose and wolf populations. Exactly how the moose and wolves arrived here is a bit of a mystery. The moose were long thought to have swam across the water, although new evidence suggests the possibility that they might have been brought here by humans. The wolves may have crossed the lake during a cold snap that froze the water. More recently, newer groups of wolves have been relocated here because the study group's population had dipped below sustainable levels, and the moose population was growing without the check of predation.

The park's forest environment contains coniferous pine, spruce, and fir, as well as deciduous aspen, red oak, and paper birch. Other landscapes include ponds, swamps, and exposed rocks and cliffs. In addition to moose and wolves, 17 other mammalian species live here—far fewer than in neighboring Minnesota and Canada, because any species living here first had to find a way across the lake. Those that did include elk, snowshoe hares, foxes, ermine, mink, muskrats, beavers, and bats. A few other residents include garter snakes and—unavoidably—black flies and mosquitoes.

Visitors arrive at either Rock Harbor on the east end or at Windigo on the west end. There are no roads; the only way to get from here to there is via trail or boat. The Rock Harbor Lodge, located on the island's eastern side, is the park's only lodging facility, with 60 rooms and 20 cottages (it also operates two primitive camper-cabins on the Windigo side of the park). There are also 36 campsites for backpackers, paddlers, and recreational boaters spread throughout the park.

With hiking and boating being the only means of transportation and limited visitor services, this is a national park for adventurers, explorers, and those seeking a more intense experience in nature. Other activities include fishing, wildlife photography, and scuba diving, especially on the many shipwrecks—which tells you something about the weather, waves, and hazards here. Scuba diving is usually done via private charters and requires advanced skills along with coldwater, deepwater, and wreck experience. The park closes in winter, which in the North Country extends from November 1 to April 15.

Rocky shoreline covered in lichen

As an aside, Lake Superior is the largest freshwater lake in the world, and Isle Royale is the largest island on it. Almost in the middle of the island is Siskiwit Lake, and the largest island on that lake is called Ryan Island—which makes Ryan Island the largest island on the largest lake on the largest island on the largest lake in the world. Urban legend adds two more layers to the Russian nesting doll image. Ryan Island is said to have an area called Moose Flats, which seasonally floods to become a "pond," out of which Moose Boulder is said to protrude to become an "island." But like most urban legends, the story is better than the evidence.

Exploring the Park

Most backpackers stay at one of the 36 designated tent campsites in the park. In addition, dispersed cross-country camping outside of designated campgrounds is permitted for those looking for solitude, adventure, self-sufficiency, and low-impact camping in a wilderness setting. Rangers strongly advise that, because of the island's swamps, rough terrain, and thick vegetation, this option is suitable only for experienced backpackers who are familiar with the landscape. (Permits are required, and additional regulations apply.) Don't assume that just because this is an island in the middle of the Midwest that the terrain is flat and easy; it's not.

➤ About 140 of the park's 165 miles of hiking trails can be connected to form a long figure eight–shaped double loop around the island. Figure between about 10 days and two weeks, depending on your fitness and hiking style. If you're not quite up for that, the classic **Greenstone Ridge Trail** traverses the island on a ridge formed by one of the earth's largest and thickest lava flows. Its 42 challenging miles (including 4,300 feet of elevation gain and loss) give hikers views of Lake Superior, forested wilderness, rocky exposed ridges, and inland lakes and wetlands.

➤ On the Windigo side of the island, the **Greenstone Ridge Trail** can also be combined with the **Feldtmann Ridge Trail** to make a 30-mile loop that features an inland lake and campsites on one

of Lake Superior's many bays as well as in the interior forest.

➤ On the Rock Harbor side of the island, a network of trails allows hikes of varying lengths, including the 4-mile **Scoville Point Loop**, which starts on the **Stoll Memorial Trail** and goes east through a coniferous forest to Scoville Point, with views across the lake. On the return along Tobin Harbor, you may be lucky enough to see moose.

➤ At both **Windigo** and **Rock Harbor**, hikers can connect trails to form day-hiking and backpacking itineraries of various lengths, but don't forget that the ferry system also makes stops around the entire perimeter of the island, allowing visitors to start their hiking adventures virtually anywhere.

OPPOSITE: Moose in a remote lake (top left); trail around peninsula near Rock Harbor Lodge (top right); kayakers paddling near Rock Harbor (bottom)

BELOW: Hiker in backwoods on Greenstone Ridge Trail

Mammoth Cave
National Park

The landscape is fractured, its forests punctuated by sinkholes, cracks, underground rivers, and springs that pop up between the rocks. But the varied landforms and rock formations only hint at the main feature of this park. Mammoth Cave National Park reserves its best displays for those willing to go beneath the surface to an underground world of massive rock amphitheaters, huge chambers, long passages, vertical shafts, and tunnels of all shapes and sizes. Along the way are virtually every other type of cave formation known—stalagmites, stalactites, gypsum needles, mirabilite flowers, and more—ranging from dramatically imposing to fine and delicate.

Mammoth Cave is part of the Mammoth-Flint Ridge Cave System. More than 420 miles of surveyed passageways make it the longest known cave system in the world, with many more—perhaps several hundred—miles of passages yet to be mapped, measured, and explored. The underground labyrinth of chambers, caverns, and tunnels was created when a long-extinct inland sea dried up and left behind its detritus—shells and bones of sea life and deposits from mineralized seawater—to create a bed of soft sandstone. Millions of years and the inexorable force of fresh water carving its way through the rock did the rest.

Human use is an integral part of the park, and dates back perhaps 4,000 years. Relics found in the cave have included human remains, including a 2,000-year-old mummified body, ancient footprints, and remnants of clothing, sandals, wooden dishes, and ancient torches made of bundles of cane. Discovery of the caves by European Americans dates to the late 1790s, according to local lore, when a hunter followed a bear he had shot into the caves. In the next century, the caves were used as a church, a tuberculosis sanatorium, and a source of saltpeter for making gunpowder used in the War of 1812.

Entrance to Mammoth Cave

The cave's path to national park status was fraught with controversy. Unlike the early large western parks, which were established before private land ownership had become the norm, Kentucky was already well settled with farms when the push to protect the caves began. Moreover, tourism had already shown its promise as an economic engine that could be more lucrative than farming the fields, hills, and ridges of the rock-strewn landscape. The so-called cave wars that ensued were the result of various landowners competing to attract tourists to cave' features beneath their land, using every tool at their disposal: roadside signs, direct solicitation, court cases, and illegally blasting entrances into the cave system. Taking notice of the unique resource, the federal government entered into the fray with the power of eminent domain, leaving locals with a protected national park, a tourism attraction, and long-lasting resentments.

Established in 1941, the 53,000-acre park preserves, protects, interprets, and studies the biological and geological features and processes of the cave. The park's foundation document also notes the park's aboveground features, which include a diverse forested landscape, and the ridges, towers, fissures, sinkholes, and other characteristic landforms that formed through the erosion and dissolution typical of a limestone karst landscape.

Exploring the Park

Exploring the park is first and foremost about what's below the surface. Above the surface, the park's 37 square miles offer both front-country and backcountry trails, a front-country campground, and 13 backcountry campsites for hikers (as well as paddlers or even equestrians).

➤ Guided national park tours into the caves visit notable cave structures such as **Grand Avenue**, **Frozen Niagara**, and **Fat Man's Misery**. Tours range from short hour-long overviews of some of the cave's most accessible features to the more in-depth **Grand Avenue Tour** (4 miles of walking and 400 feet of climbing, all of it underground). For the even more adventurous, some tours explore more authentic, historic caving experiences. One tour eschews modern lighting in favor of using old-style paraffin lamps carried by visitors. Another tour departs from the developed parts of the cave and includes a more authentic cave-exploring experience: crawling in the mud, squeezing through tunnels, and negotiating uneven rock surfaces.

➤ For day hikers, the south side of the Green River has 18 miles of trails leading to ridgelines, rivers, sinkholes, cave-fed springs, and historic sites. Seven miles of trails are clustered around the visitor center, including the popular **River Styx**, where the water emerges from the caves. One of Mammoth Cave National Park's unique offerings is the Beneath Your Feet program, which makes a connection between the land that visitors are walking on above the surface and the mystery and magic of what lies below. Fourteen wayside signs on the trails and paths near the visitor center include images, information, and videos (via smartphone-accessible QR codes) about what features, formations, passageways, and chambers are buried 20,100 or more feet below the earth. Eleven additional miles of trails (most of them short) can be accessed from various trailheads along the park road. The names give some idea of their main features: the **Cedar Sink**, **Sand Cave Trail**, **Sloan's Crossing Pond Trail**, **Turnhole Bend Nature Trail**, and the **Mammoth Cave Railroad Bike and Hike Trail**.

➤ Backpackers (as well as day hikers looking for longer hikes) should head to the park's northern region, which is laced with trails that can be interconnected in myriad ways. The trails are fairly short; among the longest are the **Sal Hollow Trail** (8.6 miles) and the **Raymer Hollow** and **First Creek Trails** (just over 6 miles each), but the interconnections, loops, and spurs make it possible to link trails together to explore a representative cross section of the geology and features of the park.

Small ice-covered pond near Maple Springs Ranger Station (top left); trail within Mammoth Cave (top right); dripping cave formations (bottom left); trees above ground near the trail entrance (bottom right)

Big Bend National Park

TEXAS

———

Designated 1944

Only five national parks sit on international borders, and four of them—North Cascades, Glacier, Isle Royale, and Voyageurs—are on the border with Canada (or Canadian waters). Big Bend is the only national park on the southern border with Mexico.

For more than 1,000 miles, the Rio Grande (in Spanish, *Río Bravo*) forms the boundary between Mexico and the United States; 118 miles of that border are in Big Bend National Park. The Treaty of Guadalupe Hidalgo decreed that the international border between the United States and Mexico was in the center of the deepest river channel as the river flowed in 1848. (Rivers often change course, which, in the case of international borders, can lead to unending problems.) In the case of the Rio Grande, paddlers generally north of the centerline (on the left side of the river, as they face downstream) are in the United States. Paddlers south of the centerline (to the right, as they face downstream) are in Mexico. Given the necessity to change course to dodge rocks and obstacles, this means that most rafters and kayakers are probably flouting a passel of international border-crossing rules as they make their way down the river.

Named after a horseshoe-shaped bend in the river, Big Bend protects the largest expanse of the Chihuahuan Desert in the United States. It is also the only park in the United States to contain an entire mountain range: the Chisos Mountains are a series of sky islands, all of which are wholly within the park. Sky islands are created when high-elevation peaks rise from a surrounding landscape of desert. The park's range of elevations (from about 1,800 feet at the lowest point of the river to 7,832 feet atop Emory Peak) and relative abundance of water (supplied by the mountains or the river itself) create a wide range of habitats. The park boasts more than 1,200 species of plants, more than 450 species of resident and migrating birds, 56 species

Rio Grande and Santa Elena Canyon Trail

FOLLOWING SPREAD: Chisos Basin (left); lizard on red rock in Tuff Canyon (top right); hiker on Grapevine Hills Trail (middle right); purple cactus in Santa Elena Canyon (bottom right)

of reptiles, and 75 species of mammals. Even among national parks, these are big numbers. Also contributing to the health of the biodiversity is the fact that the adjacent Mexican states of Chihuahua and Coahuila are now protecting the Maderas del Carmen and the Cañón de Santa Elena regions to preserve their flora and fauna.

The Rio Grande's route along the international border in the park is dramatic. Three spectacular canyons—Santa Elena, Mariscal, and Boquillas—slice through sheer walls of limestone. Elsewhere, the river's influence spreads into the surrounding desert via creeks and arroyos, supporting plant and animal species. In the center of the park, the mountains rise in the middle of what is the largest expanse of roadless public land in Texas. More than 150 miles of trails ramble around the park's 800,000 acres, from river bottom to mountaintop. This is an ideal destination for backpackers and hikers who have the know-how to cope with the sometimes extreme changes in temperature and an arid environment.

A rafting trip down the Rio Grande is one of the highlights of visiting the park. It can be booked as a day trip or as an overnight; some rafting itineraries include side hikes into canyons that are only accessible from the river.

Exploring the Park

Most of the park's trails are concentrated in three areas. The majority of the trails are accessed from trailheads in the Chisos Basin area. A second set of trails are found on the eastern side of the park, in the Rio Grande Village area. And a third series of trailheads are located near and along Ross Maxwell Scenic Drive.

➤ The Chisos Basin area of the park gives hikers lots of options, with interconnecting trails and backcountry campsites for backpackers. The **Chisos Basin Loop Trail** is a family-friendly, 1.8-mile loop with views of Emory Peak, the Pinnacles, and the Window. Middling-length day hikes include the 4.8-mile **Lost Mine Trail** and the 5.6-mile **Window Pour-Off Trail**. The main feature is a notch in a rock face, which serves as the "window"—but the window is almost beside the point because the entire trail is full of views. Longer, more challenging all-day hikes include **Emory Peak**, the park high point, which is about a 10.5-mile round trip with 2,400 feet of elevation gain and some rock scrambling before the summit. Another strenuous trail is the **South Rim Trail**, sometimes described as the most scenic hike in the park. With 2,000 feet of climbing and sweeping desert views, it's a 12-mile hike, 15 miles if the detour to Emory Peak's summit is added in.

➤ In the Rio Grande Village area, the 0.75-mile **Rio Grande Village Nature Trail** is a good family choice, with views of the river, sand dunes, and cliffs and the possibility of wildlife viewing. The highlight hike here is the **Hot Springs Trail**. Don't just stop at the springs: the mile-long trail (each way) offers beautiful views of the river and the mountains in the distance. Highlights include wildflower blooms in spring and pictographs, not to mention stopping to soak in the perfect 105-degree springs.

➤ Ross Maxwell Scenic Drive links the center of the park with the southwestern river side of the park; along the route there are a number of trailheads. Taking off from the drive's southwestern end point, Santa Elena Canyon Drive leads to the **Santa Elena Canyon Trail**, one of the park's premier short hikes, with its sky-piercing 1,500-foot canyon walls. The 1.6-mile, round-trip trail sometimes runs next to (or even into) the river bottom, and sometimes climbs up the canyon walls. Heading back along Ross Maxwell Scenic Drive toward the center of the park, the **Mule Ears Spring Trail** is named after two volcanic plugs that poke up out of the desert. Starting at the Mule Ears Overlook, located off of a spur road that turns off the main road, the trail leads to a spring in which the gray and brown Chihuahuan Desert turns into a green oasis of cottonwoods and other plants. This shadeless 3.8-mile round-trip hike is best avoided in the summer or on hot days. The **Chimneys Trail** is a mostly level 4.8-mile round trip that leads through the desert to ancient volcanic spires where, at the base, petroglyphs created hundreds of years ago still whisper their mysteries.

Balanced Rock

Virgin Islands
National Park

VIRGIN ISLANDS

───

Designated 1956

Hiker on Ram Head Trail

FOLLOWING SPREAD: One of many sheltered bays in the national park (left); Trunk Bay Beach (top right); hawksbill turtle swimming along the Trunk Bay Underwater Snorkel Trail (bottom right)

When Christopher Columbus arrived in the Virgin Islands in 1493, he was greeted by the Taíno people who lived in this region of white sand beaches, lush vegetation, sea turtles, and coral reefs. His arrival marked the beginning of a process that would destroy much of the Indigenous culture. Today, Virgin Islands National Park preserves the islands' outstanding scenic features, the Caribbean tropical marine and terrestrial ecosystems, and the cultural heritage from pre-Columbian through colonial times.

Virgin Islands National Park takes up about 60 percent of the island of St. John, including 5,500 acres of surrounding ocean, as well as almost all of Hassel Island, a small island located near the capital city of Charlotte Amalie on St. Thomas. An additional 13,000 acres of coral reef, sandy bottoms, seagrass beds, and mangrove forests are protected under the auspices of the adjacent Virgin Islands Coral Reef National Monument.

Nature is the highlight here, with beach walking, snorkeling, scuba diving, and boating among the most popular activities. Some of the park's beaches are regularly featured on "best beaches" lists. Inland from the beaches, the park offers the opportunity to explore the complex tropical rain-forest ecosystem. The park also contains scores of prehistoric and historic sites dating from perhaps as early as 840 BC. Petroglyphs and other artifacts provide information about the lives of pre-Columbian people and how their culture developed from early hunter-gatherers to villages to the more complex ceremonial culture of the Taíno people who met Columbus here in 1493. Adding to the sense of history are the remains of the homes and graves of both the Europeans who exploited the land and the enslaved Africans who were brought to toil on the plantations.

Exploring the Park

Trailheads are found on the roads around the park, leading either downhill to beaches or uphill to green-and-blue views of the surrounding forest and ocean. Historic sites are found throughout. Note that on some trails the sun can be fierce; bring sun protection, bug protection, and plenty of water.

➤ Among the easier trails are two that wind either a half mile or a mile around the **Cinnamon Bay Plantation**, one of the earliest and most successful plantations on the island. Other short hikes include the 1-mile **Lind Point Trail** from Cruz Bay to Lind Point and Honeymoon Beach. Also starting in Cruz Bay, the **Caneel Hill Trail** leads steeply up to the observation deck on Caneel Hill, where views on a clear day extend all the way to Puerto Rico. Another mile-long trail is the **Ram Head Trail**, which begins at Salt Pond Bay and leads to the southernmost point on St. John. Hikers looking

for a challenge can take the **Bordeaux Mountain Trail** to bag the island's 1,277-foot high point. It's another short trail—only a mile—but it is steep (25 percent grade, with a 1,300-foot ascent), rocky, and not maintained. There are several viewpoints along the way, but disappointingly none from the forested summit.

➤ Several longer trails take two to four hours (or more, depending on how much time is spent on beach sitting, snorkeling, and general exploration). The 2.6-mile, one-way **L'Esperance Trail** follows a historic Danish road past ruins of some of the island's earliest plantations to a beach at Reef Bay. Also ending at Reef Bay is the 3-mile **Reef Bay Trail**, which combines hiking, history, and beach sitting. The trail leads down through forests and past a waterfall and pool, ancient petroglyphs, an old sugar mill, a beach, and the chance to snorkel on the Genti Bay coral reef. The Reef Bay and L'Esperance Trails can be combined to make a sort of horseshoe.

OPPOSITE: Annaberg Sugar Plantation (top left); donkeys resting near the sugar mill (top right); Hawksnest Beach (bottom)

BELOW: Sailboats in Hawksnest Bay

Haleakalā
National Park

HAWAI'I

Designated 1961

Halemau'u Trail

FOLLOWING SPREAD: Pīpīwai Trail through bamboo forest (top left); endemic silverthorn tree within Haleakalā Crater (middle); bay along the road to Hāna (bottom left); 'Ohe'o Gulch along Kūloa Point Loop Trail (right)

At its lowest point, mountain meets sea, and a tropical monsoon climate warms and waters the intersection of cliffs, beaches, and surf. At its highest point, an alpine desert climate is superimposed on a 10,023-foot-tall volcano. In between, some of the most diverse ecosystems in the national park system contain more endangered species than any other national park. Most notable are the Dr. Seuss–like silversword plant and the *nēnē*, the Hawai'i state bird, which had once died out in the park but was reintroduced with the help of local Boy Scouts who returned the young endemic geese to the mountain by carrying them in their backpacks.

Measured from its base on the ocean floor, which is 19,680 feet below sea level, to its summit 10,023 feet above sea level, Haleakalā clocks in at 29,700 feet from bottom to top, making it the second-tallest mountain on earth, behind only Mauna Kea. (Measured from base to summit, the Big Island's Mauna Kea is about 33,500 feet—4,500 feet taller than 29,032-foot Mount Everest; Haleakalā beats Everest by about 700 feet.) Haleakalā last erupted sometime between 1480 and 1600. The mountain is usually considered dormant, which means that while there is no evidence of imminent eruption or activity, the underlying geology and hot spot could still support a future eruption.

Haleakalā is a shield volcano—a type of wide, gently sloped volcano created by large, very hot liquid lava flows—that rose from the ocean perhaps 750,000 years ago. At first, it was a lifeless rock desert of molten lava, basalt, ash, and pumice. But gradually, organic detritus from the ocean might have washed over its shoreline, collecting in tidal pools or clinging to the rock. Over millennia, a bird might have visited, shedding a few insects it carried in its feathers or dropping fecal matter with seeds or other bits and pieces of yesterday's lunch. At some point, enough organic matter collected on the volcanic debris for seeds to

sprout and grow into plants. An insect survived. A few more birds arrived and decided to stay, perhaps eating fish from the ocean, or the insects that made a home here, or seeds from the plants that grew from the seeds another bird dropped. More seeds, more insects, more birds. Ecosystems developed, each adapting to the microclimate, elevation, and exposure. As in the Galápagos Islands, isolation led to the evolution of endemic species found nowhere else on earth. Fast-forward to today, when many of them are threatened or endangered by feral animals, exotic plants, agriculture, and land development.

Haleakalā's entry into the national park system predates its official designation date of 1961; it was actually part of Hawai'i National Park, which was established in 1916 and included Haleakalā on Maui and the volcanoes of the Big Island of Hawai'i. In 1961, the two parks were split, and Haleakalā National Park was given its own separate status.

The park is divided into two sections: the peak and surrounding highlands, and the lower Kīpahulu, a section on Maui's southeast coast, just southwest of Hāna. The mountain region and Kīpahulu are not connected by roads, and Kīpahulu is remote, so visiting both is a multiday project. Most visitors focus on the summit, which is accessible via a well-maintained, switchbacked road that goes all the way to the top. The most popular activities are photographing the sunrise or sunset, star gazing, bicycling down the road, or hiking into the crater. (It is technically not a volcanic crater, but rather an eroded valley 2,600 feet deep and filled with lava, cinder cones, and other volcanic features, such as the wildly colored rock formations of Pele's Paint Pot.) A unique forest known as Hosmer Grove contains exotic trees from the Himalayas, Japan, Australia, and different parts of North America, which were brought and planted here as an experiment.

Exploring the Park

Haleakalā's most popular hiking trails are in the summit area, but there are also waterfall trails in the Kīpahulu District. Trails in the summit area are challenging because of high elevations (altitude sickness is a possibility) and changing weather. Regardless of how much of a tropical paradise the seafront can be, mountain weather loses temperature with elevation and can be below freezing.

➤ The summit area has short trails to viewpoints, as well as trails into the crater (three cabins are available for overnight stays; permits are required). The two main trails that lead from the summit into the crater are the **Halemau'u Trail** (the trailhead is on Crater Road) and the **Sliding Sands Trail** (which begins at the visitor center near the summit). Both trails lead to the network of interconnecting loops in the middle of the crater. Hikes leaving from the summit area start downhill; be sure to factor in twice as much time to hike back up. Also, factor in extra time for hiking on the soft and sandlike cinder trails, which can make for slow going.

➤ The Kīpahulu District offers the best waterfall hike on Maui, the 4-mile, round-trip **Pīpīwai Trail**, which gains 800 feet as it passes Makahiku Overlook and a bamboo forest, and arrives at Waimoku Falls. The 0.5-mile **Kūloa Point Trail** goes to 'Ohe'o Gulch, sometimes called the Seven Sacred Pools. To get to Kīpahulu, visitors must drive either the famed winding Hāna Highway clockwise around Maui's northeast coastline, or take the Piilani Highway counterclockwise along Maui's southeast coastline.

➤ For hardcore hikers, the **Kaupo Trail** links the **Kaupo Gap Trail** in the crater area near the summit with the Piilani Highway on Maui's southeast coast. However, the part of the trail that connects the summit crater area with the highway near the coastline is outside of the park boundaries and is not maintained by the National Park Service. It can be difficult to navigate, brush-covered, muddy, and steep, and is recommended for experienced hikers only, or hikers with guides. It can be done downhill or uphill. Another reason to use a guide: transportation logistics are tricky, as the trailheads are on top of the mountain and on the far back side of Maui's remote southeast coast. Some car-rental companies do not permit travel on dirt and gravel roads.

Hiker on Halemau'u Trail

Petrified Forest
National Park

ARIZONA

———

Designated 1962

Francisco Vázquez de Coronado wasn't looking for petrified rocks when he came this way in 1540; he was seeking gold and the fabled Seven Cities of Cibola. Instead, his expedition found what they called *el desierto pintado*—the Painted Desert—a variegated landscape of colors and shapes created by tectonic plates and erosion. The Painted Desert sprawls across northern Arizona, southeast of the Grand Canyon and east of Flagstaff. Its vast mesas and buttes contain historic artifacts, such as detailed petroglyphs and the remains of Pueblo sites. They also contain geological treasures, such as the trees-turned-to-stone that are the core feature of Petrified Forest National Park. From the air, the landscape looks like a God-sized abstract canvas painted in striated hues ranging from purple to pink to orange to gold. Up close, the petrified wood looks like gemstones sized for giants.

At least nine species of fossil trees have been identified in the Petrified Forest; all are extinct, but rendered immortal in stone. The slow process of turning wood to stone began 200 million years ago, when what is now an arid dryland was located much closer to the equator in a tropical, wet environment. Fallen trees were covered with water, ash, and mud—materials that slowed decomposition. As the cellular structures of the wood slowly dissolved, minerals such as silica filled the spaces left behind. The minerals replaced the original striations, rings, and burls, then crystallized in those shapes to re-create the patterns of the living tree. The shapes and forms came from the trees, but the colors came from the stone. If copper cobalt or chromium filled the spaces, the wood was rendered in not-very-woody-looking green or blue; if manganese filled the space, it became an equally untreelike pink. And while all this was going on at the cellular level, plate tectonics were carrying the entire region from the tropics to northern Arizona.

Trail through Blue Mesa

FOLLOWING SPREAD: Petrified trees broken down in a small canyon (left); spiral petroglyph at Martha's Butte (middle); fallen petrified tree (top right); Agate House (bottom right)

Located on both sides of I-40 near Holbrook, Arizona, Petrified Forest National Park is on a convenient travel path for visitors to northern Arizona's monuments and parks, as well as those traveling between Flagstaff, Arizona, and Albuquerque, New Mexico. With about 650,000 annual visitors, Petrified Forest is about middling in terms of national park visitation numbers, so it feels less crowded than some of the better-known parks. Somewhat unusual for national parks, not all of the land within the national park boundary is owned by the National Park Service; instead, there are inholdings of private lands, and maps of some parts of the park show ownership in the old checkerboard pattern that dates to the early days of western settlement and the Homestead Act. The park has slowly been acquiring titles to some of these inholdings. The south and south-central parts of the park, accessed from the Rainbow Forest Museum, and the northern section, accessed from the Painted Desert Visitor Center, are the prime visitor areas; the two are connected via the 28-mile main park road, which has frequent overlooks and spurs to points of interest.

Exploring the Park

Much of the Painted Desert within Petrified Forest National Park is protected as Petrified Forest National Wilderness Area, where motorized travel is limited. Backpacking is allowed (though off-trail hiking requires good navigation skills). Camping at large (by permit) is allowed a mile or more from a parking area.

➤ North of I-40, the **Tawa Trail** leads 1.2 miles between trailheads at the Painted Desert Visitor Center and Tawa Point for day hiking; for longer hikes, add on the connecting 0.5-mile **Painted Desert Rim Trail**, which can also be connected with the 0.5-mile **Kachina Point Trail**.

➤ South of I-40 is where most of the petrified wood is on display, along with Puebloan sites and ancient petroglyphs. The 0.75-mile **Crystal Forest Loop** is named for the crystalline displays in the logs here. The 1.6-mile **Long Logs Loop** has an ancient logjam that looks like some giants abandoned a game of pick-up sticks. And **Giant Logs Trail** has some of the largest and most colorful logs in the park. Off the **Blue Mesa Scenic Loop**, the 1-mile **Blue Mesa Loop Trail** descends from the mesa into blue badlands decorated with petrified wood; numerous plant and animal fossils have also been found here.

➤ The south side also features short trails to some of the park's important archaeological sites: **Puerco Pueblo** (a 0.3-mile loop to a 100-room pueblo), **Agate House** (a 2-mile round trip to a small home entered through the ceiling; it also can be connected with the **Long Logs Trail**), and **Newspaper Rock** (a short spur to rocks covered with more than 650 petroglyphs made as many as 2,000 years ago).

OPPOSITE: Desert flower on Long Logs Loop (top left); petrified tree that has turned into stone agate (top right); Giant Logs Trail near Painted Desert Visitor Center (bottom)

BELOW: Part of a petrified tree along Giant Logs Trail

Canyonlands
National Park

UTAH

———

Designated 1964

It's a maze of rock lying on the bed of what was once a sea, with a crater thought to be the work of asteroids. Author and frequent visitor Edward Abbey, who knew a thing or two about the otherworldly southwestern landscape, called Canyonlands "the most weird, wonderful, magical place on earth." Its patchwork of colors and shapes was formed by the combination of an inland sea, tectonic forces, salt deposits, gravity, and the implacable scouring of the Colorado and Green Rivers. The 337,598 acres of colorful canyons, mesas, buttes, fins, arches, and spires that make up Canyonlands National Park is part of a connected complex of federal lands that also includes Capital Reef National Park and the Glen Canyon National Recreation Area. A host of other national monuments and national forests extend in a sprawling patchwork north to Arches National Park and the Colorado border and southwest—past Bryce Canyon and Zion National Parks—all the way to the Grand Canyon in Arizona.

Moab, Utah, is the jumping-off point for most visitors to Canyonlands. The main part of the park is divided into four distinct and different districts: the Island in the Sky, the Needles, the Maze, and the two rivers—the Green and the Colorado—that meet in the park. Planning a trip here means choosing which part of the park to explore, because navigating from one section to another can be a time-consuming (and bone-rattling) challenge due to the large area, the dirt roads, and the roundabout routes required to cross the canyons and rivers in order to get from here to there. As a practical matter, most visitors explore one region of the park at a time.

From Moab, the Island in the Sky area is closest, which is one reason it attracts about 75 percent of the visitors to the park. Its broad, level mesa sits in the triangle formed by the Colorado and Green Rivers; from afar, it looks like a long, flat island rising above a sea

Elephant Hill in the Needles region

of desert. Main features in this part of the park include Island in the Sky Road, with its many viewpoints and trailheads; the White Rim, which is a sandstone bench 1,200 feet below the mesa; and the rivers, which are another 1,000 feet below the White Rim. White Rim Road, which requires a four-wheel-drive vehicle, traverses the White Rim Sandstone level of the park between the rivers and the Island in the Sky. Since 2015, day-use permits have been required to drive or bike on White Rim Road.

Located just south of the Island in the Sky on the east side of the Colorado River, the Needles region is the next most popular section of the park, with about 20 percent of the visitors. The district's name refers to the needles of rock—red- and white-banded pinnacles—that are the distinctive features of this part of the park, although other formations—such as grabens, potholes, and arches—also vie for attention. There are also petroglyphs left by Ancestral Puebloans, most notably on Newspaper Rock on the Needles access road. The Needles is more remote than the Island in the Sky, and many of its features require four-wheel-drive treks on dirt roads or long hikes, some of which require day-use permits.

The Maze, the rivers, and the Horseshoe Canyon day-use areas divide up the remainder of the visitors, so those looking for isolation will find it in one of these sections. As its name suggests, the Maze is remote and jumbled. It is considered one of the most remote parts of any of the national parks, at least in the contiguous states, and requires considerably more time and effort to visit, along with a four-wheel-drive vehicle and traditional map and compass navigation skills (the National Park Service recommends NOT relying on GPS). The rivers part of the park is the haunt of kayakers and rafters. It can actually be divided into two segments: above and below the confluence. Above the confluence, the water is calm and can be floated, rafted, or paddled by rafts and kayaks. But the force of the flow increases exponentially as the two rivers join into one. Cataract Canyon, just below the confluence, is fed by snowmelt. As the river squeezes through the narrow walls, it develops powerful natural rapids. In spring and summer in a heavy snow year, this section of river has some of the fiercest white water in North America.

Off to the northwest is Horseshoe Canyon, a non-contiguous parcel of the park set aside as a day-use area. The canyon is home to some of the oldest—and what have been called some of the most important examples of—Indigenous rock art in the country, some of which was made as much as 4,000 years ago by hunter-gatherers who predated the ancient Puebloans of the region, and some of which was made after the Spanish introduced domesticated horses to the Americas in the mid-1500s.

Recreational activities include four-wheel driving, mountain biking, horseback riding, river running, hiking, and backpacking. Permits are required to access many parts of the park, even if only for day use.

Exploring the Park

Canyonlands National Park has hundreds of miles of hiking trails. In the Needles region, hikers must stay in designated campsites. In other parts of the park, at-large camping is permitted with restrictions: tent sites must be on bare rock, in sandy washes, or in areas devoid of the fragile biological soil crusts. Campsites must also be at least 1 mile from a road and at least 300 feet from an archaeological site, historic site, or water source. Four-wheel-drive vehicles are recommended to get to many of the more remote trailheads—and necessary to get to a few. Water is an issue in much of the park; get information about seasonal sources at the ranger stations, and bring more water than you think you need.

➤ At the Island in the Sky area, popular short hikes include **Mesa Arch**, one of the park's most iconic sites (especially at sunrise). The arch perches on a cliff, overlooking views of White Rim Road, the canyons, and the La Sal Mountains in the distance. **Grand View Point** lies at the southern end of Island in the Sky Road, featuring views of the White Rim, the Maze and Needles areas, and distant mountains. For more, continue past the first viewpoint on a mile-long trail that leads to a second viewpoint. **Aztec Butte** is a 1.2-mile hike that starts off Upheaval Dome Road, just off Island in the Sky Road, and climbs to a scenic viewpoint where you'll see Ancestral Puebloan structures called granaries. The 1.6-mile,

Hiker on Joint Trail to Chesler Park in Needles region (top left); Island in the Sky region (top right); Mesa Arch at sunrise in Island of the Sky region (bottom)

round-trip trail to the **Upheaval Dome Overlook** is short but steep, leading to views of one of the most interesting features in the park. Upheaval Dome is either a salt dome or a meteor crater, but so far its origins remain a mystery. For longer hikes, the 8.3-mile **Syncline Loop Trail** also starts from the Upheaval Dome Trailhead and takes five to seven hours to wind through the canyons around the dome. (Note that getting a view of the dome requires detouring on the Upheaval Dome Overlook Trail.) Two other longer (and more difficult) day hikes, which can also be done as overnights, are the view-filled 11.2-mile **Alcove Spring Trail** and the 10.8-mile **Murphy Trail**, which leads from the Island in the Sky to White Rim Road and back.

➤ In the Needles, popular short hikes include the easy 0.6-mile **Cave Spring Trail**, which features the region's cultural history and desert plant life. Another easy 0.6-mile hike, the **Pothole Point Trail**,

interprets the cycles of desert potholes and is especially good for small children. The 2.4-mile **Slickrock Foot Trail** is an easy trip through park geology. For longer hikes, the 5.4-mile **Chesler Park Loop** is a moderate scenic loop (a four-wheel-drive vehicle is required to reach the trailhead). **Lost Canyon** is an 8.6-mile loop with some of the best scenery in the Needles. Finally, the 10.6-mile **Druid Arch Trail** is difficult, but its scenery and spectacular arch make it one of the park's most popular hikes.

➤ The unmarked and primitive trails of the Maze are recommended for experienced hikers who have good navigation skills. That means knowing how to use paper maps and a compass, since digital service is not reliable. Some canyon routes are marked by cairns, but routes through washes are often not marked at all and newcomers will need topographic maps to tell the canyons apart. Sections of slickrock and other rock present obstacles on some routes, including the **Maze Overlook Trail**; basic rock-scrambling skills may be needed, as well as ropes (to pull your backpack up after you). Trailheads can be accessed via dirt roads. Another way for backpackers to reach the Maze is via a two-hour jet-boat shuttle from Moab, which lets hikers off at Spanish Bottom on the Colorado River. From there, a foot trail climbs more than 1,000 feet to the **Dollhouse Area**, from which trails lead north to explore the wilds of the Maze.

➤ The highlight of the Horseshoe Canyon unit is the **Great Gallery**, with some of the most significant rock art in North America, including a well-preserved panel depicting life-sized figures standing in remarkably rendered perspective. The gallery is framed by sheer sandstone walls and mature cottonwoods shading the intermittent stream in the canyon bottom. This difficult 7-mile hike features uneven terrain, slogging through sand, and scrambling on steep rock. It begins with a descent of nearly 800 feet—meaning that a climb of nearly 800 feet is waiting for you at the end of the day. Figure five hours or more.

Guadalupe Mountains National Park

TEXAS

———

Designated 1966

What is now an arid rocky land punctuated by cholla and prickly pear cactus was once part of a 400-mile-long U-shaped coral reef. Where there are now rocks and rattlesnakes, there was once a habitat for anemone and fish. The Capitan Reef—made of fossils that were left behind when the sea receded—is a remnant of an inland ocean that covered the area perhaps 260 to 270 million years ago. Today, much of what's left of the Capitan Reef is underground. The longest exposed stretch runs from Guadalupe Mountains National Park in West Texas to Carlsbad Canyon National Park, almost 40 miles away in southeastern New Mexico. Rising more than 3,000 feet above the surrounding Chihuahuan Desert, the Guadalupe Mountains contain the four highest peaks in Texas, including the state high point at 8,751 feet, Guadalupe Peak, and the prominent silhouette of 8,085-foot El Capitan, which once served as a landmark beacon for travelers crossing the Southwest.

In 1978, Congress formally designated 46,850 acres of the park's backcountry as wilderness, which is defined by the Wilderness Act of 1964 as "an area where the earth and its community of life are untrammeled by man, where man himself is a visitor who does not remain." However, humans have left their mark on these mountains for some 10,000 years, with early Indigenous hunter-gatherer communities leaving evidence such as projectile points, baskets, pottery, and rock art.

Spanish explorers traveled through the region in the late 17th century but found the arid climate and remote location unappealing for settlement. Until the mid-1800s, the region was settled and used primarily by Indigenous peoples. More European Americans arrived in the mid-1800s via the Butterfield Stage, which carried mail and passengers on the only route that crossed the Continental Divide in the American Southwest. As ranchers settled in, conflicts with the resident Mescalero Apache people increased; by 1880, the Apache had left, or been forced out, and more ranchers had arrived. Much of the land that became the national park was donated by or bought from some of the large early landowners and their families.

Exploring the Park

Campgrounds are available at Pine Springs and Dog Canyon. Water is one of the watchwords for hiking in Guadalupe Mountains National Park: surface water here is uncommon, and summer temperatures and the dry air make dehydration and heat exhaustion a constant threat.

➤ The Pine Springs area is one of the major trailheads for hikes leading into the high country. The route to **Devil's Hall** is 3.8 miles round trip, but don't be fooled by the modest mileage; this hike is rated difficult, with a rocky wash and a natural rock staircase up a "hallway" of steep canyon walls. The route offers views of geological formations, steep canyons, tall trees, and mountaintops, but the scrambling over boulders and debris can make for ankle-twisting, slow-going travel. Trails to state high points are always popular, but the **Guadalupe Peak Trail** makes visitors work for their bragging rights. Also starting in the Pine Springs area, this trail ascends more than 3,000 feet on a rough and rocky route through pinyon pine and Douglas fir forests. The reward is expansive views of El Capitan and the desert lowlands.

➤ The McKittrick Canyon area was the home of Wallace Pratt, a geologist who later donated his land to the park. The **McKittrick Canyon Nature Trail** is a short mile-long interpretive trail. Longer

View of El Capitan at dusk

trails in the area include the 10-mile, round-trip **Notch Trail**, which goes through McKittrick Canyon (figure four to six hours). Solitude lovers might head to the 9-mile **Permian Reef Trail**. One of the least used trails in the park, it climbs the north side of McKittrick Canyon to sweeping views atop the Wilderness Ridge.

➤ In addition, there is a network of trails spreading out from **Dog Canyon** on the northern edge of the park, which can be accessed from secondary roads from the New Mexico side of the border. On the western side of the park, the white **Salt Basin Dunes** are also a scenic highlight, shimmering sands contrasting with the dark mountains. A 3- to 4-mile hike (round trip, mileage depends on your route) up and over the dunes is a fun challenge, but hiking on the sand can require scrambling; hikers should keep track of their energy and water for the return trip.

➤ For backpackers, there are 10 backcountry campgrounds, most of them in the Pine Ridge area; backpacking itineraries can be made of varying lengths by combining trails. According to the National Park Service, the trek to the top of **McKittrick Ridge** is "the toughest hike in Texas" and is best attempted as an overnight, with a rest and stargazing stop at the McKittrick Ridge Wilderness Campground.

OPPOSITE: Rocky outcrop on Guadalupe Peak Trail (top left); hiker on Guadalupe Peak Trail (top right); Salt Basin Dunes (bottom)

RIGHT: Guadalupe Peak Trail

North Cascades National Park

One of many cascading waterfalls in North Cascades National Park

FOLLOWING SPREAD: Diablo Lake (top left); deer in forest along Thornton Lake Trail (middle left); bell flowers along Thunder Creek Trail (middle); Thornton Lake (bottom left); Mount Shuksan reflected in Picture Lake (right)

For outdoor adventurers, North Cascades National Park is one of the pristine wilderness jewels of the national park system. In some places, its mountainside meadows seem reminiscent of the pastoral European Alps, while elsewhere enormous glaciers and steep, ice-scoured cirques look like they belong in fierce and raw Alaska. High mountains (some rising above 9,000 feet), glaciers that feed hundreds of streams and lakes, a vast range in elevations, and abundant rainfall create a landscape of immense biological diversity. Most species of North America's mountain wildlife can be found here, including a small population of grizzly bears. It is the only place grizzlies are found in the contiguous United States apart from the Greater Yellowstone and Northern Rockies (Bob Marshall Wilderness/Glacier National Park) Ecosystems.

It all starts with water, in flowing and frozen form. Whether it's snow or ice or rain doesn't matter; as soon as water hits the earth, it finds its way downhill. Glaciers creep downhill, streams cascade, and rivers roar down through valleys, carrying fine glacial silt that turns the creeks and lakes—hundreds of them—that soft, milky blue green. At the higher elevations, abundant snowfall replenishes the largest concentration of glaciers in the contiguous states—although even here, the snowfall is not enough to forestall the effects of climate change. (The park's long-running research program monitors climate change and glacial retreat. Forty-four monitored glaciers are undergoing significant retreat; three have disappeared.) Lower down the mountain slopes, rainfall sustains old-growth forests of enormous western red cedar, Douglas fir, and western hemlocks, some of which are 1,000 or more years old. Between the forests and the glaciers are the upland meadows, where the timeline of life is compressed as tiny flowers paint the landscape in purples, reds, pinks, and yellows, all of them jostling to complete their life cycles between the last snowfalls of spring and the first snowfalls of autumn.

At 500,000 acres, North Cascades is the largest but least visited of Washington's three national parks, perhaps because Seattle, the nearest major population center, has two other famed parks—Mount Rainier and Olympic—within shorter driving distances. Much of North Cascades is wilderness. Additionally, it is surrounded by other protected lands—several national forests and wilderness areas, as well as provincial parks in British Columbia—which imparts even more of a sense of wild isolation.

It is also part of a complex of three cooperatively managed national park units. Ross Lake National Recreation Area is a long, thin swath of land that surrounds and follows the Skagit River. The river, along with Highway 20, which parallels it, runs east to west and cuts the park into southern and northern sections. On the eastern side, the highway leaves the park, and the river (and the recreation area) turn north and head to Canada, forming the park's northeastern border. Lake Chelan National Recreation Area forms the park's southern border; the lakeside town of Stehekin gives access to the national park, although not as conveniently as Ross Lake and Highway 20. Located at the north end of Lake Chelan and near the southern end of the park, Stehekin is reachable by seaplane, boat, ferry, horse, or foot, but not by car or bus or Uber or taxi—there are no roads.

Exploring the Park

Much of the interior of North Cascades National Park is inaccessible to day hikers because of the distances from trailheads; most day users, including hikers, boaters, and fishermen, access the park through the Ross Lake and Lake Chelan National Recreation Areas.

But there are several day hikes accessible from Highway 20 and from Stehekin. Backpackers have their pick of lakes, passes, forests, and some of the steepest mountain scenery in the national park system.

➢ From Stehekin, several trails branch out. The popular **Rainbow Loop Trail** is not really a loop; it's a 4.4-mile trail that starts and ends at two trailheads that are 2 miles apart from each other on Stehekin Valley Road. (The "loop" can be completed by hiking those 2 extra miles, but there's also a shuttle bus.) The trail features views of the Stehekin River Valley and the head of Lake Chelan. Backpackers can use the Rainbow Loop Trail to access the **Rainbow Creek** and **Boulder Creek Trails**, which veer off into more remote parts of the park.

➢ Some work is required to reach the trailhead for one of the park's most popular day hikes, the **Cascade Pass Trail**. From Highway 20, it takes about an hour on Cascade River Road to cover 23 mostly unpaved miles to the trailhead. From the parking area, hiking choices include the 2-mile, out-and-back trail to the scenic pass (don't be fooled by the easy-sounding mileage: it starts with 30 switchbacks). More ambitious hikers can continue on spur trails to either the **Sahale Glacier** or **Horseshoe Basin** (mileage depends on the combination of trails selected). Backpackers can continue on the **Cascade Pass Trail**, then pick up the **Stehekin Valley Trail** to head toward the Stehekin Valley and the town of Stehekin (a total of 22 miles from the Glacier Pass Trailhead).

➢ Another highlight hike is the **Thunder Creek Trail**, although spectacular Park Creek Pass is 20 miles away, so out of reach for day hikers. Nonetheless, the first few miles offer a chance to climb through the beautiful old-growth forest, following glacier-fed Thunder Creek. Multiday backpackers can hike to Park Creek Pass, and either turn around or continue all the way to the Stehekin Valley.

➢ North Cascades is one of only a few parks that can boast two national scenic trails. From the southwest, the **Pacific Crest National Scenic Trail** enters the park near Lake Chelan; it exits to the east of the park, then continues north through the Pasayten Wilderness to E. C. Manning Provincial Park in Canada. The **Pacific Northwest National Scenic Trail** crosses the park from east to west. From the east, it enters from the Pasayten Wilderness, then follows the western shore of Ross Lake southward before crossing the Skagit River and heading into the northern heart of the national park.

Redwood National Park

CALIFORNIA

———

Designated 1968

The sequoias (*Sequoiadendron giganteum*) of Sequoia and Yosemite National Parks are the most massive organisms on earth—think of them as the football players of the plant kingdom. But their taxonomic cousins, the redwoods (*Sequoia sempervirens*) of Redwood National and State Parks are the tallest—we'll call them the basketball players of the plant kingdom. The tallest redwood on record is a tree named Hyperion, at 379.1 feet. To put that in perspective, consider that this one single tree grows higher than the 345-foot high point of the entire state of Florida.

Redwoods grow only in Northern California and southern Oregon, and they are irreplaceable. Some of them sprouted more than 2,000 years ago, and it's taken from then until now to create the rich and complex environment that sustains not only redwoods, but also the equally impressive Douglas firs and Sitka spruces and the lush community of epiphytes, ferns, and flowering plants that grow on and around them. A century of logging between the late 19th century and the 1970s reduced two million acres of old-growth forest to a mere 100,000 acres. Today, about half of those acres are preserved in a unique partnership between the National Park Service and California State Parks, which together preserve some 40,000 acres of old-growth redwood forest, along with another 90,000 acres of second-growth forests, prairies, oak woodlands, meadows, the wild and scenic Smith River, sand dunes, and rugged cliff-lined beaches from which visitors might see whales, dolphins, sea lions, porpoises, orcas, and seals.

Archaeological evidence suggests that the region was hunted and grazed by Indigenous peoples some 3,000 years ago; the Tolowa, Yurok, Chilula, Wiyot, and Karuk peoples all have strong historical ties to the region, but the Yurok apparently outnumbered the others, with as many as 55 villages supporting more than 2,500 inhabitants. When European Americans

Hiker on trail among redwoods

FOLLOWING SPREAD: Carruthers Cove on Coastal Trail (left); Tall Trees Grove (top right); Fern Canyon (bottom right)

arrived, they exploited the region for trapping, gold, timber, and, later, tourism. Fortunately, what attracts tourists is the spectacle of the enormous trees, so there is an economic motive, as well as an ecological one, for protecting the trees and the environment that sustains them.

The federal-state partnership oversees three state parks—Del Norte Coast Redwoods, Jedediah Smith Redwoods, and Prairie Creek Redwoods—and Redwood National Park. The move toward preservation began as early as 1910, when early activists lobbied to preserve the remaining stands of redwoods; eventually, the state of California decided to protect crucial tracts of the redwoods that remained by forming state parks. In 1968, the national park was established; in 1978 it was expanded with the addition of lands purchased from timber companies.

Exploring the Park

Walking—and stopping to look up—is perhaps the best way to appreciate the scope and size of the enormous and ancient trees in Redwood National Park. The park's trails can be divided into "Big Trees" and "Pacific Coast"—both impressive in their own, very different ways. Day hikers will want to decide which section of the park to explore—the north, south, or coastal section. Note that many of the trailheads require travel on challenging dirt roads, and some of the parking areas are not suitable for trailers and RVs. The park can be generally divided into north and south by Bald Hills Road, which cuts the park in half and connects with Highway 101, also roughly in the center of the park.

➤ Some of the park's best-known trails are on the south side. The **Tall Trees Grove** is one of the most famous, although the road to its trailhead is four-wheel drive only, and the hike requires a permit and includes some steep elevation gain and loss. The reward is one of the most impressive forest walks in the world. There are two options for arriving at the grove: the direct 1.3-mile **Tall Trees Access Trail**, or the longer 3-mile (also less used and more beautiful) **Emerald Ridge Trail**, which leads to Redwood Creek, which hikers can then follow to the grove. Putting the access trail and the Emerald Ridge-Redwood Creek hikes together into a loop, then adding in the short loop around the grove itself, results in about a 7-mile hike.

➤ Also on the south side of the park, two of the more easily accessed big trees trails are the flat and accessible **Karl Knapp-Foothills Trail**, a 2.5-mile loop trail that combines big trees and a scenic creek, and the 2.6-mile **Trillium Falls Trail**, a family favorite that switchbacks to rise about 200 feet as it passes through forests of old-growth redwoods, maples, ferns, and fir trees. It also passes a small waterfall and lush carpets of the trail's eponymous trillium, and there is a chance of spotting one of the park's Roosevelt elk herds. Also in the south is the **Lady Bird Johnson Grove**, which offers an easy walk to an iconic grove (although the logistics of getting to its trailhead can be a challenge).

➤ On the north side is the just over 0.5-mile **Stout Memorial Grove Trail**. This is another trail where most of the work involves logistics to the trailhead; the trail itself features a majestic grove, and the chance to while away a day watching the Smith River flow by. The 5.5-mile **Boy Scout Tree Trail**, on the north side of the park, is a mostly moderate hike interrupted by some steep grades and switchbacks. And the 13-mile **James Irvine-Miners Ridge Loop**, one of the most popular longer trails in the park despite its river wading and predictable wet feet, takes in Fern Canyon and Gold Bluffs Beach. Hikers not up for the full 13 miles can do a shorter loop around the Fern Canyon segment.

➤ While the big trees are the named attraction in Redwood National and State Parks, a 70-mile **Coastal Trail** showcases the Pacific cliffs and beaches and makes for spectacular coastal backpacking. (Most of the trail is continuous, but to cross the Klamath River and get around Klamath requires arranging transportation.) Coastal day hikes include the 5-mile **Klamath Section** of the coast to False Klamath Cove, Hidden Beach's tide pools, and the Klamath River Overlook—a whale-watching and sea lion paradise. The **Crescent Beach Section** is kid-friendly, with pristine beaches and occasionally glimpses of elk grazing on the grasslands just inland from the beach.

Coiled fern along Stout Memorial Grove Trail (top left); Bald Hills Road (top right); hiker on fallen redwood on Damnation Creek Trail (bottom left); rhododendron along Lady Bird Johnson Grove Trail (bottom right)

Arches National Park

Dry, dusty, rocky, harsh: the rocks, deserts, canyons, and buttes of intermountain America seem as old as time, permanent fixtures in our imagination of our landscapes. But in fact, many of the remarkable landforms we see in the western national parks began as the detritus of a literal inland sea, shaped by cataclysmic changes. The caves of New Mexico's Carlsbad Caverns, the ridges of Texas's Guadalupe Mountains, the dune fields of Colorado's Great Sand Dunes: all of them began with water. The same is true of the arches, natural bridges, windows, spires, balanced rocks, and sandstone fins of Arches National Park.

Sometime around 300 million years ago, a sea flowed into what is now the Colorado Plateau of eastern Utah. When it receded and evaporated, it left behind a salt bed that was thousands of feet thick in places. Then came the forces of air, gravity, tectonic movement, water, and—of course—time. Windblown sediment deposited successive layers of sandstone. Continuing erosion, changing climate, and gravity metamorphized what came before. The weight of new deposits of rock pressed down with so much force that the old salt underneath was liquefied, the crashing of continental plates shifted some land formations up and let others sink down, and ice formed in cracks and expanded to break apart the rock. The result is a landscape of varied colors and textures, fantastical landforms, and more than 2,000 natural stone arches—the highest density of natural arches in the world.

The arches are instantly recognizable, among the marquee images of the national parks. Delicate Arch frames a mountain view lit by red sunrise that reflects off of red rock. Landscape Arch spans an incredible 306 feet, perhaps the longest stone span in the world. Not to be outdone, the Double O Arch seems to do petrified calisthenics: one arch sits atop another, like a pair of figure skaters striking an intertwined pose.

In this landscape of rock, rock, and more rock, vast expanses of seemingly unyielding, hard, dry ground stretch in all directions. But the ecosystem is, in reality, extremely fragile. A thin, breakable soil crust—made up of different combinations of cyanobacteria, algae, fungi, and lichens—regulates water flow into the earth and returns nutrients to the soil. Human traffic disturbs, compresses, and breaks up that crust; the scarce rainfall and paucity of organic material means recovery time is slow. As part of southern Utah's arc of national parks famed for their geological features, Arches has attracted nearly two million visitors in recent years. To manage the impact of visitors on the environment—and on each other—the national park has been implementing a timed-entry system over the last few years.

Arches is not the most backpacker-friendly park in the national park system. Backpacking is allowed, with permits, but few maintained trails access the backcountry, so travel requires navigation skills. Lack of water is a predictable challenge, and the fragility of the land requires hikers to carry approved toilet bags for packing out human waste.

The park is, however, a day hiker's paradise, with numerous short trails leading to one or more of the park's famous arches. Hikers wanting to spend multiple days on the park's trails should make reservations well in advance to stay in the park's campground; those who don't score a campsite in the park have a choice of hotels and campgrounds in and around nearby Moab, Utah.

Exploring the Park

The main park road runs south to north through most of Arches National Park, starting at the visitor center on the southwest side of the park and ending at the

Delicate Arch

FOLLOWING SPREAD: Turret Arch in Windows Section (left); Landscape Arch (top right); hiker on Devils Garden Trail (bottom right)

Devils Garden Campground and Trailhead. Trailheads and viewpoints are strung along the road; in addition, unpaved roads veer off, leading to other features in the park.

➤ On the south side of the park near the visitor center, the **Park Avenue Trail** (1 mile, one way) descends north steeply into a spectacular canyon and continues down the wash to Courthouse Towers at another trailhead on the main road.

➤ Two of the park's iconic landmarks are in the middle of the park. The easy **Balanced Rock Trail** takes visitors on a short loop hike that begins with an accessible paved path, but then changes to gravel slickrock. If you squint and tilt your head, the Balanced Rock looks a little like Seattle's

BELOW: Balanced Rock

OPPOSITE: Navajo Arch

Space Needle—a giant ball sitting atop a spire. Also moderate, the 3-mile, round-trip **Delicate Arch Trail** leaves from a trailhead on Delicate Arch Road, roughly midway through the park. It follows rock cairns across open slickrock with no shade, then climbs steadily before traversing a narrow rock ledge to reach a bowl. At the top of one of the park's sandstone fins, one of the most famous arches in the park stands in solitary splendor to catch the sunrise.

➤ At the far north end of the main park road, a network of trails branch out from the **Devils Garden Trailhead.** A relatively flat 2-mile, round-trip trail takes hikers to **Landscape Arch**, which, at 300 feet long, is the largest in the park—that's about the size of a football field. Side trips are possible to Tunnel and Pine Tree Arches. For more challenges and a longer hike, the **Devils Garden Primitive Trail** takes off from Landscape Arch Trail and makes a loop that gives access to numerous spur trails and viewpoints to other arches, including the famed Double O Arch, Private Arch, Partition Arch, Navajo Arch, Wall Arch, the Dark Angel Pinnacle, and more. Narrow ledges, uneven surfaces, and slickrock scrambling make this a trail for adventurous hikers comfortable with heights—and even so, it's not a good choice in rain or snow, when the slickrock is, well, too slick for safety. The trail is 7.8 miles; figure at least four hours, or more if you wander off on all the spur trails.

➤ Often described as a maze, **Fiery Furnace** (a bit south of the Devils Garden area) is one of the park's most popular hiking destinations, but it's also a challenging hike, with hard-to-see trail markers, some tricky scrambling and footing, and frequent opportunities to wander into a labyrinth of dead-end canyons where GPS signals will be of no help. The National Park Service recommends that first-time visitors go on a guided ranger hike (tickets should be booked well in advance; the 2-mile trip takes about three hours); experienced hikers wanting to hike on their own can apply in advance for a self-guided exploration permit and must watch a safety video on arrival.

Capitol Reef
National Park

UTAH

———

Designated 1971

A 65-million-year-old wrinkle in the earth's crust is the central feature of Capitol Reef National Park in south-central Utah. At 100 miles long, the Waterpocket Fold is the largest exposed monocline in North America, a steplike dip that was probably created by colliding continental plates. Newer and older layers of earth folded over each other in an S-shape, creating a long, skinny swath of striated rock formations. Weathering and erosion exposed the underlying layers, fashioning a variegated landscape of red-rock buttes, sandstone cliffs, monoliths, cliffs, canyons, bridges, arches, and a prominent line of white domes, which gave the park the first part of its name. Early settlers thought the domes resembled the US Capitol building. The reef part of the name came from the fact that the formations were a barrier to travel; even today, few paved roads traverse the rugged rock terrain. Sixty miles of this unusual formation are protected in the national park.

Human history is in evidence here, from ancient petroglyphs to the remains of orchards planted by Mormon immigrants. (The National Park Service staff maintains the orchards, and for a fee, visitors can harvest whatever is in season: apples, peaches, pears, apricots, and cherries.)

Capitol Reef's rock formations resemble those of Zion, but it is a much younger park (designated in 1971), less well known, and slightly farther away from the Big 3 triumvirate of southwestern parks: Grand Canyon, Zion, and Bryce Canyon. With only about one-quarter of the annual visitation of Zion, and 60 percent more land, Capitol Reef gives visitors more room to spread out among its many miles of unpaved roads and twisting canyons.

Activities include auto touring (four-wheel-drive vehicles are highly recommended) or bicycling on the paved and unpaved roads (bicycling is not permitted off-road). Road choices include Scenic Drive, which passes

Hickman Bridge

major points of interest; Notom-Bullfrog Road, which follows the eastern side of the Waterpocket Fold (10 miles is paved; the rest is not); and unpaved Cathedral Road in the northern part of the park, which goes to the Cathedral Valley and the Temples of the Sun and Moon. The primary campground is at Fruita, in the northern part of the park (there are restrooms, but no hookups).

Exploring the Park

Numerous trails are available for hiking and backpacking in Capitol Reef National Park. Heat and dehydration are risks during the hot summer months.

➤ Many of the park's most popular day-hiking trails start near the visitor center and campground closest to Highway 24 across the northern part of the park. The 3.5-mile, round-trip **Cassidy Arch Trail** is a steep and arduous hike to an overlook of the Cassidy Arch, where canyoneers start their adventures with a 175-foot-deep rappel. For a longer hike, the **Frying Pan Trail** is an 8.8-mile round trip that passes the Cassidy Arch as well as Grand Wash and Cohab Canyon. **Hickman Bridge Trail** is a 2-mile round trip leading to the natural bridge.

➤ In the far southern section of the park, the **Halls Creek Narrows**, **Muley Twist Canyon**, and **Grand Gulch Route** can be combined to make a strenuous multiday backpack laced with side canyons and creeks, with plenty of opportunities to wade through high water or scramble through rocky slots. A good choice for experienced canyon-country hikers, this route is usually done as a two- or three-day camping trip, depending on the number of trails linked together and how hard the hikers want to work.

➤ In addition to traditional hiking and backpacking, canyoneering trails wind though the park's slot canyons. Canyoneering involves rock scrambling, climbing, and rappelling, and often requires swimming or wading as well as the use of ropes and other technical climbing equipment. **Cassidy Arch Canyon** is one of the park's most popular canyoneering routes. It is approximately 2.3 miles long, with eight rappels, and takes up to four-and-a-half hours to complete. Free day-pass permits (specific to each route) are required for canyoneering in the park. Visitors not experienced with the technical demands of canyoneering should hire a guide.

OPPOSITE: Cathedral Valley (top); Hickman Bridge (bottom left); rocks in front of Pectols Pyramid (bottom right)

BELOW: Hiker on bentonite hills

Voyageurs National Park

MINNESOTA

———

Designated 1971

BELOW: Lake Kabetogama

OPPOSITE: Rocky point along Lake Kabetogama

FOLLOWING SPREAD: Kayak resting on the shore (left); trail through the woods near Kettle Falls (top right); kayaker approaching a small waterfall (bottom right)

About equally divided between water and land, northern Minnesota's Voyageurs National Park is not immediately known as a hiking destination. The park's name refers to the voyageurs, French Canadian fur traders who were the first Europeans to travel through this region of cliffs and rocky ridges, wetlands and forests, streams and lakes, and shorelines. But they did so by boat, their paddling periodically interrupted by the need to portage across the land separating one body of water from the next by hiking while carrying their canoes.

Today, Voyageurs National Park is spread over nearly 220,000 acres of land and water, islands, marshes, streams, inlets, coves, ponds, and bays; to the east of the park is the Boundary Waters Canoe Area Wilderness. In summer, Voyageurs is especially popular with canoeists, kayakers, other types of boatmen, and fishermen. The park is divided between the car-accessible mainland to the south, and the heart of the park—the water-laced Kabetogama Peninsula—to the north, which is only accessible by water in the summer. Hiking trails on both the mainland and the peninsula allow hikers to explore this transitional landscape, which combines aquatic and terrestrial ecosystems, coniferous and deciduous forests, and habitats for loons, moose, wolves, and black bears. In winter, a plowed ice road gives access to the peninsula and its trails for skiers, snowshoers, ice fishermen, and snowmobilers.

Exploring the Park

Boating is definitely the premier activity in Voyageurs National Park. Canoe and kayak camping allow visitors to access the water-laced park's interior, set up camp, and use the trails to explore. A few trails are accessible from the mainland side; boats are not required.

➤ From the mainland, day hikers can check out the **Blind Ash Bay Trail** near the Ash River Visitor Center. For backpackers, the lightly used 28-mile **Kab-Ash Trail** offers a wilderness experience as it traverses much of the mainland side of the park from the Ash River to Kabetogama. Interconnecting loops and four trailheads allow visitors to fashion hikes of various lengths. Fall is the best time to hike; in summer, the trail is often overgrown, hot and humid, and full of mosquitoes.

➤ Toward the eastern side of the Kabetogama Peninsula, the 9.5-mile **Cruiser Lake Trail** is considered the park's premier hike. It includes several additional miles of spurs and traverses the peninsula from south to north, past ponds and lakes, to a classic North Country view of Anderson Bay. Other trails and trailheads in the system include the **Mica Bay Trailhead**, the **Anderson Bay Trail**, and **Little Shoepack Trail**.

Badlands National Park

Designated 1978

Extreme variations between heat and cold, a lack of reliable water, and an exposed, rugged landscape prompted the Lakota people to call this part of South Dakota the *mako sica*—or bad lands. French Canadian fur-trappers—the first Europeans to spend appreciable time here—agreed, and described the region as *les mauvaises terres pour traverser*, or "the bad lands to cross." Ever the contrarian, Theodore Roosevelt said nonsense to that. Seduced by these wide-open spaces punctuated by eroded buttes and pointy pinnacles, he always referred to his adopted home as "the so-called badlands."

Almost 250,000 acres of Badlands National Park encompass a mazelike landscape of mesas, buttes, and canyons, combined with the largest undisturbed tract of mixed-grass prairie remaining in the United States. Like almost all the western national parks, Badlands is only the most recent entity to occupy a region that had previously been used and lived in by a long series of Indigenous peoples. What is different about Badlands National Park is that its southern unit, also known as the Stronghold District, is today managed in partnership with the Oglala Lakota, who revere it as a sacred ceremonial site.

Most visitors enter through the northern section of the park, which has easier access via proximity to Interstate 90. The main visitor area is at the far eastern side of the North Unit, with the Ben Reifel Visitor Center, the Cedar Pass Lodge, dining, and a campground. From there, Badlands Loop Road bisects the park (it's not a loop within the park itself, but it makes a loop outside the park by connecting via Highway 240 and Interstate 90). The gravel-dirt Sage Creek Rim Road gives access to the Sage Creek Campground and leads to the 64,000-acre Sage Creek Wilderness. Wildlife ranges from small (including the black-footed ferret, one of the most endangered species in North

Big Badlands Overlook

FOLLOWING SPREAD: Notch Trail (left); hiker on trail through Yellow Mounds (top right); Yellow Mounds Overlook (bottom right)

America) to enormous (a herd of more than 1,200 bison, which have thrived in the park since 50 of them were introduced here in 1963).

In addition to its geological and wilderness features, the park is known for fossils, particularly of early mammals from the Eocene and Oligocene eras, dating back approximately 33 million years, when mammals including camels and the early ancestors of deer and cattle roamed over North America.

Exploring the Park

Most of the day-hiking trails start out from the visitor center area of the eastern side of the North Unit of Badlands National Park. Off-trail hiking is permitted, though hikers should be sure to have adequate gear, water, sun protection, and navigation skills. (Cell phones are unreliable in much of the park.)

➤ For short trails, the quarter-mile **Fossil Exhibit Trail** follows an accessible boardwalk with replicas of fossils and interpretive information about animals that once roamed here, making it a great hike for families. The 0.5-mile **Cliff Shelf** follows

boardwalks, but is not as accessible, with log stairs and 200 feet of elevation gain. Features include the possibility of seeing wildlife such as deer or bighorn sheep, especially when intermittent water sources are full. The more challenging 1.5-mile **Notch Trail** can be acrophobia-inducing and treacherous in wet weather as it winds through a canyon, then negotiates a log ladder and a ledge to arrive at the Notch, with views of the White River Valley.

➤ For longer day hikes, the 4-mile Medicine Root Loop connects a section of the Castle Trail and the **Medicine Root Trail** to explore the mixed-grass prairie and views along some of the badland formations. The 5-mile, one-way **Castle Trail** is the longest in the park, beginning at the Door and Window Parking Area and connecting with the **Fossil Exhibit Trail**.

➤ For backpackers, the **Sage Creek Wilderness**, in the northwestern section of the North Unit, offers experienced hikers a chance to test their backcountry and navigation skills. Trails, such as they are, are mostly social trails and animal trails and are not maintained. At-large camping is allowed.

OPPOSITE: Bighorn sheep in Cedar Pass

BELOW: Ground squirrel along Badlands Loop Road (left); animal fossil in the dirt along Castle Trail (right)

Theodore Roosevelt
National Park

NORTH DAKOTA

———

Designated 1978

Wild horse in a field near
Peaceful Valley Ranch

FOLLOWING SPREAD: Badland
hoodoos (left); Theodore
Roosevelt's original cabin
(top right); bison near Wind
Canyon (bottom right)

There is only one national park in the entire system named after a single person, and it seems appropriate that the honor went to Theodore Roosevelt. After becoming president in 1901, Roosevelt used his authority to create the US Forest Service; he also signed the 1906 Antiquities Act, which allowed for the subsequent establishment of national monuments. His administration oversaw the establishment of 150 national forests, 51 federal bird reserves, four national game preserves, five national parks, and 18 national monuments. The National Park Service estimates that during his presidency, Roosevelt protected approximately 230 million acres of public land.

Roosevelt's eponymous park is not large—only about 70,000 acres—and it is divided among three separate sections. The largest is the South Unit, immediately abutting Interstate 94. The slightly smaller North Unit is about 80 miles to the north. In between is a third, much smaller parcel, Roosevelt's much-loved Elkhorn Ranch. The winding Little Missouri River and the multiuse (hiking, horse riding, mountain biking) Maah Daah Hey Trail connects the three sections.

The park showcases the wildlife of the North Dakota badlands—bison, mule deer, white-tailed deer, elk, feral horses, longhorns, pronghorns, coyotes, bobcats, prairie dogs, beavers, and porcupines—and the area's geography: plateaus cut by rivers, peaks and valleys, and expansive vistas of rolling prairie. It was a landscape that changed the trajectory of Roosevelt's life. He arrived in North Dakota as a skinny bespectacled New Yorker just shy of his 25th birthday, intending to enjoy a vacation hunting bison. His response to the land was immediate; within two weeks he had entered the cattle business and turned himself into a westerner-in-the-making. His experiences here—bison hunting, cattle ranching, and simply sitting and taking in the western landscape—set him on his lifelong path of conservation.

Today, the ranch offers visitors a chance to step back in time: part of the road to the ranch is unpaved, and the last 3 miles of the route sometimes require four-wheel-drive, high-clearance vehicles. And—just like in Teddy's day—if you get stuck, there's no cell phone signal.

Exploring the Park

One hundred miles of foot and horse trails wind through the three units of Theodore Roosevelt National Park, offering wildlife viewing and camping.

➤ The network of trails that cross the South Unit can be accessed from either of the two visitor centers, both of which are located near the park's southern boundary, right off of Interstate 94. Trails can also be accessed from Scenic Loop Drive, which makes a 32-mile circle through the park, and from secondary roads that lead to trailheads on either side of the park. Highlights include the **Petrified Forest Loop**, which connects to the **Maah Daah Hey Trail** to form a 10.5-mile loop taking in what's left of what was once a forest, now frozen in stone, along with prairie, badlands, meadows, and wildlife. The trailhead is accessed via dirt roads on the western side of the park. A shorter favorite hike is **Burning**

Coal Vein Trail, accessible from a trailhead on Coal Vein Road, which veers off of Scenic Loop Drive. It's a short loop (less than an hour) that offers a variety of park landscapes: juniper forests, butte edges, gorges, and meadows.

➤ In the North Unit, the **Little Mo Nature Trail** is a 30- to 45-minute self-guided nature trail through a river bottom. Walkers can choose between a 0.7-mile slightly graded hike on the paved inner loop or a slightly longer (just over a mile) hike on an unpaved outer loop. About the same length, but leading through badland terrain and dry washes, is the **Caprock Coulee Nature Trail**, which is only about a mile, but can be extended into the more strenuous 4.3-mile **Caprock Coulee Trail**, where a stiff climb offers the reward of a ridgeline with beautiful views of the badlands.

➤ In between the two larger units, at the **Elkhorn Ranch** homesite, a 0.7-mile mowed pathway leads from the parking area to the cabin site. Not much more than the cabin's foundation stones remain.

➤ In addition to the trails in the individual park units, the **Maah Daah Hey Trail** system connects all three units of the national park on its 144-mile route through the North Dakota badlands.

OPPOSITE: Wind Canyon Trail (top left); Wind Canyon (top right); scenic view from main park road (bottom)

BELOW: Coyote near Peaceful Valley Ranch

Channel Islands National Park

CALIFORNIA

_____

Designated 1980

Its geology features cliffs and sea caves; its ancient historic sites reveal evidence of some of the oldest human remains in North America; its contemporary history includes being the site of an oil spill that spurred the establishment of the Environmental Protection Agency. Channel Islands National Park, off the coast of Southern California, is a place where archaeology, history, geology, and environment intersect.

Dates for the earliest human settlements of North America are subject to ever-changing scientific debate, which catapults backward as new evidence is discovered. In 1959, human thighbones were discovered on Santa Rosa Island, one of eight islands that make up the archipelago of the Channel Islands. Radiocarbon dating suggests that the so-called Arlington Man walked around the island some 13,000 years ago. Other artifacts—middens, burned mammoth bones, shell mounds, fire pits, and fishhooks—also date back that far, or even farther, suggesting that some of the earliest inhabitants of Pacific North America may have arrived in the Channel Islands following a coastal migration route from Siberia. Early settlement sites have produced some of North America's earliest evidence of seafaring and island colonization, some of the oldest shell middens, and the earliest examples of basketry from the Pacific coast. (Meanwhile, prehistory continues to be rewritten. In 2021, ancient footprints were discovered in New Mexico's White Sands National Park; carbon dating the surrounding sediments suggests they were made 21,000 to 23,000 years ago—give or take—which further pushes back our understanding of when humans might have arrived in the Americas.)

Parts or all of the northernmost five islands are included in Channel Islands National Park; the Nature Conservancy manages most of the rest. The park's foundation document notes the importance of the park's cultural and historic resources, as well as its natural, scenic, wildlife, marine, ecological, and scientific importance. What this means for the visitor is a varied island environment featuring an abundance of sea life (with activities like whale watching, scuba diving, snorkeling, and spearfishing), as well as landforms ranging from cliffs to beaches to a spectacular series of sea caves, best explored by kayak.

In addition to its importance as a site of prehistoric human settlement, the Channel Islands also claim a role in 20th-century history. In 1969, a blowout on a Union Oil rig resulted in what was then the largest oil spill in American waters: 200,000 gallons of crude oil created an oil slick covering about 800 square miles. (Only the Gulf Coast Deepwater Horizon and Exxon Valdez oil spills were larger.) Following the spill, tides carried the oil onto the beaches of Anacapa, San Miguel, Santa Rosa, and Santa Cruz Islands, killing birds, seals, dolphins, and other sea life. The resulting media attention—combined with environmental issues that had gained media and political attention during the 1960s—helped spur the establishment of the Environmental Protection Agency in 1970.

Despite its proximity to densely populated Southern California, Channel Islands National Park has the lowest visitation of any of California's nine national parks, perhaps because of the inconvenience of getting there via ferry or private boat, or perhaps because visitor infrastructure is largely undeveloped, making the islands an appealing option for those looking for a more primitive experience, but not as attractive to those looking for developed facilities, restaurants, and lodges. Most visitors arrive in the summer, but winter and spring are good times for wildflowers and whale migrations, and calm waters in the autumn are good for scuba divers and snorkelers.

View from eastern side of
Anacapa Island

Exploring the Park

Because of ferry schedules and prevailing ocean conditions, most visitors arrive to Channel Islands National Park at Santa Cruz Island. Four-wheel-drive roads on the map notwithstanding, there is no transportation available on the islands. The islands are also not accessible to visitors in wheelchairs or to those who cannot climb ladders to embark and disembark from the ferries.

➤ The eastern portion of Santa Cruz Island is managed by the national park and is accessible to hikers via its network of trails and four-wheel-drive roads. Most visitors planning to camp arrive at Prisoners Harbor on the north shore of Santa Cruz Island and stay at the Del Norte Campground 3.5 miles from the landing area; from there, it is possible to link the roads and trails to explore the entire island, including hiking all the way to **Scorpion Anchorage** on the east side. From Scorpion Anchorage, a network of roads and trails fans out, including the strenuous 7.5-mile **Smugglers Cove Trail** and the 10-mile **Montañon Ridge Loop**, featuring good views but challenging, unmaintained trail.

➤ Several trails and roads traverse Santa Rosa Island, providing visitors with spectacular hiking opportunities. These trails and roads range from the relatively flat route to **Water Canyon Beach** to the rugged, mountainous path to **Black Mountain**.

➤ Somewhat farther away from the other four islands, **Santa Barbara** has about 5 miles of trails that circle and loop around the entire island. Highlights include elephant seals, sea lions, wildflowers, and scrambling up and down the cliffs that lead from the higher interior to the ocean.

➤ Most of **Anacapa Island** is closed to hikers to protect wildlife habitat. East Anacapa has about 2 miles of interconnected looping trails that scale the cliffs using a stairway from the landing cove. Overlooks feature coastal views; camping is permitted in primitive camping areas.

➤ A permit (including a liability waiver) is required to visit and hike on **San Miguel Island**, which is owned by the US Navy and is open only when National Park Service personnel are on the island. Visiting most of the island requires being accompanied by a park ranger. (There are concerns about the possibility of unexploded ordinance from old tests done by the Navy on some parts of the island.) The island features a unique combination of tidal pools; habitat for sea life; and a strange caliche forest made up of the fossilized remains of ancient roots and tree trunks that grew on the island during periods of colder and wetter climates.

OPPOSITE: Kayakers at Scorpion Bay off Santa Cruz Island (top left); lighthouse on Anacapa Island (top right); kayaker in sea caves along Santa Cruz Island (bottom left); pelicans on rocks near Anacapa Island (bottom right)

BELOW: Montañon Ridge Trail

Biscayne National Park

FLORIDA

———

Designated 1980

Boca Chita Lighthouse

FOLLOWING SPREAD: Kayakers on Biscayne Bay (left); great egret just offshore of Boca Chita Key (middle); walking path near Dante Fascell Visitor Center (top right); boat arriving at Boca Chita Key (bottom right)

Biscayne National Park is at the northern end of the Florida Reef; Dry Tortugas National Park is at the southern end. The two parks could not be more different. While Dry Tortugas is 70 miles from the nearest of the Florida Keys, Biscayne is within sight of glittering, sky-scraping Miami.

But even though Biscayne inhabits one of the most metropolitan locations in the national park system (Cuyahoga Valley, Saguaro, Gateway Arch, and Indiana Dunes being other parks with serious cosmopolitan credentials), it preserves a rare combination of shipwrecks, coral reefs, and mangroves. Originally designated as a national monument to protect the bay and marine environment from the effects of proposed power plants and increasing urban development, the park today protects 72,000 acres of the northernmost range of the Florida Reef.

With 95 percent of its acreage underwater, this is largely a water activities park. The visitor center, accessible by car on the mainland side of the bay, is the embarkation point for most park activities. The park's two campgrounds—located on the other side of the bay, on Elliott Key and Boca Chita Key—are only accessible by boat and are very basic. Known for its waterfront views, Boca Chita Key has a grassy camping area, picnic tables, grills, and toilets, but no running water for drinking or bathing. Elliott Key steps up the facilities with cold-water showers and drinking water (mostly reliable; check with rangers or bring a backup supply), as well as picnic tables and grills.

If you want to canoe, kayak, or paddleboard, you'll have to bring your own boat, rent from an outfitter outside the park, or join a tour offered by the Biscayne National Park Institute. The tours include activities such as cruises to Boca Chita Key and the lighthouse, sailing and exploring Jones Lagoon, snorkel and paddle tours, and heritage tours.

Exploring the Park

Biscayne National Park is primarily a water-based park, with marked paddling trails. But there are some hiking trails available, both on the mainland and the islands. There's a price to pay for the natural beauty of the coves, the water trails, and the shoreline views: the park is mosquito infested in spring, summer, and early autumn and can be buggy in the cooler months as well. Bring bug repellent and wear protective bug clothing.

➤ The park lists four paddling trails, all of which begin at the visitor's center at Convoy Point on the mainland (but note that one of them, the **Elliott Key Paddling Trail**, is rather ambitious for most paddlers—six hours or more one way).

➤ In addition to the paddling trails, the **Maritime Heritage Trail** is a boating-snorkeling-diving trail that visits six marked shipwrecks (which act as artificial reefs, attracting colorful coral and fish life) and the Fowey Rocks Lighthouse. Of the shipwrecks, the *Erl King*, *Alicia*, and *Lugano* are best suited for scuba diving, while the shallower *Mandalay* offers spectacular snorkeling.

➤ For hikers, Elliott Key offers a hefty 7-mile, one-way hike on the **Spite Highway Trail**, but to get to it, you have to first get to Elliott Key by boat. Originally a six-lane highway down the center of the barrier island, the trail has now been reclaimed by the forest. What is left is a wide, flat hiking thoroughfare with no elevation change.

➤ On the mainland, just outside the visitor center at Convoy Point, the short and easy **Jetty Trail** follows the mangrove-lined shoreline to the Colonial Bird Protection Area.

➤ **Adams Key**, **Elliott Key**, and **Boca Chita Key** each also have short loop trails.

Katmai National Park and Preserve

ALASKA

_____

Designated 1980

Path to Devil's Cove

FOLLOWING SPREAD: Angler in a small river (top left); harbor seal in Kukak Bay (middle left); red fox on shore of Kukay Bay (middle); view of alpine lake from bush plane (bottom left); grizzly bear at Brooks Falls (right)

The scene at Brooks River looks like Mother Nature's equivalent of a thru-hiker's all-you-can-eat buffet. The animal equivalents of thru-hikers are the 20, 50, sometimes 70 or more enormous brown bears (and some not-yet-enormous cubs) galumphing along the banks and, in some cases, cavorting in the river itself. The all-you-can-eat buffet is the seemingly endless stream of sockeye salmon that are on a mission of their own: to swim upstream to their spawning grounds. Some succeed. Others jump into waiting ursine paws and mouths. As a general rule, 1,000-pound brown bears rarely hang out in such close quarters with one another, but the abundance of easy pickings in the rich fishing hole of the Brooks River and Falls overrides any antisocial proclivities. In this feeding ground, there is enough for all.

Katmai National Park and Preserve is one of seven Alaskan parks that entered the national park system in 1980 as part of the Alaska National Interest Lands Conservation Act (ANILCA). Located about 290 miles southwest of Anchorage on the remote Alaska Peninsula (a place where it is said that there are more brown bears than people), Katmai is the westernmost of five Alaskan national parks arrayed in an arc along the coast of the Gulf of Alaska.

While the image of dozens of brown bears gorging on summertime salmon feasts has become a symbol of the Alaskan wilderness, the park was founded not for its wildlife, but for its geological drama. Mount Katmai is the park's centerpiece (though not its highest peak), a 6,716-foot stratovolcano that was one component of the 1912 eruption that led to the creation of the park. The strongest part of that event took place 6 miles away when what would come to be known as Novarupta (it means, quite accurately, "new eruption") exploded in what would turn out to be the largest volcanic event of the 20th century. Measured by volume, Novarupta

released 30 times as much magma as Mount St. Helens did in 1980. It formed a 40-square-mile pyroclastic flow known as the Valley of Ten Thousand Smokes. And it caused the entire summit of Mount Katmai to cave in on itself, forming an enormous caldera that is now a lake.

Designated a national monument in 1918, the park and preserve protect the area around the eruption, as well as 18 other active volcanoes. As a remote national monument with no roads or trails, Katmai was initially undeveloped and rarely visited. But gradually, the region became known for its wildlife; in addition to being one of the premier areas in the world to view brown bears, Katmai is known for moose, caribou, wolves, lynx, wolverines, red foxes, river otters, mink, martens, weasels, porcupines, snowshoe hares, red squirrels, and beavers. ANILCA expanded the park to four million acres, making it the fourth-largest national park. Unlike most Alaska parks and preserves, which allow subsistence hunting and fishing throughout both the park and preserve units, Katmai allows subsistence hunting (as well as sport hunting) only on the designated preserve.

This is a wilderness park, with opportunities to travel by foot, kayak, canoe, and raft. But unlike Gates of the Arctic or Kobuk Valley, Katmai does have lodges, cabins, and developed camping areas. Access is usually via the town of King Salmon, where park headquarters are located. There are no roads into the park, so depending on the destination, visitors travel via boat or bush plane.

Exploring the Park

Most of Katmai National Park and Preserve is wilderness, with no maintained trails, although the volcanic high country can (in places) be easier to walk across and navigate than some of the waterlogged lowland

trails in parks like Gates of the Arctic and Kobuk Valley. It is possible to arrange to be dropped off and picked up by bush taxis in different parts of the park. Katmai's wilderness is best explored by backpackers with advanced skills in communications, first aid, navigation, glacier travel, river crossings, foul weather, and self-rescue. Hired guides can also be arranged.

➤ For day hikers, the Brooks Lodge area, near the bear-viewing platforms, is one of the most developed parts of the park and the most visited area, especially in the prime bear-viewing period (late June through July and September). The viewing platform is limited to 40 people, and if others are waiting, visitors are limited to an hour of bear watching. The busiest times are from about 10:00 a.m. to 4:00 p.m., when day-trippers arrive by boat or plane; travelers who stay overnight will have uninterrupted viewing early in the morning and in early evening. A short, 1.2-mile, round-trip trail leads from the lodge to the viewing platforms at Brooks River. Also in the Brooks River area is

the **Dumpling Mountain Trail**, a 3-mile, out-and-back hike to the Dumpling Overlook. Beyond, it is possible to continue another 2.5 miles to the summit of Dumpling Mountain via a cross-country route. There is no maintained trail beyond the overlook.

➤ Tours from Brooks Lodge include a guided bus tour to the **Valley of Ten Thousand Smokes**, 23 miles away, which includes the opportunity to do some day hiking. It is also possible to arrange for one-way transportation to and from the **Overlook Cabin**, and then hike and backpack from there.

➤ In the general area of the Valley of Ten Thousand Smokes, some key features and destinations include the Buttress Range (Katmai Pass and the Southwest Trident lava flows), Mount Griggs, Mageik Lakes, and the Novarupta Dome itself. Hiking to the **Katmai Caldera** is a peak experience for those with endurance and off-trail travel skills; all routes to the caldera require travel on snow and glaciers with crevasses.

BELOW: Fireweed in remote area of the park

OPPOSITE: Islands and mountains in Kukak Bay

Glacier Bay
National Park and Preserve

———

Designated 1980

Humpback whale breaching in Icy Strait

FOLLOWING SPREAD: Icebergs near Johns Hopkins Glacier (left); Forest Trail near park headquarters (middle); view of remote lake from bush plane (top right); boats moored in Bartlett Cove (bottom right)

At the point where ice meets sea, titans collide. Enormous icebergs calve off from the main glacier, crashing into the bay. Elsewhere in the 3.3-million-acre Glacier Bay National Park and Preserve, more than 1,000 other glaciers carve their way across and around the highest coastal mountain ranges on earth. Most of the glaciers are receding, but even global climate change has not yet been able to diminish the grandeur of this Narnia-like world.

Sculpted in ice, replenished by snow, the wintery landscape at first obscures the fact that this is a biologically rich ecosystem that joins mountains, forests, and sea. The resulting marine and terrestrial wildernesses are globally significant, making up one of the largest internationally protected biosphere reserves in the world.

Like most Alaska national parks, Glacier Bay is not accessible via road. So it might be logical to assume that the same factors that keep visitation numbers down in other Alaska parks—distances, the logistics and expense of private plane flights and ferries, few maintained trails, and limited visitor infrastructure—would keep visitors away here too. But while Glacier Bay may not have access by road, it does have access by cruise ship. Some 80 percent of the park's 600,000 annual visitors arrive as part of an Inside Passage cruise itinerary.

Large ships do not disembark passengers for shore excursions. Instead, visitors see the park's key features—the enormous calving glaciers and the wildlife—from the water. Smaller adventure-oriented cruises do off-load passengers for excursions, which can include kayaking, whale watching, catamaran rides, and hiking.

The main point of entry is Bartlett Cove, on the east side of the park, which has a landing strip, anchorage dock and fuel station, a lodge with guest cabins, a campground, and all of the park's marked and maintained hiking trails. The nearest town is Gustavus, which also has lodging and dining options; lodges can arrange for excursions, including boat tours and flightseeing.

In addition, whitewater rafting trips are another way to experience the interior. Six- to 10-day trips are available on the Tatshenshini River. Starting in Canada's Yukon Territory, the route passes through the Yukon's Kluane National Park and Reserve and British Columbia's Tatshenshini-Alsek Provincial Park and ends at the Dry Bay Ranger Station in the Glacier Bay National Preserve (on the west side of the park).

Technically, the park is open year-round, but cruise ships only operate in the summer, and most of the park facilities close in the off-season.

Exploring the Park

Glacier Bay National Park and Preserve's key features are the glaciers feeding into the bay, so a boat tour is a must. For hikers, Bartlett Cove has the park's only developed trails; however, it is also possible to hike off-trail in the forests and along the shorelines. The cove has a walk-in first-come, first-served campground, but the park also has hundreds of miles of shorelines, beaches, and islands that are open to camping. Some of these can be accessed via the park's tour boat, which can drop off and pick up passengers at designated locations.

➤ Bartlett Cove trails include the mile-long, round-trip **Tlingit Trail**, an easy stroll along the forested shoreline, with educational features such as a traditional Tlingit canoe, a complete whale skeleton, and information about Tlingit culture and native plants. The mile-long **Forest Loop**

Trail, an easy trail on dirt, gravel, or boardwalk, traverses both the temperate rain forest and beach environments of Bartlett Cove.

➤ Longer trails include the 4-mile, round-trip **Bartlett River Trail**, which passes an intertidal lagoon where ducks, geese, and other waterfowl congregate, then enters a spruce hemlock forest before reaching the Bartlett River estuary. Wildlife sightings might include coyotes, moose, bears and river otters along the beach, and seals, which follow the salmon as they travel up the river in late summer. The 8-mile, round-trip **Bartlett Lake Trail** is a full-day excursion that climbs a moraine on a trail whose wilderness character presents some footing and route-finding challenges. For lovers of shorelines, there is a long coastal stretch that starts at the Bartlett Cove Dock and goes 6 miles south to Point Gustavus. Features include land, shore, seabirds, humpback whales, sea otters, and bald eagles.

BELOW: Steller sea lion near Johns Hopkins Inlet

OPPOSITE: Coastal wolf along inner Glacier Bay Basin

Gates of the Arctic
National Park and Preserve

ALASKA

_____

Designated 1980

BELOW: Grizzly bear in a remote area of the park

OPPOSITE: View of remote river from bush plane

American national parks are sometimes said to be in danger of being loved to death. Certainly, that was true during the COVID-19 pandemic, as cabin-fevered Americans rediscovered national parks and outdoor recreation. Some of the most popular national parks implemented new policies: reservations and ticketing, quotas for campsites, and lotteries for permits for popular hiking trails.

Such is not the case at Gates of the Arctic National Park and Preserve. The far northernmost and the second-largest park in the entire system is also the least visited. Visitors have a number of challenges when they plan a trip, but overuse and overcrowding won't be among them.

This is a wilderness writ large: 8.4 million acres of large mountains, large valleys, large expanses of trailless, roadless terrain, and large swings in climate and weather. When combined with the adjacent Noatak

National Preserve and Kobuk Valley National Park just to the west, it is part of one of the largest expanses of wild parkland in the world.

The park's name, Gates of the Arctic, refers to two peaks: Frigid Crags and Boreal Mountain. Wilderness advocate Robert Marshall (better known for the eponymous Bob Marshall Wilderness, just south of Glacier National Park in Montana) traveled here between 1929 and 1939 and referred to these mountains as the "gates" that led from the Brooks Range to the Arctic.

The park is oriented in a roughly east-to-west direction, following the general trend of the Continental Divide as it snakes its way through the middle of the park to divide the watersheds of the Pacific and Arctic Oceans. On the north side of the park, the precipitous Brooks Range also trends east to west, the gateway to the Arctic tundra. Wind, water, temperature, glaciers, and plate tectonics have created a dramatic landscape. Steep granite and limestone pinnacles reach straight for the sky, towering over lowlands laced with hundreds of miles of streams and rivers, their slow winding paths to the oceans confounded by the almost nonexistent gradient.

The park is habitat for brown and black bears, as well as wolves, moose, Dall sheep, wolverines, musk oxen, and some of the Western Arctic caribou herd. In summer, migratory birds from southern climes join the few year-round resident avians. Vegetation depends on elevation and location. In the taiga forests, black spruce live in sparse groves that dot the shaded north-facing slopes, while boreal forests of white spruce, aspen, and birch cover the sun-catching south-facing slopes. As elevations climb toward the tree line, krummholz appears—"crooked trees" twisted and stunted by cold and wind. In the valleys, tussock grasses, alder thickets, and soaked, spongy ground create obstacles for anyone trying to make their way

across the enormous floodplains; experienced hikers consider 5 or 6 miles a day to be a high-mileage day.

Looking from a bush plane at endless miles of terrain seemingly unmarked by humans, it seems improbable that people have lived in this challenging and unforgiving environment for more than 13,000 years. But people did live here—and still do. For many centuries, nomadic hunter-gatherers roamed among the mountains, the tundra, and the sea. Today, a Nunamiut Iñupiat village lies just inside the park at Anaktuvuk Pass, with one of the park's three visitor centers and a museum.

Access to the park is via private charter from Fairbanks to either Bettles, Anaktuvuk, or Coldfoot. The latter is also accessible via car by driving 280 miles on the Dalton Highway from Fairbanks.

Exploring the Park

This is not terrain for beginners. The same precautions and warnings that apply to other Alaskan parks apply here: there is no cell service, there are no trails, it can snow any day of the year, and help can be days away. Inside the park boundary, there are no visitor facilities—no restrooms, no lodges, no roads, no boat rentals, no last-minute shopping for forgotten gear, no snack shops. Nor are there any trails or developed campsites—just mountains surrounded by vast plains filled with bogs, tussocks, alder thickets, and river crossings. For most people, the best way to explore Gates of the Arctic National Park and Preserve is with a guide service, which will arrange the necessary plane drop-offs and pickups with an air taxi service.

➤ From **Anaktuvuk** and (less conveniently) from **Coldfoot**, it is possible to hike into the park; from **Bettles**, visitors can arrange for a bush taxi to drop them off. They can then continue by hiking or (if they brought a boat) paddling down one of the park rivers to a prearranged pickup spot.

➤ Local air taxis provide flightseeing trips, day trips, overnight campouts, or multiday expeditions into the park, which may include both hiking and paddling through remote locations. Air taxis will also take visitors into neighboring Kobuk Valley National Park to get a park passport stamp.

➤ The **Arrigetch Peaks** are the most famous section of the Brooks Range. The name means "fingers of the outstretched hand" in the Iñupiat language, which described the fingers (jagged granite spires) forming a cirque around the "hand." Guide services offer both flightseeing day-trip tours of these mountains, or longer multiday expeditions.

OPPOSITE: Red fox in the backcountry (top left); caribou antlers in the backcountry (top right); rocky peaks in remote area of the park (bottom)

BELOW: Kayakers on Noatak River

Kenai Fjords
National Park

ALASKA

———

Designated 1980

By Alaska standards, Kenai Fjords National Park is downright accessible. Just outside the city of Seward and about a two-and-a-half-hour drive south of Anchorage, it is one of only two Alaska national parks that are reachable by road, bus, and train. But this is still Alaska: the park is largely wilderness, with only one road, which penetrates the park to reach the Exit Glacier, the park's prime destination. The remainder of the park is accessible by boat, bush plane, and hiking.

Like most Alaska national parks, Kenai Fjords has a prominent key feature. One of the largest in the United States, the 700-square-mile Harding Icefield feeds some 40 glaciers that carve their way downhill to end on patches of land, or in lagoons, lakes, or the Gulf of Alaska. In the process, the glaciers have sculpted the park's namesake coastal fjords, which are fringed by northern forests, home to brown and black bears, moose, beavers, coyotes, lynx, mountain goats, martens, mink, river otters, and snowshoe hares—not to mention little brown bats, hoary marmots, meadow jumping mice, and northern bog lemmings. Where ice meets water, the rich north Pacific sea life has supported human communities for thousands of years; today's visitors may glimpse sea otters, harbor seals, sea lions, humpback whales, and killer whales.

Kenai Fjords entered the national park system as a national monument in 1978 and was upgraded to a national park with the passage of the Alaska National Interest Lands Conservation Act in 1980. The combination of (relative) accessibility and Instagram-worthy glacial landscapes makes Kenai Fjords the most visited Alaskan national park—although that still puts it in the bottom 15 of all US parks. A campground at Exit Glacier and three public-use cabins are available for camping. Hiking to Exit Glacier and kayaking are among the park's most popular adventure activities; flightseeing and boat tours can be arranged in Seward.

Stand-up paddler in
Bear Glacier Lagoon

While the park is open year-round, the best time to visit is from June through August. Many of the park's main attractions are inaccessible during the winter due to rough seas and heavy snow.

Exploring the Park

As with all Alaska national parks, marked and maintained trails are in short supply in Kenai Fjords National Park and wilderness is widely available. To go beyond the marked trails requires all the usual backcountry skills (navigation, self-rescue, and communications) as well as glacier skills if traveling on the glaciers.

➤ The only marked and maintained hiking trails are in the Exit Glacier area. Access is by private car or a 12-mile bus ride from Seward. From the parking lot, the easy 2.2-mile **Glacier Overlook Loop Trail** leads to the toe of Exit Glacier. The **Harding Icefield Trail** is about an 8.2-mile round trip to see the enormity of the ice field up close and personal. Allow plenty of time: the trail includes a massive 3,800 feet of elevation gain.

➤ Glacier hiking is possible, but those with no (or limited) glacier experience should go with a guide. National Park Service literature cautions visitors

about sliding, flooding, and other unexpected movements of the glaciers and ice fields, as well as dangers such as falling into a crevasse. Depending on the hike, visitors will need traction devices and ski poles (at a minimum), and possibly crampons, skis, snowshoes, ice axes, and ropes—and the skills to use them for safety and self-rescue.

➤ For those whose backcountry skill set includes kayaking, a series of primitive campsites on the Gulf of Alaska coastline are accessible via kayak; short off-trail hikes to viewpoints can be done from many of these campsites. However, because the fjords are exposed to the Gulf of Alaska (with only a few coves to provide shelter from surf, swells, and potentially high winds), inexperienced kayakers are strongly advised to travel with a guide. For day kayakers, one of the most popular destinations is **Bear Glacier Lagoon**, which can be done with a guide service, or, for more advanced paddlers, can be accessed via a 12-mile water taxi from Seward. Bear Glacier is the largest glacier in the park. Its proto-lagoon is a lake that filled between the glacial moraine and the glacier itself; kayakers can view the glacier and paddle around the giant icebergs that have calved from it.

OPPOSITE: Rocky sea mountain with trees in Aialik Bay (top left); kayaker in Bear Glacier Lagoon (top right); hikers on Godwin Glacier (bottom)

BELOW: Harbor seals on small iceberg

Kobuk Valley
National Park

ALASKA

—————

Designated 1980

Alaska's national parks celebrate Alaskan icons: Denali encircles the highest peak on the North American continent, Wrangell-St. Elias is known for its calving glaciers, and Katmai is famed for its congregations of grizzly bears fishing for salmon. Kobuk Valley National Park's central feature is a bit unexpected. Located 25 miles north of the Arctic Circle, this far northern national park preserves the Great Kobuk Sand Dunes. Yes, sand dunes in Alaska.

The Great Kobuk Sand Dunes, the Little Kobuk Sand Dunes, and the Hunt River Dunes are made up of deposits that were finely ground and left behind by retreating glaciers, then blown into dunes by strong winds. Most of the original dune fields are now anchored in place by forest and tundra vegetation, but about 20,500 acres of active dunes—some as high as 100 feet tall—remain just south of the Kobuk River.

The park is also famous for its annual caribou migration. Twice each year, the 400,000-strong Western Arctic caribou herd migrates between summer calving grounds north of the Baird Mountains and winter homes south of the Waring Mountains. En route, the caribou traipse over the sand dunes and cross the Kobuk River, where they are hunted by Indigenous people, as they have been for thousands of years. Other wildlife in the park includes brown and black bears; wolves and coyotes; Arctic and red foxes; caribou, moose, and Dall sheep; Canadian lynx and wolverines; and martens, beavers, and river otters.

The park's almost 1.8 million acres also include about 81,000 acres of lands owned by Alaska Native corporations and the state of Alaska. South of the Kobuk River, nearly 175,000 acres are managed as the Kobuk Valley Wilderness. Kobuk Valley is also part of a much larger protected ecosystem that extends almost all the way across northern Alaska. To the north and west, the park is bordered by the Noatak National

Small stream near Great Kobuk Sand Dunes

FOLLOWING SPREAD: Point where the sand dunes meet the forest (left); view of barren hills and meandering river from bush plane (top right); animal bone on the sand dunes (bottom right)

Preserve, which extends almost to the Chukchi Sea. The Selawik National Wildlife Refuge lies to the south of the park. To the east of Noatak is Gates of the Arctic National Park and Preserve, and to the east of Gates of the Arctic is the Arctic National Wildlife Refuge, which extends east to the Canadian border and north to the Arctic Ocean.

There are no roads or designated trails into the park, so visitors must fly in via private charter, usually from Bettles (the jumping-off point for Gates of the Arctic) or Kotzebue (a small city about 100 miles west of Kobuk Valley on the coast of the Bering Sea). Kotzebue houses the Northwest Arctic Heritage Center as well as the park's headquarters. There are also two seasonal ranger stations (at either end of the park), but no supplies or facilities. Visitors must fly in with all of their camping gear, food, boats (if they plan to travel by river), fuel for cooking, and emergency communications equipment. Like Gates of the Arctic, this is big, remote wilderness. The National Park Service recommends that all independent backpackers have communications, navigation, and self-rescue skills, and the ability to cope with changing weather and conditions. Guide services are available.

The park is open year-round; planes will fly visitors into the park even in winter, but flight plans are subject to weather and often change (meaning that a group waiting to be picked up at a prearranged date and time may have to wait until the weather allows planes to fly). Snow is possible year-round, although in summer, rain and wind (and mosquitoes) are more common. Summer days and winter nights are both long. In early July, the sun never dips below the horizon, and in late December and early January, the sun is only visible for a couple of hours a day, with long hours of twilight on either side—and the possibility of seeing the aurora borealis at night.

Exploring the Park

The fishing town of Kotzebue (population 3,000) is the closest full-service town to Kobuk Valley National Park. The National Park Service office provides information about air taxi companies operating in the area.

➤ Depending on the length of the trip, visitors can plan to hike through the tundra, climb the peaks of the Baird Mountains, or walk across the sand dunes. Hiking is more difficult in the lowlands because of spongy wet ground, frequent river and stream crossings, and alder thickets. But planes cannot land high in the mountains, so most hikers start at the lower elevations and then head up to the drier ridgelines—though the distances are deceptively long and may require navigating through both tundra and forest.

➤ The most popular camping destination is the **Great Kobuk Sand Dunes**. Backpackers can land directly on the sand dunes or hike to them from the Kobuk River.

➤ The **Onion Portage** on the north bank of the Kobuk River (so named for the wild onions growing along its banks) is another popular destination, especially in late summer, when caribou can be seen swimming across the river as they migrate to their winter homes south of the Waring Mountains. Hikers can also climb the bluff for views of the Jade Mountains.

OPPOSITE: Semicircular river that separates the sand dunes from the forest

BELOW: Hiker on the sand dunes

Lake Clark
National Park and Preserve

ALASKA

_____

Designated 1980

It's not much farther as the crow flies from Anchorage to Lake Clark National Park and Preserve than it is from Anchorage to Kenai Fjords National Park—only about 100 miles—but in the case of Lake Clark, it's one of those "can't get from here to there" situations, at least by road. Google Maps refuses to even consider the question. A visitor's only choice is a plane. It is not surprising, then, that in any given year this park is another one of Alaska's competitive entries for least visited in the entire national park system.

But visitors who do take the effort to get there are rewarded with superlatives. Located southwest of Anchorage on the Cook Inlet of the Gulf of Alaska, Lake Clark sits at the intersection of the Alaska Range and the Aleutian Range. With four million acres of jagged mountains rising as high as 10,000 feet, two volcanoes (one of them recently active), and glaciers, lakes, river valleys, tundra, coastal rain forest, and salt marshes, Lake Clark National Park and Preserve is almost a microcosm of everything Alaskan.

The wildlife is equally impressive, with virtually every major Alaskan species represented. Perhaps most importantly, both ecologically and commercially, the park supports one of the largest salmon runs in the world. The salmon run attracts large groups of brown bears, making this one of the world's premier places to see large groups of brown bears in their natural habitat. Top places for bear viewing include Chinitna Bay (on the coast of Cook Inlet), Crescent Lake (in the heart of the Chigmit Mountains; also a top fishing spot), Silver Salmon Creek (halfway down the Cook Inlet coast; another famous fishing spot), and the less visited Cook Inlet sites of Shelter Creek and Tuxedni Bay (where brown bears may be less habituated to humans and potentially more dangerous).

Like so many national parks, Lake Clark is a place where different environments and ecological habitats intersect to create edge communities rich in biological diversity. And, as in many national parks, there is also an intersection between human and natural histories. The archaeological record goes back 9,000 years; more recently, the Alaska Native Dena'ina people have lived here for hundreds of years, and more recently still, Russian and European American explorers, homesteaders, and miners have settled in the region. The major settled area near the park is Port Alsworth on Lake Clark; several other communities, mostly of Dena'ina, are spread around the park.

As with most Alaska national parklands added to the system when the Alaska National Interest Lands Conservation Act was passed in 1980, subsistence hunting, trapping, and fishing are allowed throughout the park and preserve, while sport hunting is only allowed in the preserve. The Dena'ina phrase *Ye'uh qach'dalts'iyi*, which means "what we live on from the outdoors," refers to the traditional knowledge about harvesting animals, plants, and fish, which has been passed down from one generation to the next.

Also typical of Alaska parks, Lake Clark makes visitors work to see its secrets. Getting there is part of the adventure, and a well-developed network of bush taxis (either boat or plane) is available to shuttle visitors into the park. (Planning needs to include considerations about the type of bush plane needed—floatplanes land on water, wheeled planes touch down on solid ground, and ski-planes land on snow; Lake Clark has all three kinds of landing areas.)

Once in the park, visitors have more choices of facilities than at most other Alaskan parks. In addition to backcountry camping, visitors can stay in privately owned bed-and-breakfasts and lodges. (The park contains more than 200 private parcels totaling nearly 200,000 acres.) Top activities include boating, kayaking, fishing, hiking, and wildlife viewing.

Coastal brown bear in Cook Inlet

FOLLOWING SPREAD: Turquoise Lake (left); kayaker on Lake Clark (top right); Silver Salmon Creek (bottom right)

Exploring the Park

Lake Clark National Park and Preserve offers a few miles of maintained trails near Port Alsworth, and almost unlimited day-hiking and backpacking opportunities starting from places that can be reached by plane or boat. The tundra provides good hikeable terrain. Alaska wilderness precautions apply. Visitors who have arranged for day-hiking drop-offs and pick-ups should have enough gear to spend the night if the weather disrupts you (or your pilot's) plans. All independent hikers should have navigation, communication, and self-rescue skills.

➤ The **Tanalian Trails** originate at a trailhead near the southern airstrip in Port Alsworth and can be combined in various configurations. The **Beaver Pond Loop Trail** and the **Tanalian Falls Trail** are roughly parallel and can be combined for about a 3.5-mile, out-and-back loop to the base of Tanalian Mountain. From there, the **Tanalian Falls Trail** continues to the 30-foot-tall falls (4 miles out and back) or to **Kontrashibuna Lake**, just past the wilderness boundary (about 5.5 miles out and back). The left fork leads to the summit ridge of **Tanalian Mountain**, a strenuous 8.6-mile round trip that offers views of Lake Clark and potential glimpses of wild sheep. (The last bit of the trail is not maintained; the trip often takes eight hours.)

➤ The only other maintained trail is the **Portage Creek Trail**, which begins at the Joe Thompson Public Use Cabin (about 13 miles north-northwest of Port Alsworth, accessible via boat or floatplane). It's a 6.5-mile, out-and-back trail that starts near the Lake Clark shoreline and climbs 1,850 feet through spruce and birch to views from the open tundra.

➤ Gravel bars, tundra, coastal beaches, and lakeshores offer good off-trail hiking for travelers with good navigation skills. However, challenges include fording rivers, navigating around bogs, and bad weather (which could delay pilots and set back your pickup time—or day). The National Park Service suggests planning for a mile per hour to cope with route finding, errors, and terrain obstacles. Some options are the **Hope Creek Route** (one to two days) or the **Low Pass Route** (one to three days) in the valley above the Richard Proenneke Cabin (accessible from Upper Twin Lake); the **Telaquana Route** (five to seven days), which follows an ancestral Dena'ina Athabascan route from Telaquana Lake to Kijik Village on Lake Clark (accessible from Telaquana Lake, Turquoise Lake, or Lower Twin Lake); or the **Upper to Lower Twin Lakes Route** (one to two days, accessible from Upper or Lower Twin Lake).

OPPOSITE: Kayaks on shore of Turquoise Lake (top left); moose antlers along Lake Clark (top right); tourist boat near Silver Salmon Creek Lodge (bottom)

BELOW: View of Lake Clark during storm from bush plane

Wrangell-St. Elias
National Park and Preserve

————

Designated 1980

Hikers on Kennicott Glacier

FOLLOWING SPREAD: Blue pool of water melting onto Kennicott Glacier (left); backpackers in remote areas of the park (top right and bottom right); Hidden Creek Lake (middle right)

At 13.2 million acres, Wrangell-St. Elias National Park and Preserve is the size of six Yellowstones. Or think of it as the entire state of Massachusetts plus the state of Vermont, with a couple of extra counties thrown in. It reaches from sea level to 18,008 feet at Mount St. Elias on the Canadian border—the second-highest mountain in both the United States and Canada and the fourth-highest peak in North America. The park contains parts of several mountain ranges, including Mount Wrangell, a recently active 14,000-foot shield volcano. Its supersized glaciers include the massive Bagley Icefield, which contains multiple glaciers that stretch 127 miles long, 6 miles wide, and as much as 3,000 feet thick. The Wrangell Glacier, with a surface area of more than 1,500 square miles, is the largest piedmont glacier in the world; the Hubbard Glacier is the longest tidewater glacier in Alaska; and the Nabesna Glacier is the world's longest valley glacier.

The park's foundation document cites protection of the natural scenic beauty of the diverse habitats, continuing access for wilderness-based recreational opportunities, and continuing access for subsistence use. As with all of Alaska's national parks, Wrangell-St. Elias is a wilderness park. Indeed, it is the largest single wilderness unit in the United States. But it has better road access than most: two unpaved roads access the park's interior, one from the northwest side and one from the west. Note, however, that the roads are gravel, and thus off-limits for rental cars from most major companies. It is possible to find local companies, and some major brands, that allow travel beyond the pavement, but visitors intending to drive into the park need to factor this complication into their planning.

On the north side of the park, Nabesna Road runs eastward for 45 miles of rough travel (a high-clearance, four-wheel-drive vehicle is recommended; figure one-and-a-half hours each way). The road was originally built to access the Nabesna Gold Mine, which operated from 1925 to 1945 and is now on a private inholding at the end of the road, off-limits to visitors. The draw for driving this road is the scenery, with views of the Wrangell, Mentasta, and Nutzotin Mountains, as well as the frequent trailheads, campsites, and pullouts for wildlife viewing.

From the west side of the park, the 60-mile McCarthy Road (figure two hours each way) follows the route of an old mining railroad that once served the long-defunct Kennecott Copper Mine. The road ends at the Kennecott River, which is crossed on a pedestrian bridge, after which visitors can walk or take a shuttle for the remaining half mile to the inholding village of McCarthy. McCarthy once served the mine; today, it does the same for tourists, with outfitters and guides, a couple of restaurants, accommodations, and flight-seeing and air taxi services. Outfitters can be used for all manner of adventures: packrafting, kayaking, ice climbing, glacier travel, and backpacking.

As with all Alaska parks, Wrangell-St. Elias presents wilderness challenges in line with its enormous size, northern latitude, and superlative geological and landscape features. Cell phone signals are unreliable to nonexistent, weather is unpredictable and variable, and backcountry travelers must have skills and gear for navigation, communication, self-rescue, food storage, and their means of travel (hiking, glacier travel, river crossings, or boat travel). Tree line is at about 3,000 feet, meaning that far-reaching views (in good weather, at least) make for easier navigating, and cross-country travel is smoother than it is lower down through alder, across rivers, and through bogs.

On the coast, some cruise ships come close to the Hubbard Glacier. Unlike Glacier Bay National Park, whose boundary extends into Glacier Bay, Wrangell-St. Elias's boundary extends only to the shoreline, not into

the Gulf of Alaska. So visits from cruise ships don't count in official park stats; without those visitors, Wrangell-St. Elias only tallies up about 75,000 visitors per year.

Exploring the Park

Most of the maintained hiking trails in Wrangell-St. Elias National Park and Preserve are in good shape for the first few miles and then turn into rougher, less easily followed routes. Day-hiking trails are found in the Kennecott area at the end of McCarthy Road and along Nebesna Road. None of the multiday/off-trail routes described below have mileages because mileages depend on each party's route selection.

➤ From the end of McCarthy Road, one of the easier day hikes in the park is the 2.4-mile, round-trip **West Kennecott Glacier Trail**. More strenuous trails include the 5.7-mile, round-trip **Root Glacier Trail**, the 8-mile, round-trip **Erie Mine Trail** (which does not, however, go all the way to the Erie Mine), and the **Jumbo Mine Trail**, an all-day round-trip hike of 10 miles (and probably that many hours, with 3,000 feet of climbing). Spectacular views are the reward.

➤ From the **Kotsina Trailhead** at about mile 14.5 on McCarthy Road, there are two multiday routes; both include off-trail route-finding challenges. The **Dixie Pass Trail** follows a creek to a high alpine pass (about 18 miles round trip; it takes two to three days). The **Nugget Creek Trail** is a fairly straightforward route, with only occasional gentle climbs, that goes 15 miles to a rustic cabin (available by reservation), a mine, and a glacier (allow three days for the round trip).

➤ From Nabesna Road, day hikes include the 12.6-mile, round-trip **Rambler Mine Trail**, the 7-mile, round-trip **Lost Creek Trail**, and the 4.2-mile, round-trip **Skookum Volcano Trail**. Multiday backcountry routes include the **Soda Lake Trail**, featuring a tundra hike to a remote lake (about a 30-mile round trip), and the **Trail Creek-Lost Creek Loop**, which adds the **Trail Creek Trail** to the **Lost Creek Trail** to make a spectacular three- to four-day loop (about 22 miles), with canyons, tundra hiking, and lots of stream crossings.

➤ Bush landing sites in the park are accessible by chartering a plane. The **Goat Trail Route** across Skolai Pass to Glacier Creek is one of the park's highlight experiences for serious backpackers; this fly-in, point-to-point hike in the remote southern part of the park takes about a week. The Glacier Creek Cabin can be used on a first-come, first-served basis. In addition, the following areas are considered premier fly-in destinations for base camping and off-trail hiking: Hidden Creek Valley, the Beaver Creek area, Chelle Lake area, the Sanford-Dadina Plateau, and the remote valley of the Baultoff Creek area.

OPPOSITE: Backpacker on glacial moraine

BELOW: Backpacker among flowers in remote section of the park

Great Basin
National Park

NEVADA

_____

Designated 1986

Great Basin National Park earned its place in the national park system in 1922 as Lehman Caves National Monument, which protected the marble Lehman Caves and their distinctive formations of stalactites, stalagmites, cave popcorn, and cave shields. In 1986, the monument was expanded and upgraded to become Great Basin National Park, which protects not only the caves but also 77,000 acres of the Great Basin and most of the South Snake Mountains, including 13,063-foot Wheeler Peak (the second-highest mountain in Nevada) and Wheeler Peak Glacier, one of the southernmost glaciers in North America.

From caves to glaciers, and with elevations ranging from 6,800 feet to more than 13,000 feet, this is a park with extraordinary diversity in terms of ecosystems. In the lowlands, communities of sagebrush, saltbrush, single-leaf pinyon, and Utah juniper predominate. On higher mountain slopes, white fir, quaking aspen, Engelmann spruce, and Ponderosa pine forests take over. On the highest peaks, there is only the rock-strewn arctic-alpine tundra of the world above tree line.

Perhaps the most spectacular and noteworthy plant resident of the park is the bristlecone pine, which thrives in the harsh weather and poor soil of higher elevations—and the Great Basin has harsh weather and poor soil in abundance. Bristlecones are stunted-looking trees noted for their tortured, twisted shapes, the result of being buffeted by the wind for thousands—yes, thousands—of years. The Great Basin bristlecone pine (*Pinus longaeva*) has the longest life span of any conifer; a grove on Wheeler Peak contains several specimens that are more than 3,000 years old, and another tree cut down in the park for research purposes, called the Prometheus tree, was dated to be just under 5,000 years old, making it possibly the oldest tree ever identified.

View of Wheeler Peak from
Snake Creek Campground

The Great Basin lies west of the Continental Divide; in the grand scheme of things, it is in the Pacific watershed. But the region is endorheic, meaning that in this thirsty, arid land, any water that falls here stays here. Rain and water from melting snow evaporate, drain into sinks, or stay in the region's few lakes. None of it flows into streams that flow into rivers that flow into an ocean.

Great Basin National Park is also one of the most remote parks in the contiguous states, near neither a major population center nor a main travel route for tourists. Located in eastern Nevada near the Utah border, it is nearly four hours from the nearest large airport (in Salt Lake City) and three-and-a-half hours in the opposite direction from the next nearest national park (Zion). One of the 10 least visited parks in the system, it is ideal for travelers seeking an off-the-beaten-path western wilderness experience.

BELOW: Parachute Formation in Lehman Caves

OPPOSITE: Bristlecone pine along Bristlecone Trail (top left); hiker on Timber Creek Trail (top right); marmot along Mountain View Nature Trail (bottom left); hiker on Bristlecone Trail in winter (bottom right)

Exploring the Park

Two areas of Great Basin National Park attract the most visitors: the main visitor center area, with its cave tours and nature trail, and the mountain-hugging Wheeler Peak Scenic Drive, which leads to a campground and trailheads from which visitors can climb to the foot of the glacier or the summit of the peak.

➤ To hike through the **Lehman Caves** requires joining a tour during which rangers explain the history, ecology, and geology of the caves; tickets are required and often sell out in advance. The hour-long **Parachute Shield Tour** travels through large rooms connected by passages and ramps. The 90-minute **Grand Palace Tour** visits the Gothic Palace, Music Room, Lodge Room, Inscription Room, and Grand Palace, including the famous Parachute Shield formation. Introduced in 2022, the 30-minute **Gothic Palace Tour** is intended for families. This shorter tour takes in the Gothic Palace, which features many of the cave's highlight features of stalactites, stalagmites, cave popcorn, and columns.

➤ Just outside, also near the visitor center, the **Mountain View Nature Trail** is an easy 0.3-mile interpretive loop trail that describes the ecology and geology of the park.

➤ Going higher, the **Summit Trail**, **Glacier Trail**, and **Alpine Loop Trail** are all accessible from Wheeler Peak Scenic Drive and from or near the Wheeler Peak Campground. (The 6.4-mile **Lehman Creek Trail** also heads off from the campground, but it goes downhill and to the east.) From the campground, the 2.4-mile, round-trip **Bristlecone Trail** leads to the alpine grove of ancient trees; turn around there, or continue on the **Glacier Trail** to the base of the Wheeler Peak Glacier for a total round trip of 4.8 miles. The Wheeler Peak Summit is accessed from Wheeler Peak Scenic Road via the **Summit Trail**, or from the campground via the **Alpine Lake Loop**, which connects to the Summit Trail. Either way, the 13,000-foot summit can present altitude sickness challenges for unacclimated hikers.

National Park of
American Samoa

AMERICAN SAMOA

———

Designated 1988

The National Park of American Samoa is the only national park in the system whose name begins with the park rather than the location, but that oddity is only one (and the least important) of many ways in which this place is unique. Located 740 miles east of Fiji and 2,600 miles south of Hawaii, this national park is closer to Australia than anywhere in the continental United States, and it is one of only two national parks that are in US territories rather than states. Spread out over the waters and reefs of four tropical islands in the Pacific Ocean, as well as 40 volcanic mountains and coral sand beaches, it is the only national park south of the equator. It is one of the least visited parks in the system.

American Samoa's range of terrestrial wildlife is small, but protecting it—particularly the islands' bat populations and the threatened rain-forest habitat that sustains them—was one of the reasons the park was proposed. The total list of land animals contains only about 25 species, and that includes modern introductions such as Norway rats, house mice, and domestic cats. Native animals include geckos, skinks, the Pacific boa, and three species of bats, among them the Samoan flying fox—a fruit bat with a wingspan of nearly three feet. What American Samoa lacks in mammals it makes up in 343 species of flowering plants, 135 species of ferns, and about 350 species of birds. Its offshore reefs and waters are home to some 950 species of fish, 250 species of coral, and larger animals such as sea turtles and humpback whales.

The park's mission turned out to be much broader than protecting the terrestrial rain forest: the park includes 4,000 undersea acres of coral reefs that surround the islands. And—unusually for an American national park—the National Park of American Samoa was charged with working to preserve not only the ecological environment, but also the region's 3,000-year-old cultural environment of Fa'a Sāmoa, which guides the

Ofu Beach on island of Ofu

FOLLOWING SPREAD: Volcanic shoreline on island of Ta'ū (top left); flying fox on Mount Alava Trail (middle left); hibiscus along Mount Alava Trail (middle); sunset on island of Ta'ū (bottom left); rocky southern shoreline of island of Olosega (right)

beliefs, customs, and etiquette of the Samoan people. Also unique is the fact that the land for the park is not owned by the National Park Service; rather it is leased from villages whose people are allowed to continue their traditional subsistence activities within the park.

Visitors arrive at the airport in Pago Pago, the island's capital city on the island of Tutuila. The park is spread out among several islands, but the visitor center for the park is located on Tutuila. To the east, the territory's Manu'a Islands include Ta'ū, Ofu, and Olosega. Ta'ū is reachable by taking a local plane from Pago Pago to the village of Fiti'uta; from there, visitors can explore Ta'ū's section of the national park, or continue on to Ofu or Olosega by hiring a fishing boat. Accommodations are available on Tutuila, Ta'ū, and Ofu. Homestays with local families, tours with local guides, and volunteer work trips aboard a fishing boat are among the ways visitors can connect with local people.

Exploring the Park

Opportunities for exploring the National Park of American Samoa are divided between land and sea, with beach walking to combine elements of both. At first sight, the park's main features—coral reefs and South Pacific tropical rain forest—seem more suited for scuba divers, beach sitters, and bird-watchers than hikers. There is, however, a network of trails, some of which can be unexpectedly challenging for those harboring ideas of a lazy tropical paradise. The weather can be hot (especially at the lower elevations) and stormy (this is, after all, a rain forest), and some of the trails have significant elevation gain along with obstacles like rock, mud, lack of obvious trail markers, and plenty of fast-growing jungle vegetation to obstruct the way.

➤ Tutuila's section of the national park, near Pago Pago, is the most convenient for visitors to access. Encircling Pago Pago Harbor, a network of trails ranges from short and easy to challenging scrambles and climbs. For dedicated hikers, the trail to **Mount Alava** offers a view of the surrounding jungle and ocean, but the 7-mile, out-and-back trail is steep and muddy in places and can be difficult in hot or rainy weather. For history

buffs, the 1.7-mile **World War II Heritage Trail** passes several World War II installations, which helped protect American Samoa from Japanese invasion.

➤ On Ta'ū, a trail runs from **Saua**, a sacred ancient site considered to be the birthplace of the Polynesian people, then around **Si'u Point**, to the southern coastline, where sea cliffs soar to around 3,000 feet—some of the tallest in the world.

➤ Much of the national park on the islands of Ofu and Olosega is underwater; with some of the healthiest reefs in the South Pacific, it's a favorite destination for snorkelers. (Diving requires private charters or liveaboards, as there are limited dive services in American Samoa; snorkeling just requires bringing your own equipment.) For walkers, the pristine coral sand beaches of Ofu offer long stretches of shoreline hiking.

OPPOSITE: Hiker on ridgeline of Mount Alava Trail

BELOW: Mount Alava Trail

Dry Tortugas National Park

FLORIDA

_____

Designated 1992

BELOW: Entrance to Fort Jefferson

OPPOSITE: Brick seawall and walkway surrounding Fort Jefferson

Seventy miles offshore from Key West, accessible only by ferry, seaplane, or private and charter boats, Dry Tortugas is among the least visited of the national parks, mostly because of how difficult it is to get there. Most of it—all but 40 acres of its 100 square miles—is underwater.

When Spanish explorer Ponce de León arrived here in 1513, the Dry Tortugas were notable for two things. There was no fresh water, making the islands uninhabitable (and hence "dry"). And there was an abundance of sea turtles (*tortugas* in Spanish). Later, as the American coast of the Gulf of Mexico was settled, it became evident that these islands were notable for another reason: their location. West of Key West and north of Cuba, the seven islands sit smack in the middle of the southern entrance to the Gulf of Mexico, within cannon-shot distance of the deep-water channel that allowed passage through the dangerous waters around the Florida Reef. (More than 200 sunken ships are found underwater in

the national park, dating from as far back as the 1600s.) That location meant that anyone who controlled these islands also controlled shipping traffic to eastern Texas, Louisiana, Mississippi, Alabama, and western Florida. In 1825, the US government built a lighthouse; in 1846, construction of a fort began.

Six-sided Fort Jefferson sprawls around almost the entire perimeter of Garden Key and is the largest masonry structure in the Americas. Its 16 million bricks were put in place by white contract workers and (mostly) Black slaves. A cistern system was built to provide the fresh water that would be needed by personnel assigned to the fort. One of the earliest proponents for building the fort was General Robert E. Lee (at the time, an officer in the US Army). But this southern fort ultimately served the Union cause; it was occupied and manned throughout the Civil War by soldiers of the Union Army. The fort was also used as a prison mostly for deserters, but also for a few others, including, most notably, the doctor who had treated John Wilkes Booth after he broke his leg during the assassination of President Abraham Lincoln. After the Civil War, the fort was infrequently used and largely abandoned to the birds, sea turtles, and sea life that had always been there—as well as the occasional brigand and pirate.

In the middle of the 20th century, the federal government took a renewed interest in the islands, in part because of their history, and in part because of their ecological importance. In 1935, Fort Jefferson National Monument was established, and in 1992 it was expanded and upgraded to Dry Tortugas National Park. One-third of the loggerhead turtles in the world nest on East Key, while Bush Key is a nesting site for some 100,000 sooty terns, along with other seabirds such as brown noddies, brown pelicans, masked and brown boobies, double-crested cormorants, frigatebirds, and roseate terns. Undersea, the variety of coral and fish

species is abundant, protected by the park's remoteness. However, it is not immune to climate change, pollution runoff, and diseases that are now affecting reefs around the world. In recent years, higher visitation numbers have become a problem (the islands are now among the Instagram targets of travelers following the trail of social media bucket lists). Other threats include pillaging of artifacts from shipwrecks and commercial fishing, which is not allowed but nonetheless occurs on a regular basis.

Exploring the Park

With only 40 dryland acres (out of the park's area of 100 square miles), Dry Tortugas National Park is not a hiking destination. It is, however, a camping destination. Visitors arrive either by the Yankee Freedom Ferry or by private charters and boats. Most ferry passengers come for day trips; ferry passengers who intend to camp must secure a camping ticket when they book their passage. (Camping tickets are limited and sell out months in advance; campers arriving by private boat do not need a ticket.) This is primitive, basic camping.

Overnight visitors must bring everything they need, including water and hard-plastic animal-proof cases.

➤ For walkers, the trek around the entire perimeter of **Fort Jefferson** is about 0.5 miles. There is also a mile-long beach walk on **Bush Key**, which is only open in late fall and early winter, from October 15 through January 15. The rest of the year, Bush Key is given over to the 100,000 sooty terns and 4,500 brown noddies that nest here.

➤ Perhaps the best way to explore the islands is underwater. The ferry does not allow air canisters, and there are no dive shops or refill stations on the island, so all diving is done via private boats, charters, or liveaboards. Snorkeling equipment is available from the ferry. The beaches right next to the fort (and the moat itself) are popular snorkeling areas with shallow waters (usually five to 15 feet), clear visibility, and an abundance of sea life. Visitors staying overnight on the island can go night snorkeling. Bring a dive light—or better, two—and scope out the area during the day so you won't be disoriented in the dark.

OPPOSITE: Shore of Bush Key near Fort Jefferson (top); royal terns near entrance to Fort Jefferson (bottom left); great blue heron on Bush Key (bottom right)

BELOW: Sea fan on beach near Fort Jefferson (left); gray snapper near Fort Jefferson (right)

Saguaro National Park

ARIZONA

———

Designated 1994

Saguaro cacti on a hillside

Put it in a picture with roadrunners, tumbleweeds, coyotes, and cowboys: the saguaro is one of the cherished symbols of the American West. Instantly recognizable, it stands 50 (or more) feet tall, with Gumby-like arms that wave—in welcome? in warning?—to visitors entering the Sonoran Desert of southern Arizona, eastern California, and northern Mexico. With its towering height and imposing profile, the saguaro can be considered a member of the exclusive "charismatic megaflora" group—plants that (like their megafauna cousins) attract attention and concern because of some combination of rarity, beauty, size, and behavior. Most such charismatic species might get on a postage stamp, or on the endangered species list, or have an organization dedicated to protecting them. The saguaro, along with redwoods and giant sequoias, has the distinction of having its own eponymous national park.

With real estate—whether for cacti or humans—success is all about location, location, location. Looking up at a cactus as tall as a five-story building, it may be hard to imagine that each of these behemoths started life no bigger than a mustard seed. It is only the luck of the draw—and the location—that determines whether the seed lives or dies. In the world of infant saguaros, the lottery winners are those that land in the shade of so-called nurse trees, other species that protect seedlings from trampling and from the desert extremes of sun, wind, and heat.

Even when a saguaro seed manages to embed itself in a sheltered spot, it has a long path to eventual grandeur. It takes six to eight years to reach a single inch in height, 50 years before it will flower, and 70 to 100 years before it sprouts its first arm. For another 50 to 80 years, most will continue to sprout additional arms, often around half a dozen, occasionally many more—but sometimes none at all. Finally, at the age of about 150, the saguaro will reach its full height (the record is 78 feet), after which it might live another 50 years if not killed earlier by infections, fire, windfall, extreme cold, extreme heat, or even lightning strikes.

Saguaros are supremely adapted for a challenging environment of heat, sun exposure, wind, and long periods of drought interrupted by short bursts of intense rain and cold. Their adaptations offer lessons to humans who live in, or hike in, this same environment. Its skin prevents excess moisture evaporation (lesson one: wear sun protection and SPF protective clothes). Its flowers bloom at night (lesson two: don't hike in the heat of the day). And a mature saguaro can soak up to 200 gallons of water after a heavy rain (lesson three: drink whenever there is a water source). In addition, saguaros have a root system that includes both one long taproot and a network of just-under-the-surface rootlets that spread as wide as the saguaro is tall, enabling the plant to collect and hoard rainwater when it falls. A system of woody ribs supports the five-story height and the two-ton weight of the mature plant.

Saguaros are notable not only for their megaflora status, but also for the fact that they are linchpin species in their ecosystem, meaning that scores of other species depend on them in some way—for shade, shelter, nesting cavities, food, and a water source. So the cycle of mutual dependence continues: the nurse trees protect the seedlings, the giants provide for their smaller neighbors, and the national park system protects the entire ecosystem.

Two noncontiguous parcels (separated by the entire city of Tucson) make up the park today. The Rincon Mountains, to the east of Tucson, were designated a national monument in 1933; the Tucson Mountains, to the west, were added in 1961. Together, the two units were granted national park status in 1994. The Rincon Mountains have the park's highest elevations; their 8,000-foot summits make them part

of the chain of sky islands that stretch from southern Colorado to Mexico. These mountain environments surrounded by seas of deserts contain species that are typically found farther north. For hikers, this often means cooler temperatures (and more shade) than are found in the surrounding lower desert landscapes.

Exploring the Park

With 165 miles of hiking trails and almost 80 percent of its acreage designated as wilderness, Saguaro National Park offers excellent opportunities for day hikers, equestrians, and (in the Rincon Mountain District) backpackers. (Backcountry camping is not permitted in the Tucson Mountain District.) This is a desert with harsh conditions. While surface water is found on some trails in some seasons, water planning should be a priority. Desert temperatures can be cool at night, so bring layers. Rattlesnakes are not uncommon; if scrambling around rocks, don't put your hands where you can't see them.

➤ The southwestern part of the Tucson Mountain District contains the visitor center and, just to the north, **Bajada Loop Drive**, an unpaved 5.2-mile auto loop. This corner of the park contains several picnic areas and trailheads that lead to a network of trails of varying lengths and difficulties. Between the visitor center and the driving loop is the **Desert Discovery Nature Trail**, a flat, wheelchair- and stroller-accessible 0.5-mile loop through a stand of large saguaros. Also along the drive is the 0.8-mile **Valley View Overlook Trail**, with views of the Avra Valley and Picacho Peak. For hikers looking to work a little harder, the combination of the **King Canyon and Hugh Norris Trail** creates an 8.4-mile loop with 1,750 feet of elevation gain and a rocky, strenuous scramble up a side spur to the summit of Wasson Peak, just shy of 4,700 feet. (Bonus: the first section of the trail leads to some petroglyphs.)

Just outside the park boundary is the Arizona-Sonora Desert Museum, which offers informative interpretive displays of the surrounding ecological systems.

➤ The Escalante Road driving loop is the main access into the Rincon Mountain District. Trailheads on the north side of **Escalante Road** lead to a large network of trails of varying lengths and difficulties. For day hikers, the long distances between the low parking areas and the summits make it difficult to reach the higher elevations in one day. With their longer mileage range, backpackers can reach the seclusion of the park's high points. The 800-mile **Arizona National Scenic Trail** also crosses the eastern side of the park, starting from the Rincon Valley in the south. Note that the Rincon Mountain District is managed for wilderness values; beyond the trailheads, there are no services.

➤ Mica Mountain is the park high point at 8,666 feet. Several round-trip routes lead to the rounded summit; one of the most popular is from the **Douglas Spring Trailhead** on the northwestern side of the park. The summit itself is largely forested, but the hike to it has lovely views. Figure 26 to 30 miles (hence, a backpacking trip, not a day hike), depending on whether you take side trips to nearby points such as Spud Rock or Man Head Rock, which offer more expansive views.

➤ The **Tanque Verde Ridge Trail** begins at a trailhead off Escalante Road and heads to the eastern half of the park. This strenuous 17-mile, out-and-back trail includes superb views, but with 4,300 feet of elevation gain, it's a stretch to complete it in one day. It's a better choice for backpackers. Day hikers, of course, can strike out on it and choose a turnaround point based on time, energy available, and the views.

Mountain lion in a cave (top left); saguaro cacti, with Baboquivari Peak Wilderness in the background (top right); hiker on King Canyon Trail (bottom)

Death Valley
National Park

The national parks are no strangers to extremes; even so, when it comes to extremes, Death Valley is *extreme*. Covering almost 3,400,000 acres (almost the same size as the entire state of Connecticut), the largest park in the contiguous states is also the hottest, driest, and lowest. Elevations range from 282 feet below sea level (at Badwater Basin) to 11,049 feet atop Telescope Peak in the park's Panamint Range. The landscape changes from sand dunes to salt flats to sunbaked valleys to snow-covered peaks, with the occasional ephemeral lake or field of super-blooming wildflowers brought to life by rare rainstorms. Temperatures range from a blistering 134 degrees (the hottest temperature ever recorded in the world) to the park's record low of 15 degrees.

The valley is essentially a below-sea-level basin that trends north-south, bounded on the west by the Panamint Range and on the east by the Black, Funeral, and Grapevine Mountains of the Amargosa Range. Most of the park is in eastern California, but a small triangle-shaped section pokes into neighboring Nevada; 93 percent of the park is wilderness.

Its name notwithstanding, Death Valley has been inhabited by a rich diversity of plants, animals, and humans. Indigenous peoples may have lived here as early as 9,000 years ago, adapting to the extremes of climate by seasonally commuting. Think of them as Indigenous equivalents of today's "snowbirds," with winter homes snuggled in the valleys and summer homes camped in the mountains. Plants and animals are similarly adapted to the harsh conditions. Creosote bushes outcompete other plants by drilling their taproots deep down for water, then hoarding it and producing chemicals that inhibit the growth of neighbors. Desert bighorn sheep have a tough digestive system that allows them to absorb nutrients from desert plants such as mesquite and catclaw. And the

Hiker in the badlands near Zabriskie Point

FOLLOWING SPREAD: Hiker admiring Artists Palette (left); footprints in the mesquite sand dunes (top right); hiker on mesquite sand dunes at dusk (middle); hiker in Devils Golf Course (bottom right)

nutritionally flexible coyote can survive on cactus fruit, mesquite beans, flowers, insects, lizards, snakes, and birds, in addition to its preferred diet of rodents, rabbits, and other small mammals. Perhaps most improbably, the desert pupfish manages to eke out a living here—even when water temperatures rise above 110 degrees, oxygen levels plummet, salinity levels are twice those of the ocean, and daily temperatures fluctuate as much as 45 degrees.

By contrast, the forty-niners who gave the region its name were not quite as adaptable: they were trapped here while seeking a shortcut to the California gold fields. Local lore tells us that, as they finally found their way out, one of the members turned and said, "Goodbye, Death Valley," perhaps memorializing the one member of their party who did not survive, perhaps memorializing the group's fear that all of them would die there. Later years brought more names: Badwater Basin, Charcoal Kilns, Dantes View, Darwin Falls, Devils Golf Course, Furnace Creek, Hells Gate, Saline Valley, and Salt Creek give some idea of the challenges of this landscape. Between 2010 and 2021, 47 people perished in the park. The top cause of death was auto accidents; other deaths resulted from heatstroke, falls, and, in one case—however improbably—drowning.

With summer temperatures averaging above 100 degrees, the park is best visited in late fall, winter, and early spring. Activities include auto touring (either on main roads or back roads) to viewpoints and trailheads. Cyclists can ride on 785 miles of roads (bicycles are not allowed in the wilderness areas). Photography is popular, especially at sunrise and sunset. There is also prime bird-watching here; Scotty's Castle and Wildrose (riparian habitats), the High Panamints region (bristlecone pine habitat), and Saratoga Springs (a desert oasis) concentrate migrating and endemic birds in areas with food and water. With nearly 3,400,000 acres to explore, hiking and backpacking opportunities are almost infinite, either on-trail or off-trail, following canyon bottoms, open washes, alluvial fans, and old dirt roads. Highlights include expansive vistas of mountains and deserts, dark night skies for stargazing, and a fair guarantee of solitude. However, hikers should be experienced in desert hiking; water availability and heat are constant issues.

Hikers among the hills of Artists Palette (top left); Badwater Basin salt flats (top right); hiker admiring view of Zabriskie Point (bottom)

Exploring the Park

Highway 190 bisects Death Valley National Park, generally east to west, making a winding horseshoe shape as it curves through the middle. At Furnace Creek, Badwater Road leaves the highway and heads south through the middle of the valley; to the north, Scotty's Castle Road leaves Highway 190 and heads to the Scotty's Castle Visitor Center and the far northern tip of the park. Note that many of the trails start at marked and named trailheads, but the trails themselves may be unmarked, following features like canyon bottoms and dry riverbeds. The ability to navigate with a map and compass is required for anyone leaving the main roads.

➤ Trails off of Badwater Road include the 2.5-mile, one-way **Golden Canyon Trail**, which goes from the Zabriskie Point Trailhead on Highway 190 to the Golden Canyon Trailhead on Badwater Road, featuring millions of years of geology and eroded badlands, all arrayed in colored layers. **Gower Gulch Loop** is a 4-mile round trip that starts about 2 miles south of Highway 190. The trail features colorful badlands, canyon narrows, and some off-trail scrambling. The 3-mile, round-trip, off-trail hike to **Desolation Canyon** is another canyon-and-narrows hike; it begins from a trailhead on a dirt road about 3.7 miles south of Highway 190. The **Natural Bridge Canyon Trail** is a short easy hike to a natural bridge (about 0.5 miles in) and a dry waterfall (just a bit farther). The trailhead is on a gravel road about 13.2 miles south of Highway 190.

➤ Almost exactly in the center of the park, the Stovepipe Wells area on Highway 190 has a lodge, campground, airstrip, ranger station, general store, and gas station, making it a good orientation point for trailheads along the highway. **Mesquite Flat Sand Dunes**, located just east of Stovepipe Wells, can be hiked to from either the highway or the unpaved Sand Dunes Road; they are the easiest dunes to access in the park. It's a 2.8-mile, out-and-back, cross-country hike to reach the top of the highest dune. Early morning, evening, and even full-moon nights are best (less heat, less or no direct sunlight, and better lighting for pictures).

Bring plenty of water. Starting 2 miles south of Stovepipe Wells, the popular **Mosaic Canyon Trail** goes 2 miles one way up a narrow, polished marble-walled canyon with some slickrock scrambling and the possibility of seeing bighorn sheep; the dramatic narrowest section is in the first half mile, after which hikers not wanting to do the full distance often turn around. The **Salt Creek Interpretive Trail** follows a boardwalk along a small stream for half a mile. About 10 miles east of Stovepipe Wells (and about 13.5 miles north of Furnace Creek), this short creekside walk is worth the detour in early spring and late winter to see the life that collects along a water source, including the rare desert pupfish.

➤ Scotty's Castle Road heads from Highway 190 to the north side of the park. Hiking choices here include both marked trails and trailless routes through canyons and washes. The trailhead for **Fall Canyon** and **Titus Canyon** is on a gravel road, 3 miles off Scotty's Castle Road; hikers have options for either canyon, with rugged mountains, colorful rock formations, petroglyphs, wildlife, rare plants, and spectacular canyon narrows. Titus Canyon is accessed on Titus Canyon Road, which goes all the way to the Nevada side of the park and is the most popular backcountry auto road in the park. The Fall Canyon option is a moderately difficult 6-mile,

out-and-back hike that starts at the Titus Canyon parking area. The route begins on an informal trail, then goes into the canyon for 2.5 miles. Hiking farther is possible for experienced climbers with scrambling skills, but most people turn around here. Eight miles west of Scotty's Castle, the 1.5-mile **Little Hebe Crater Trail** loop starts from the Ubehebe Crater parking area and features a series of dramatically eroded volcanic craters.

➤ For summer visitors, hiking in the valley itself is not advised; temperatures often soar above 120 degrees. But the park's elevations rise to more than 11,000 feet, and the higher elevations offer at least somewhat cooler temperatures (usually temperatures drop about three to five degrees for every gain of 1,000 feet in elevation). While midsummer is likely to still be unpleasantly hot, spring and fall are good times to climb. High-elevation trails may be closed due to snow in winter. The **Wildrose Peak Trail** is 4.2 miles one way, and gains 2,200 feet to the 9,062-foot summit, with excellent views as the reward for a very steep final mile. Peakbaggers will want to take on **Telescope Peak Trail**, the 7-mile, one-way trail that gains 3,000 feet to reach the park's 11,049-foot high point. In winter, the climb requires ice axes, crampons, and the skills to use them. The mountain is usually snow-free by June.

OPPOSITE: Ubehebe Crater

BELOW: Hiker in Titus Canyon (left); rare desert gold superbloom (right)

Joshua Tree National Park

CALIFORNIA

_____

Designated 1994

They rise from the dun scrub of the Mojave Desert, something of a cross between a cactus and a tree. Legend tells us that they were named by Mormon emigrants, who were journeying, Bibles in hand, to find their promised land. The desert trees, they thought, were waving to them, like Joshua, who directed the Israelites as they crossed the desert to conquer Canaan. The story is undocumented, but that hasn't stopped it from being repeated often enough to attain the status of truth.

Nomenclature aside, *Yucca brevifolia*—also known as the yucca palm, tree yucca, palm tree yucca, and, in Spanish, *izote de desierto* ("the desert dagger")—is not a tree; it's in the yucca family. Fibrous trunks divide into a system of branches that support dense circular bunches of evergreen, bayonet-shaped leaves, each of which can be as much as three feet long. The largest yuccas grow to about 40 feet in height, sometimes more, and can live for hundreds of years (although without the evidence of tree rings, their longevity is at best an estimate). Deep taproots reach as much as 35 feet underground to find groundwater. As adaptive as they are to their harsh environments, Joshua trees may not be able to adapt to the most recent threat: climate change. Research suggests that their range is being reduced, and even moving; their numbers could decrease by as much as 90 percent by the end of the 21st century.

With nearly 800,000 acres (more than half of which is officially designated wilderness), Joshua Tree is one of the largest national parks in the system (eighth, among the contiguous states; 15th overall). It is also one of the more heavily visited—number 11—in part because it is located only about two hours east of the populated Los Angeles metropolitan area.

The park's ecosystems range from the montane forests of the surrounding ranges to sandy soil grasslands and sand dunes found in the southeast of the park, from cactus gardens to high desert. At the lower elevations on the eastern side of the park, the Colorado Desert features habitats of creosote, ocotillo, saltbush, yucca, cholla, and prickly pear. Joshua trees thrive in the higher elevations of the Mojave Desert ecosystem; in addition to California, they are also found where the Mojave pokes into adjoining areas in Nevada, Utah, and Arizona. The park is also noted for its superbloom; it is one of California's mountain-desert areas that occasionally come alive with spring wildflowers that carpet the desert with color.

The intersection of desert and mountain climates creates an ecological edge effect, where species that rarely live near one another share a habitat. In the plant world, some of the park's Joshua trees live within sight of Ponderosa pines; in the animal kingdom, the park is home to dryland species such as large herds of desert bighorn sheep, coyotes, black-tailed jackrabbits, kangaroo rats, and seven species of rattlesnakes, but also mountain species like bobcats, mountain lions, black bears, and southern mule deer. Located along the Pacific migratory bird flyway, Joshua Tree is also an excellent bird-watching destination, with more than 350 species of birds recorded.

Much of the landscape is wide open, with broad swaths of desert punctuated by rock outcroppings and the fantastical shapes of the Joshua trees themselves. The surrounding mountain ranges, the striking granite formations, the rock mazes, and five oases whose water supports fan palm—California's only indigenous palm—make this a multifaceted landscape.

Joshua Tree National Park can be visited year-round, but summers are often brutally hot, especially for active pursuits like hiking. Hiking beyond the well-marked nature trails requires attention to desert details (water and heat exhaustion), as well as navigation (maps

Joshua tree in front of rocks

FOLLOWING SPREAD: Grove of Joshua trees (left); Skull Rock (middle); rock formations near Jumbo Rocks Campground (top right); flowering desert cactus in the backcountry (bottom right)

and compasses in addition to digital apps and backup batteries). Sun exposure, high temperatures, and lack of surface water create the risk of heat exhaustion and dehydration. Fall and spring offer more manageable temperatures; visiting between February and April adds the possibility of seeing desert wildflowers.

Three visitor centers are located by entrance stations on the northwestern side of the park; there is also a visitor center at the south entrance, which is accessible from Interstate 10. A network of roads (paved and unpaved) crosses parts of the park. Day hikers base camping at one of the campgrounds should take advantage of being on-site and get in a few miles before the heat of the day.

Exploring the Park

Joshua Tree National Park's large network of trails includes everything from tenth-of-a-mile-long nature trails to multiday expeditions. For day hikers, the trail networks around the Black Rock Nature Center and the West Entrance Station offer the most choices of interlocking loops. Several campgrounds in the park's northwestern section also have nearby networks of trails. The northwest section of the park is in the higher Mojave Desert environment characterized by the Joshua trees; the eastern side is in the lower (and hotter and drier) Colorado Desert.

➤ The **Black Rock Nature Center** and campground area offers a large network of loops that can be combined in almost endless permutations. Trails wind out from the campground; mileage depends on how they are connected. The 1.3-mile **Hi-View Nature Trail** is an interpretive trail, with a guide to vegetation and ecology available from the nature center. Longer trails include **Eureka Peak**, the **West Side Loop**, and the **Black Rock Canyon-Panorama-Morongo View Loop**. The **Warren Peak** side trail climbs steeply to the 5,103-foot high point in this part of the park, with views of the Santa Rosa Mountains, San Jacinto Mountains, and

San Bernardino Mountains. At the nearby **West Entrance Station**, the **Northside** and **West Access Trails** also lead to a network of loops.

➤ From the Hidden Valley Campground, the **Hidden Valley Nature Trail** is an easy mile-long trail with interpretive signs; the **Hidden Valley Connector** leads to Barker Dam and the Old Queen Valley Historic Road, which features giant rock formations, large groves of Joshua trees, and opportunities for photos of classic Joshua Tree landscapes.

➤ At Sheep Pass Campground, the **Ryan Mountain Trail** can be accessed either from the park road near the campground, or from the campground via the **Sheep Pass Spur**. The 5,456-foot peak is a strenuous 1.5-mile climb; 360-degree views of the park are the reward.

➤ Heading south from Ryan Campground, the **Lost Horse Loop** is shaped like an upside-down lollipop; the loop part of it circles Lost Horse Mountain, where one of the park's more profitable old mines once produced gold and silver. What is left are crumbling structures and collapsing shafts; the mines themselves are off-limits.

➤ The Jumbo Rocks Campground features the **Skull Rock Nature Trail**. Just northeast of the campground is a picnic area with a trailhead for the **Split Rock Loop Trail**. The **Split Rock Connector** leads southeast to connect with trails in the Belle and White Tank Campground areas.

➤ For backpackers, the almost 40-mile-long **California Riding and Hiking Trail** crosses virtually all of the northwest section of the park and is perfect for a multiday trip. Going west to east, it enters the park near the Black Rock area, where it can be accessed from the **Boundary Trail**. Inside the park, it can be accessed via several park roads and Ryan, White Tank, and Belle Campgrounds. It exits the park near the North Entrance Station.

Barker Dam Nature Trail

Black Canyon of the Gunnison
National Park

COLORADO

_____

Designated 1999

It's not the deepest canyon in the national park system. The 2,000-foot gash that the Gunnison River slices through the earth to create the Black Canyon is less than half the depth of the Grand Canyon. Lengthwise, the Black Canyon doesn't compete either: the Grand Canyon is 277 miles long; the Black Canyon a mere 48 miles.

But this sheer cleft in the earth is a different sort of canyon entirely. The Grand Canyon sprawls in a maze of side canyons and can turn into a virtual sun-baked convection oven in the summer. In contrast, the Black Canyon is a thin, single-minded, vertical slice, and depending on the season, some parts of it get as little as 33 minutes of sunlight in an entire day. Shrouded in shadow, at times no more than 40 feet wide, the vertigo-inducing Black Canyon is sheer, narrow, dark—and mesmerizing. Its 12-mile-long center section is the heart of Black Canyon of the Gunnison National Park. The Ute people, who lived in the region when Europeans arrived, referred to the river here as "much rocks, big water" and stayed away from it, perhaps out of superstition, perhaps out of good sense.

The rapids cannot be rafted; some sections are runnable for expert whitewater kayakers (but other sections have killed people who tried). The rapids are squeezed into narrow passages with water raging over truck-sized rocks; some of the portages are seemingly no less impossible, with treacherous ledges edged by monster-sized poison ivy. The Gunnison River drops an average of 34 feet per mile over its entire length, making its rate of descent the fifth steepest in North America; in one particularly impossible spot, at Chasm View, the drop is 240 feet per mile. By comparison, the average gradient of the Colorado River through the Grand Canyon—known for its adrenaline-producing rafting and its thrills of a lifetime—is about seven-and-a-half feet per mile.

Despite its drama, Black Canyon of the Gunnison is among the least visited of the national parks and the least visited park in Colorado. Its far-flung location is one reason, but lack of visitor infrastructure is another; the most luxurious lodgings in the park are a couple dozen RV hookups (although they do have electricity).

Exploring the Park

Black Canyon of the Gunnison National Park has two entrances. The South Rim entrance, 15 miles east of Montrose, is open year-round; the North Rim entrance, 11 miles south of Crawford, is closed in the winter. Hikers have a choice of hiking along the rim or dropping into the canyon to go all the way down to the river. Most visitors stay on the rim, hiking or driving to the overlooks. The inner canyon is a designated wilderness area, and trails leading to the bottom require close to 2,000 feet of descent (and ascent) on trails that are steep, with loose rock, scree, and mud. All inner canyon trips—even day use—require permits, along with above-average fitness, route-finding skills, and a certain insouciance when it comes to acrophobia.

➤ From the North Rim, the **Chasm View Nature Trail** is a 0.5-mile loop leading from the North Rim Campground to one of the park's most famed overviews of the narrowest part of the canyon. For more ambitious hikers, the **North Vista Trail** is a 7-mile, out-and-back hike that includes nearly 1,200 feet of climbing (and descending), starting from the North Rim Ranger Station and alternating between woodlands, overlooks, and the summit of Green Mountain, from which there is a sweeping view of the canyon.

➤ The South Rim has several short trails to overlooks: the 0.75-mile **Warner Point Nature Trail**

View of Gunnison Point near South Rim Visitor Center

FOLLOWING SPREAD: Deer at bottom of canyon (left); view of Gunnison River from East Portal Road

offers views of the San Juan Range, and the 0.3-mile **Pulpit Rock Overlook Trail** has views straight down the precipices into the river. The slightly longer 2-mile **Rim Rock Nature Trail** to Tomichi Point and the **Oak Flat Loop Trail** (also 2 miles) offer a bit more challenge, as well as views into the canyon.

➤ For those who want to explore the canyon up close and personal, the 6.5-mile, round-trip **Red Rock Canyon Route** drops (and ascends) just over 1,300 feet from a parking area on Bostwick Park Road. With mountain views and fly-fishing opportunities at the bottom, this is one of the most popular backcountry hikes in the park, but it is steep and rough. The **Gunnison Route** is a short, extremely steep route to and from the river that includes nearly 1,800 feet of elevation loss in its 1.3-mile descent (and the same in reverse). That gradient means that this is more of a scramble than a hike, and the steep drop and unmaintained trail conditions present plenty of obstacles, including rocks, mud, slippery spots, and poison ivy. Views and riverside campsites are the reward.

Cuyahoga Valley
National Park

OHIO

———

Designated 2000

Trail leading to Brandywine Falls

FOLLOWING SPREAD: Brandywine Creek from Brandywine Gorge Loop (left); bridge along Ohio & Erie Canal Towpath (top right); rock atrium along Ledges Trail (bottom right)

In 1969, Cleveland's Cuyahoga River garnered the attention of the American public—by catching fire and burning. As flames spread across the river and blazed a path through national media, it would have been inconceivable that this embattled corner of northeastern Ohio would someday be in the same league as mighty Yellowstone National Park.

Located in the densely populated Great Lakes region, Cuyahoga Valley National Park demonstrates how the definition of a national park has expanded and changed in the 150 years since Yellowstone was protected for the American people. It shows how even an area once decorated with a scrim of oil-covered industrial debris can be reclaimed. And it also shows the flexibility of the national park system, which has adapted to the different on-the-ground realities of use of the American landscape. Unlike the traditional western wilderness parks that formed the early core of the national park system—but similar to national parks in countries like England or huge state parks like Adirondack in New York—Cuyahoga is integrated and enmeshed with local communities, roads, highways, and developments, and includes partnerships with regional land-management agencies, parks, nongovernmental organizations, and private landowners.

The chain of events that led to this new vision for the National Park Service may have been lit when a spark from an overpassing train dropped down to the river and set its backlog of detritus aflame. The ensuing fire lasted for less than a half hour and caused only minor damage to the railroad bridges, but its results were long-lasting: the burning river became one of the enduring symbols of the environmental movement. Media coverage called attention to the environmental degradation of rural lands scoured by industrialization, mining, poor farming practices, hazardous waste, soil erosion, deforestation, damming, and other damage.

Time called the Cuyahoga a river that oozed rather than flowed. It was indeed a most unlikely place for a national park.

In 1974, President Gerald Ford signed legislation to create a new national recreation area, which protected 22 miles of the river and the surrounding landscape just a few miles away from where the fire had burned. Over the next 26 years, the National Park Service and its partners engaged in an aggressive program of remediation: replanting trees, taking down dams, and cleaning up waste. In 2000, the recreation area was upgraded to national park status, joining a small collection of parks immediately adjacent to large metropolitan areas.

With 2.8 million visitors in 2021, what was once one of America's most unlikely national parks is now one of the most visited in the entire system, second in the East only to Great Smoky Mountains National Park, and ranking in popularity with Yellowstone, Yosemite, Grand Canyon, Zion, Rocky Mountain, and Grand Teton. Cuyahoga Valley's popularity is even more striking when considering its size—a mere 32,000 acres, less than two percent of Yellowstone's 2.3 million acres. Like Great Smoky Mountains National Park (but unlike the big western parks), entrance is free.

Exploring the Park

Touched by three interstates (Interstate 80, Interstate 271, and Interstate 77), Cuyahoga Valley National Park is more of a day-hiking destination than a backpacking park. However, several backcountry campsites are available by permit.

➤ Approximately 40 miles of the 1,444-mile **Buckeye Trail** cut across the park. The Buckeye Trail is a horseshoe-shaped long-distance trail that makes a long southward arc around the state; it is also part of the **North Country National Scenic Trail**. In the national park, the terrain on the Buckeye Trail is varied, through forests of pine, oak, and hemlock; past orchards, creeks, and ravines; and to numerous viewpoints. A popular day hike is a 3-mile, out-and-back trail to Blue Hen Falls on the Buckeye Trail.

➤ Many of the park's day-hiking trails feature a combination of waterfalls, creeks, rock ledges, and overlooks. The 2.2-mile **Ledges Trail** encircles a plateau of rock formations and ledges made of moss-covered sandstone layers, caves, and narrow passageways through the rock mazes; it can be connected with the **Pine Grove Trail**. The 1.4-mile **Brandywine Gorge Loop** features the deep ravine carved by Brandywine Creek and dramatic views of Brandywine Falls. It can be connected with the 4-mile **Stanford Trail to Brandywine Falls Trail**, one of the park's most popular paths. Another creek-and-cascade hike is the 2-mile, out-and-back trail from **Bridal Veil Falls to Tinker's Creek Gorge**.

➤ A section of the **Ohio & Erie Canal Towpath Trail** also crosses the park. With canals, locks, waterfalls, and wildlife, the towpath is popular with walkers, runners, bikers, and families.

OPPOSITE: Rock structure along Ledges Trail

BELOW: Everett Covered Bridge

Congaree National Park

_____

Designated 2003

Boardwalk leading to
Weston Lake Loop Trail

What's in a name? And does size matter? These are two questions national park visitors might well ponder when planning a visit to 26,000-acre Congaree National Park—one of the smallest parks in the system. Originally designated in 1933 as Congaree Swamp National Monument, Congaree got an instant facelift in 2003 when its designation was changed from "monument" to "park" and its name dropped the mostly misleading word "swamp." (Congaree is not, in fact, a swamp, but rather an ecosystem of bottomlands that are subject to periodic flooding from the Congaree and Wateree Rivers.)

Despite its size, Congaree has enough space to provide habitat for one of the tallest hardwood canopies in the world, which gives it some of the most important ecological diversity in the American East. Small it may be, but in addition to its national park status, it has been named an international biosphere reserve (by UNESCO), a globally important bird area (through a program administered by the Audubon Society), a national natural landmark (through a National Park Service program), a federally designated wilderness area (by Congress), and an outstanding national resource waters designee (by the state of South Carolina). Animal inhabitants include bobcats, coyotes, deer, feral pigs, armadillos, turkeys, otters, turtles, snakes (of both venomous and nonvenomous character), and even the occasional, though rarely seen, alligator.

The rich biodiversity is courtesy of nutrient-dense floodwaters, which create seasonal swamplike conditions and support a primeval forest of stunning size and diversity. In the last two centuries, lumber operations cast covetous eyes on the enormous trees here, but the land was too remote and difficult to harvest. As a result, the park has one of the world's largest concentrations of so-called champion trees (a name given to the largest examples of their species, whether in a state, region, country, or the world). Champion trees are measured by points—the total sum of their trunk circumference (in inches) plus their height (in feet) plus one-quarter of their average crown spread (in feet). Champions of Congaree include loblolly pine, sweetgum, cherrybark oak, American elm, swamp chestnut oak, overcup oak, and common persimmon.

The park is managed for its wilderness and ecological values; there is only one short road, which leads to a car campground, a visitor center, and a 2.4-mile boardwalk that leads through the wetlands. The boardwalk provides a jumping-off point for most of the other trails, which are the only means to access the rest of the park. As a result, this is a park with a quieter, less touristic atmosphere and with fewer visitors. Except, that is, during firefly season. Along with Great Smoky Mountains National Park, Congaree is one of the only places to see the magical light shows of synchronous fireflies, a species that synchronizes its flashing lights, putting on a show just after dark in late May and early June. A newly adopted lottery permit system is now in effect to control crowds and preserve the unique experience.

Exploring the Park

Day hiking, canoeing, and kayaking are the only ways to explore Congaree National Park. Expect wet feet because most of the trails go through the floodplain, which is seasonally under water. Backpacking is permitted, but camping is restricted to disperse impact and keep tent sites away from water courses and known flooding hazards. (Additionally, backpackers should check local water-level reports and ranger recommendations for advice on choosing campsites.) There isn't much here in the way of elevation gain and loss, but in this environment, even elevation changes of a few feet

create a startling variety of ecological diversity (and can help keep tents out of the water). But don't confuse a lack of elevation with a lack of difficulty—Congaree's seasonal floods cause fallen trees that obscure the trail and create sloughs of mud to wade through. Closures are not uncommon, so check your itinerary at the visitor center. Early spring and fall are best; late spring and summer are humid and buggy.

➤ The wheelchair- and stroller-accessible **Boardwalk Loop** is the park's most popular feature. This 2.6-mile loop keeps hikers' feet out of mud and puddles. It winds through the bottomlands among some of the towering champion trees and passes a lakeside observation deck. Just off of the boardwalk is the **Firefly Trail**, an easy 1.8-mile trail; note, however, that the firefly displays take place in the evening, when the park is only open to ticketed visitors for that event.

➤ Beyond the visitor center and boardwalk, the trail network offers a combination of loops and spurs that intersect and connect so that visitors can create a hike suitable for their fitness, exertion level, and interests. The **Weston Lake Trail** hits the sweet spot for many day hikers. About 5 miles long, it offers a good introduction to the ecological diversity of the park. More enthusiastic day hikers can combine trails in various configurations to create longer hikes. On the west side of the park, the secluded **River Trail** is the only trail leading to the Congaree River itself. On the east side of the park, the **Kingsnake Trail** borders Cedar Creek and is popular with bird-watchers and photographers.

➤ In addition to hiking trails, the park also offers the 15-mile **Cedar Creek Canoe Trail** for canoeists and kayakers. (Boat rentals are offered by outfitters outside the park boundaries.)

OPPOSITE: Flooded trail (top left); tree stumps in flooded waters (top right); moss-covered tree stump (bottom left); hiker on elevated boardwalk along Weston Lake Loop Trail (bottom right)

BELOW: Flooded trail among hardwood trees

Great Sand Dunes
National Park and Preserve

COLORADO

———

Designated 2004

Only two national parks in the contiguous states are both a national park (where the focus is on recreation and preservation) and a national preserve (which allows hunting and some commercial enterprises). Located in south-central Colorado, Great Sand Dunes National Park and Preserve is one of them; the other is West Virginia's New River Gorge. The two parks could not be more different. The centerpiece of New River Gorge is a 1,000-foot-deep cleft in the earth; the centerpiece of Great Sand Dunes is an enormous 30-square-mile dune field that rises 750 feet above the plane—the tallest dune system in North America. But that elevation is writ in sand, not stone: the continually shifting winds make high-point honors a moving target.

The Great Sand Dunes were created by a sequence of erosion, sedimentation, evaporation, and wind. Rivers and snowmelt brought sediment from the surrounding mountains down to lakes in the valley. Over the course of many millennia, natural climate changes dried up the lakes, leaving behind sediments and sands. Then, prevailing winds blew the sands toward the Sangre de Cristo Mountains, where they formed the dune field. The result is one of the national park system's unique and fantastical landscapes: 30 square miles of shifting white sand dunes framed by 13,000-foot peaks.

The boundary of Great Sand Dunes National Park and Preserve encircles the four primary components of the geomorphological system that created and sustains the dunes. First is the dune field itself, which contains the active, shifting dune forms. The names—reversing dunes, transverse dunes, star dunes, barchan dunes, parabolic dunes, and nebka—refer to the different shapes created by two opposing forces: winds, which move the sands, and vegetation, which holds some parts of some dunes in place while allowing other parts to move.

The dune field contains some 6.5 billion cubic meters of sand, but that is only about 10 percent of the sand in the park. The rest lies in the sand sheet, the second component of the system, which surrounds the dune field on three sides. Much of the sand sheet is hidden by a deceptive layer of grasslands. Just beyond is the third element, called the sabkha. The Arabic word refers to salt flats, which are created when seasonally rising groundwater saturates sand and dissolves minerals, which form a hard white crust when the water evaporates.

Finally, east of the park boundary, the national preserve contains the enormous alpine wall of the Sangre de Cristo Mountains, the fourth element of the system. The mountain watershed provides a dramatic backdrop for the otherworldly sand-dune landscape. But it functions as more than a dramatic picture frame. The wide variation in elevation creates changing ecosystems: alpine tundra, forests, and riparian. It also causes an orographic effect in which prevailing winds ascend the slopes and then deposit rainfall on the rain-shadow side of the range, which is where the dunes are located. This rain-shadow effect supports the dune ecosystem as well as the diverse landscapes around it: grasslands, wetlands, forests, and tundra. The effect of the mountain water on what would otherwise be a desert ecosystem is especially striking during the spring snowmelt. In a landscape of blinding white sand and glistening white snow, the variegated colors of the spring flowers—cactus in the lowlands, wildflowers in the higher meadows—stand out in shocking contrast.

The 30-square-mile dune field is open to hiking, but there are no trails. Because the dunes are constantly shifting, the routes to their high points are constantly changing as well. No matter: hiking the dunes is one of the reasons people come here, and it is even possible to camp out in the dunes (bring your own water and

Light and shadow among Great Sand Dunes

FOLLOWING SPREAD: Great Sand Dunes, with Sangre de Cristo Mountains in the background (left); dunes shaded pink during sunset (top right); hikers on the tallest dunes in North America (bottom right)

binoculars for stargazing). Note that in summer, the surface temperature of the sand can reach 150 degrees, thunderstorms are common, and heat exhaustion is a risk. All of these risks can be lessened by hiking in the early morning or later in the evening. For some dunes, having a four-wheel-drive vehicle gives visitors the option of driving farther into the park and shortening the approach hikes to the dunes. Sand wheelchairs are available for loan at the visitor center; their fat inflated tires allow access into the dunes. (Note that they are not motor powered; they require someone to push them.) Sandboards and sand sleds are also available from outfitters just outside the park.

Understandably—given the drama of the dunes— the park's grasslands, shrublands, and wetlands are less visited parts of the park; much of the park does not have marked and maintained hiking trails. Nonetheless, many of these areas are also open to hiking, and even where there are no established trails, visitors can follow animal paths, cross-country routes, and social trails for views of wildlife, migrating dunes, and panoramic mountains.

Exploring the Park

For most people, a visit to Great Sand Dunes National Park and Preserve breaks down into hiking the dunes, hanging out at the creek, and everything else. For dune hiking, figure at least an hour for each mile— perhaps longer. And bring lots (and lots) of water and sun protection.

➤ **High Dune** on the first ridge is not the highest in the park, but at about 690 feet, it is certainly a respectable height; it is also the most impressive dune seen from the parking lot. The two- to four-hour round trip (depending on how often you stop and how easy you find climbing on a sand dune) provides expansive views of the entire dune field. High Dune can be done as an out-and-back hike, or it can be combined with a trek to (approximately) 750-foot-tall Star Dune, the distinctive pyramid-shaped dune that vies for high-point honors among the dunes. Star Dune can also be hiked (more directly and with less up-and-down walking) on its own from its base along Medano Creek.

➤ In contrast to High Dune (which beckons to visitors), **Hidden Dune** is more circumspect, even though its height of about 750 feet vies with Star Dune for the high-point title. Hidden behind other dunes, with a false summit to make it even more reclusive, it's a 7-mile round trip from the Dunes Parking Lot, less if you have a four-wheel-drive vehicle and can drive farther into the park to start at Sand Pit or Castle Creek Picnic Area.

➤ Regardless of which dune a visitor chooses, hanging out at the creek is a given; to get to the dunes from the parking area requires crossing **Medano Creek**. In spring, the creek is fresh with snowmelt and the flow of water combines with the shifting sands in the creek bed to create something called a surge flow—periodic fast-moving waves appropriate for children's tubing, paddleboarding, or boogie boarding. This is a perfect spot for families looking for a day at the beach, and for hikers coming off the dunes looking for a place to cool off and refresh.

➤ Mountain trails enter the national preserve. Near the visitor center, the 3.5-mile **Mosca Pass Trail** heads up Mosca Creek to 9,737-foot Mosca Pass;

OPPOSITE: Hikers dwarfed by grand scale of sand dunes (top left); Zapata Falls (top right); hikers among the many layers of dunes (bottom)

BELOW: Desert flowers among the dunes

the shaded creekside hike is a good choice on a hot day. For those going higher and farther, the 11-mile **Sand Ramp Trail**, located between the dunes and the mountain range, is most often used as an approach trail to reach other trails leading into the preserve's mountains. Trailheads for the Sand Ramp Trail are found in the campground or the Point of No Return parking area. Parts of this trail have some stretches of deep sand while winding up and down the foothills, so it can be slow going.

➤ On the northern end of the Sand Ramp Trail, the **Sand Creek Trail** leads to the alpine zone, with spurs veering off to Little Sand Creek Lakes, Lower and Upper Sand Creek Lakes, Milwaukee Peak (13,522 feet), and Music Pass (11,380 feet). Mileage varies according to your starting trailhead, which depends on whether you have a four-wheel-drive vehicle. The alpine zone is also accessible from four-wheel-drive Music Pass Road on the northeastern side of the preserve. The trail to **Medano Lake** and **Mount Herard** (13,297 feet, with a spectacular view of the dunes) is accessible via a trail from the parking area in the dunes section of the national park, or by Medano Pass, accessible via four-wheel-drive Medano Pass Road on the eastern side of the preserve.

OPPOSITE: Leading lines of sand dunes created by light and shadow

BELOW: Hiker walking among the dunes at sunset

Pinnacles
National Park

CALIFORNIA

———

Designated 2013

At just under 27,000 acres, Pinnacles National Park is the seventh-smallest park in the system. But it is the product of enormous seismic activity. The Pinnacles are thought to be remnants of the Neenach Volcano, which erupted 23 million years ago—200 miles away. The volcanic eruption spewed out the rock that became the Pinnacles; faulting turned these formations topsy-turvy, and plate tectonics carried them along the San Andreas Fault and deposited them in their current location about 80 miles southeast of San Jose. Erosion, weathering, wind, and rain did the rest, carving the formations into their present-day shapes.

One unique feature of the park is its talus caves, created not by the usual process of cave formation—water eroding soft rock—but by gravity. Deep narrow gorges between some of the Pinnacles were covered by enormous rocks that fell from above. The fallen rock jammed in crevices and created a sort of ceiling; the open spaces that remained below became a labyrinth of caves.

At least 13 species of bats live in the caves. Outside, mammals include cougars, bobcats, coyotes, gray foxes, skunks, and raccoons; bird species include great horned owls, California quail, prairie falcons, wild turkeys, golden eagles, peregrine falcons (which have recently returned to the park to breed, in small numbers), and endangered California condors (which were reintroduced here in a program that began in 2003). Wild pigs (a hybrid of feral domestic pigs and imported wild boars) have been destructive here, but have recently been eliminated via a 26-mile fence that runs around the center of the park. The fence does double duty: it keeps the pigs out, and one section, known as the "Pig Fence," is also used as a handhold by hikers trying to haul themselves up a steep pitch on a portion of the South Wilderness Trail.

High Peaks Trail

FOLLOWING SPREAD: Rocks reflected at Bear Gulch (left); trail out of Balconies Cave (middle); rock tunnel (top right); Balconies Cave Trail (bottom right)

More than 80 percent of the park is protected as wilderness. No park roads connect the east and west sides of the park; getting from one side to the other by vehicle requires driving a circuitous loop around the park. The majority of visitor facilities are on the east side of the park. Features include the Pinnacles rock formations, the talus caves, views of the San Andreas Fault, and wildflower displays (primarily in March and April).

Exploring the Park

The trail network is not large, but Pinnacles National Park is old school. Visitors won't find many facilities; instead, the focus is on interesting scenic and geologic features, and lots of trails suitable for all levels of hikers. Interlocking loops and spurs make it possible to fashion hikes that circle the center of the park, or even cross from one side of the park to the other. The Pinnacles Campground is located on the east side of the park. Highlights of hiking here include exploring the caves and geological formations in the park's mountainous interior. Bring flashlights if the trail you choose goes into any of the talus caves.

➢ On the east side of the park, the Bear Gulch Nature Center has numerous trailheads. **Lower Bear Gulch Cave** is open to visitors, except during the breeding season for Townsend's big-eared bats and when the caves are flooded. Longer trails head into the interior of the park and can be combined: the **Condor Gulch Trail** and the **High Peaks Trail** form a 5.3-mile loop around the park's mountainous interior.

➢ From the West Pinnacles Visitor Contact Station, the **Prewett Point Trail** leads to the **Jawbone Canyon Trail**. From the end of Chaparral Road, several trails lead into the park interior and can be linked to trails that cross the park to the east side; the longest of these is the **North Wilderness Trail**, while the **Juniper Canyon Trail** leads to an intersection with the **High Peaks Trail**. The trail to **Balconies Cave** also starts at the end of the road; the cave can be explored by visitors except when it is closed due to flooding or the bat-breeding season. (Balconies Cave can also be accessed from the **Old Pinnacles Trailhead** on the east side of the park, via the Old Pinnacles Trail to Balconies Cave, a 5.3-mile round trip.)

BELOW: Trail to Bear Gulch (left); Bear Gulch Cave Trail (right)

OPPOSITE: Juniper Canyon Trail

Gateway Arch
National Park

ILLINOIS AND
MISSOURI

Designated 2018

Urban, small, and with only a city park to offer outdoor opportunities, Gateway Arch National Park, established in 2018, challenges our definition of exactly what a national park is. Some critics have suggested that it would have been better designated a national historic park, calling it a poor fit with classic parks like Yellowstone and Yosemite, or even with new national parks like White Sands, Indiana Dunes, and New River Gorge. It is the only truly urban national park in the system. Arguably, Saguaro is bookended on two sides by Tucson, Arizona; Indiana Dunes bumps up against Gary, Indiana; Biscayne is a quick kayak paddle from Miami, Florida; and Cuyahoga lies between Cleveland and Akron, Ohio. But Gateway Arch is an urban park, plain and simple. It is also the smallest national park—its 91 acres would fit into the nation's largest national park (Wrangell-St. Elias) more than 90,000 times.

The park was established to commemorate the Louisiana Purchase, the Lewis and Clark Expedition (which started nearby), the subsequent westward migration of American explorers and settlers, the first civil government west (if only by a few feet) of the Mississippi River, and the debate over slavery that was raised when the Dred Scott case was argued in the Old Courthouse, which is now part of the park.

Despite its departure from the image of the typical American national park, Gateway Arch has a deep connection with the trails that enabled easterners to travel to and trade with the American West. The 630-foot arch is a monument to westward expansion. The museum at its base interprets the stories of some of America's most iconic national historic trails: the Lewis and Clark, Santa Fe, Mormon Pioneer, Pony Express, Oregon, and California Trails. Visitors might not be able to get much hiking done here, but this most urban of parks shares a treasure trove of information about just what it takes to walk 2,000 miles or more.

Gateway Arch

Exploring the Park

You can leave your hiking gear at home when you visit Gateway Arch National Park. The Gateway Arch itself, of course, is the prime attraction: the tram to the top takes visitors to the best view in town.

> For hikers and history lovers, the **Museum at the Gateway Arch** is fascinating. In addition to learning about the various historic routes of America's westward migrations, visitors can consider how contemporary gear differs from the supplies and equipment needed by the 19th-century pioneers as they embarked on their 2,000-mile journey on foot and by oxcart.

> Outside the museum, **Gateway Arch Park** has about 5 miles of interlocking pathways that offer views of the arch and the Mississippi River. The paths here also give access to the more hike-worthy 12.5-mile **Mississippi Greenway**, used by walkers, joggers, and cyclists. Also at the river are several riverboats that offer excursions.

BELOW: Reflection sculpture at the entrance to Gateway Arch

OPPOSITE: Explorers' Garden at Gateway Arch, with buildings of St. Louis in the background

Indiana Dunes
National Park

Only 50 miles from Chicago, Indiana Dunes National Park is located smack between the steel-mill city of Gary to the west and Michigan City to the east. Yet despite its proximity to industrial Gary (not to mention densely populated Chicago) and despite its size—at just over 15,000 acres, it is one of the smallest parks in the system—Indiana Dunes is one of the most biologically diverse of all the national parks, especially when its size is factored into the equation. Its variety of environments extends far beyond its eponymous, and admittedly impressive, sand dunes (which rise to heights of more than 200 feet). The park includes forests, wetlands, bogs, marshes, grasslands, beaches, and ponds. More than 1,100 plant species live here, ranging from arctic plants (which are suited to the cold and blustery lakeside winters) to desert species (which make their homes on the dry sandy dunes). More than 350 species of birds have been recorded, either as year-round inhabitants or migrants.

Indiana Dunes had a century-long journey to its current national park status. Inspired by reports of the botanical diversity found on the dunes, Stephen Mather, the first director of the National Park Service, held hearings in Chicago in 1916 to consider establishing a Sand Dunes National Park. Over the next 100 years, a push and pull between development, resource use, and preservation interests stalled the establishment of a national park. Indiana Dunes State Park was set aside in 1926; the Indiana Dunes National Lakeshore followed in 1966. In 2019, the lakeshore was finally reclassified as a national park. The park's eastern unit, its largest section, surrounds the state park, which has its own network of trails. The national park also contains a noncontiguous western section, which is closer to Gary, as well as several other small, disconnected parcels, which were included in the park for their ecological or historic significance.

Trail leading to Mount Baldy at sunset, with Lake Michigan in the background

FOLLOWING SPREAD: Paul H. Douglas Trail in Miller Woods (top left); boardwalk to beach near Dorothy Buell Visitor Center (bottom left); vehicle tracks in the sand along Central Avenue Beach (right)

An interesting sidenote: Some of the western national parks were initially supported by railroad entrepreneurs eager to establish train lines that would be used by tourists. But while very few national parks are now served by trains, Indiana Dunes is one of them: the South Shore Line from Chicago to South Bend makes several stops near the park.

Exploring the Park

Fifty miles of hiking trails allow day hikers access to the park's eight beaches, 15 miles of Lake Michigan shoreline, and varied ecosystems. This is more a day-hiking destination than a backpacking one, but those wanting a primitive camping experience can stay in one of the tent-only sites at the Dunewood Campground and venture out from there. There are, additionally, other trails for equestrians and bicycles.

➤ The Diana of the Dunes Dare follows the route of West Beach's **Dune Succession Trail** and honors Indiana Dunes advocate Alice Mabel Gray. Known as "Diana of the Dunes," Gray spent nine years in the early 1900s in the then-wilderness of the dunes. The hike named after her gives expansive views—all the way to Chicago—as well as an opportunity to examine, up close, the succession, fragility, and detail of the dune environment.

➤ The 4.7-mile **Cowles Bog Trail** is one of the park's longer, more rugged day hikes, highlighting an outstanding area of plant diversity where Henry Chandler Cowles conducted a landmark study of the dunes' vegetation succession. The trail passes through several distinct habitats including ponds, marshes, swamps, wooded dunes, and a quiet beach on Lake Michigan.

➤ The **Glenwood Dunes** trail system is an extensive network of trails and interconnected loops that allow visitors to tailor their hike to their fitness and interests, from less than a mile to 15 miles. In addition, the 4.4-mile, round-trip **Dunewood Trace Campground Trail** connects the Glenwood Dunes trail system to the Dunewood Campground to the east, and the 2.6-mile, round-trip **Glenwood Dunes Extension Trail** connects to the Dune Park South Shore Railroad Station to the west.

➤ Located in the park's western unit, the Paul H. Douglas Center for Environmental Education is the gateway to the **Paul H. Douglas Trail** through Miller Woods, which winds through a series of wetlands, globally rare black oak savanna, open dunes, and beaches, with views of the lake and the dunes.

OPPOSITE: Small entrance to the beach along Lake Michigan

BELOW: White plant along Cowles Bog Trail (left); great white egret in Cowles Bog (right)

White Sands
National Park

_____

Designated 2019

Just when it seems that the national park system has identified, designated, and protected every conceivable American landscape in every possible setting, a new park shows us something we've never seen before. White Sands National Park, designated in 2019, covers approximately 150,000 acres—almost half of the world's largest field of gypsum sand dunes. And while it is common for national parks to be surrounded by other public lands—national forests, Bureau of Land Management lands, or state lands—this one is entirely surrounded by the White Sands Missile Range, a military testing site under the command of the US Army.

Located in the Tularosa Basin of southern New Mexico, White Sands is a shining, blinding, ever-shifting landscape of fine white gypsum sand dunes—an inland beach without an ocean. But it was in fact an ocean that began the creation of these dunes. The ancient sea that once covered this region deposited the gypsum on land that rose to become mountaintops surrounding what is now the Tularosa Basin. Rain dissolved the gypsum, washing it into ancient Lake Otero in the closed basin. When the lake evaporated at the end of the last ice age about 12,000 years ago, it left behind a playa—a dry lake bed—filled with gypsum that solidified into crystals. Wind and friction pulverized the crystals into fine white particles that were picked up, swirled around, and put down by the winds to form ever-shifting new dunes in an ever-shifting landscape. The process continues today. Rain that falls in the mountains dissolves and washes down yet more gypsum into the basin. When water evaporates, crystals form; they are shredded and polished by wind and friction to become more dust to form yet more dunes.

Today, the basin and its sand dunes sit between the San Andres Mountains to the west and the Sacramento Mountains to the east. Part of what is now the Chihuahuan Desert Ecosystem, White Sands itself is

Layered white gypsum dunes

FOLLOWING SPREAD: Hiker on Alkali Flat Trail, with San Andres Mountains in the background (left); white dune layers (top right); hoary rosemary mint creating a pedestal (bottom right)

home to some 800 species of animals that have found a way to live here, including mammals, reptiles and amphibians, birds, one fish (the White Sands pupfish), insects (including 40 endemic moths), some specially adapted species of insects, spiders, scorpions, lizards, toads, and mammals, whose colorings have evolved to light or white in order to provide camouflage. Occasionally, visitors may spy a few controversial oryx—an antelope native to Africa's Kalahari Desert. Oryx were imported into the White Sands Missile Range in the 1970s as part of a project to provide big-game hunting opportunities. The desert-hardy antelope thrived, quickly overpopulating and spreading to adjacent areas—including what is now the park—whether they were welcome or not. Today, the oryx are mostly contained outside of the park.

The main artery of White Sands National Park is Dunes Drive, a 16-mile round-trip scenic road that links the visitor center with the hiking trails at the end of the park. The first half of the road is paved, after which it becomes hard-packed gypsum—passable for ordinary automobiles, but often a slow ride due to washboarding, potholes, and sand drifts forming on the road surface. Bicycling is a popular activity. Mountain bikes and fat-tire bikes handle the challenges better than road bikes. However, if the road is iced over or slick with snow mixed with sand, even a fat-tire bike may not be up to the job. While driving or biking, visitors are likely to see sledders gliding down the dunes; if the idea of climbing up the dunes then throwing yourself down appeals to you, buy an inexpensive dune sled from the visitor center (you can return it for a small remittance when you're done).

Exploring the Park

White Sands National Park contains five trails, all of them short, but each revealing different aspects of the park's ever-shifting morphology, wildlife, and ecosystem. If you'd like the landscape explained, sign up for a ranger-led tour—they include guided moonlight hikes, sunset tours, and morning photography tours. For those striking out without a guide, rangers caution that on all but the accessible boardwalk trail, shifting sands can obscure trails and footprints, so hikers should carefully monitor the color-coded stakes that lead through the dunes. Also, water and salty snacks help prevent heat exhaustion, hyperthermia, and electrolyte depletion.

➤ For casual day hikers, the short **Interdune Boardwalk** is fully accessible for people using wheelchairs and strollers, with displays about the science, geology, and ecology of the park. The **Playa Trail** (marked with green hearts) is a short trail with interpretive information about the playa—the dried lake beds—that are a crucial part of the process that creates the dunes. The slightly longer **Dune Life Nature Trail** (marked with blue clubs) is a favorite family hike, with interpretive information about animal life and some trail sections that scramble up and down the dunes.

➤ For overnighters and more serious hikers, the orange-spade markers of the **Backcountry Camping Trail** lead to the park's backpacker campsites. Bring plenty of water, because there isn't any. And finally, red-diamond markers of the misnamed **Alkali Flat Trail** (there's nothing flat about it) lead hikers along the edge of what is left of ancient Lake Otero. The trail is probably the park's best backcountry experience, but bring water and sun protection because it's also strenuous, with 5 shadeless, constant up-and-down miles.

OPPOSITE: Hiker on Interdune Boardwalk Trail (top); flowering soaptree yucca in the backcountry (bottom left); soaptree yucca near Dunes Drive (bottom right)

BELOW: Great horned owl near White Sands Visitor Center

New River Gorge
National Park and Preserve

Sunset over Beauty
Mountain and New River

FOLLOWING SPREAD: Hiker on
Castle Rock Trail (top left);
steps leading to Turkey Spur
Overlook (bottom left);
kayakers paddling toward New
River Gorge Bridge (right)

Southern West Virginia is a three-dimensional land-scape of gorges, ravines, and shady "hollers." Pockets of old-growth forests hold their secrets, and fast-growing second- and third-growth forests reclaim the landscape, covering remnants of old coal-mining and lumber towns whose saws and mills and dynamite once challenged the trees and left the hilltops bare. The regenerative power of this forest has overcome its logging history to become one of the most biologically diverse river systems in the southeastern United States. The river is the ineptly named New River—actually one of the world's oldest rivers. It flows 1,000 or more feet through the gorge it has carved, exposing rocks that are 300 million years old. What is new is the gorge's epony-mous national park. It is the newest park in the system.

Logging- and mining-supported communities were once hidden in the folds and creases of the mountains. Hunting and fishing have been a way of life here, from Indigenous peoples to the present. Since 1978, when the New River was certified as a wild and scenic river, the region has blossomed as an outdoor destination, with more than a thousand rock-climbing routes on cliffs that sometimes surpass 1,000 feet and 50 miles of free-flowing white water that offer adrenaline-fueled chal-lenges for rafters and paddlers.

Certified as America's 63rd national park in 2021, New River Gorge is the ninth national park east of the Mississippi River and one of only two units outside Alaska to be designated as both a national park and preserve. The "national park" designation confirms its status as a world-class recreational resource, with approximately 7,000 acres set aside for uses such as kayaking, hiking, mountain biking, and rock climbing. The "preserve" designation recognizes the region's long traditions and uses and allows the majority of the park—about 65,000 acres—to be used for hunting and fishing, as well as commercially guided whitewater rafting.

The New River Gorge is the longest and deep-est canyon in the Appalachian Mountains, and from precontact times until the present, it created a consid-erable impediment for those who wanted to get from one side to the other. The straight-line distance from the top of the canyon on one side to the top of the can-yon on the other is only about a mile. Before the New River Gorge Bridge was built in 1977, getting from here to there—even in a car—could take 40 minutes on narrow switchbacked mountain roads. The bridge cut the journey down to about a minute—assuming a driver didn't slow down to take in the view from the 3,030-foot-long bridge, the longest steel span in the Western Hemisphere and, at 876 feet above the river, the third-highest bridge in the United States.

In fact, the bridge is so high it is possible to BASE jump from it and plummet past hundreds of millions of years of geologic history. (BASE is an acronym for Buildings, Antennae, Spans, and Earth—the things thrill-seekers jump from.) BASE jumping is not permit-ted in national parks, but as another nod to the park's unique history, the legislation that established it set aside one day a year to allow jumpers to hurl them-selves into the gorge. On the designated Bridge Day (the third Saturday of every October), the bridge is closed to car traffic and opened to hundreds of parachutists, who leap into the gorge below while thousands more watch, walk the bridge, shop at the food and craft ven-dors, listen to music, or rappel from the nearby cliffs as part of what the National Park Service calls the "larg-est extreme sports event in the world."

Exploring the Park

Three activities take center stage at New River Gorge National Park and Preserve: hiking, climbing, and pad-dling. Hiking highlights include views of the gorge,

remnants of historic structures that remind visitors of how life here was once lived, and endless streams of cascades and waterfalls, seasonally punctuated by spring flowers and autumn foliage. Trails range from less than a mile to 7 miles in length, but also offer spurs and loops that can be combined to make longer excursions.

> The Grandview area offers views of the deepest section of New River Gorge on the **Grandview Rim Trail**, or a chance to hike 1,400 feet down to the river via the **Little Laurel Trail**, which follows an old woods road past the site of an abandoned coal mine. Not far from the Grandview area, the trails along and near Glade Creek offer waterfalls, swimming holes, and catch-and-release fishing; the **Glade Creek Trail** is one of the most popular.

> On the southern end of the park, the Sandstone area offers the wheelchair-accessible **Sandstone Falls Boardwalk Trail**. The Sandstone Falls range from only 10 to 35 feet tall, but what they lack in height, they make up for in width: spanning 1,500 feet across the river, divided by islands, they make up the largest waterfall system on the New River.

> One of the more extensive trail systems in the park is found in the Fayetteville area. One standout is the **Long Point Trail**, with its panoramic view of the gorge and bridge; across the gorge are the cliffs of the Endless Wall. And from the **Endless Wall Trail**, hikers can get a glimpse of how the other recreationists live, with views of rock climbers and rafters.

BELOW: Sandstone Falls

OPPOSITE: Rocks along Castle Rock Trail

With more than 1.6 million members and supporters, the **National Parks Conservation Association** is the voice of America's national parks, working to protect and preserve the nation's most iconic and inspirational places for present and future generations. It celebrates the parks—and works tirelessly to defend them—whether on the ground, in the courtroom, or on Capitol Hill. From its national headquarters in Washington, DC, and field offices nationwide, it calls on its program and policy experts, committed volunteers, staff lobbyists, community organizers, and communications specialists to ensure that national parks are well protected. For more information, please visit www.npca.org.

First published in the United States of America in 2023 by
Rizzoli International Publications, Inc. | 300 Park Avenue South | New York, NY 10010 | www.rizzoliusa.com

Publisher: Charles Miers
Associate Publisher: James Muschett
Managing Editor: Lynn Scrabis
Editor: Candice Fehrman
Design: Susi Oberhelman
Endpaper Map: Steven Gordon, Cartagram

Printed in Hong Kong

2023 2024 2025 2026 / 10 9 8 7 6 5 4 3 2 1

ISBN: 978-0-8478-9923-4

Library of Congress Control Number: 2022946539

Visit us online:
Facebook.com/RizzoliNewYork
Twitter: @Rizzoli_Books
Instagram.com/RizzoliBooks
Pinterest.com/RizzoliBooks
Youtube.com/user/RizzoliNY
Issuu.com/Rizzoli

PAGE 1: High Peaks Trail, Pinnacles National Park, California

PAGES 2-3: Dunloup Creek Falls, New River Gorge National Park and Preserve, West Virginia

PAGES 4-5: Hoodoos, Bryce Canyon National Park, Utah

PAGES 6-7: Swiftcurrent Lake, Glacier National Park, Montana